Security, Ethnography and Discourse

This interdisciplinary book analyses different contexts where security concerns have an impact on institutional or everyday practices and routines in the lives of ordinary people.

Creating a dialogue between the fields of International Relations, Peace and Conflict Studies, Sociolinguistics, Education and Anthropology, this book addresses core themes associated with conflict and security – peacebuilding, refugee settlement, nationalism, surveillance and sousveillance – and examines them as they manifest in everyday spaces and practices. Seven empirical studies are presented that bring ethnographic and/or close-up interactional lenses to practices of security in schools, refugee centres, care homes, city streets and roadsides. Drawing on fieldwork and data from Cyprus, Croatia, Bosnia-Herzegovina, Sweden, Germany and the US, the chapters explore what notions of suspicion, peace, conflict and threat mean and how they are manifested in people's lived experiences.

This book will be of much interest to students of Critical Security Studies, Anthropology, Sociology, Sociolinguistics and International Relations in general.

Emma Mc Cluskey is a Lecturer in Criminology at the University of Westminster, UK.

Constadina Charalambous is Assistant Professor of Language Education & Literacy at the European University Cyprus.

Routledge Studies in Liberty and Security
Series editors: Didier Bigo, Elspeth Guild
and R.B.J. Walker

This book series will establish connections between critical security studies and International Relations, surveillance studies, criminology, law and human rights, political sociology and political theory. To analyse the boundaries of the concepts of liberty and security, the practices which are enacted in their name (often the same practices) will be at the heart of the series. These investigations address contemporary questions informed by history, political theory and a sense of what constitutes the contemporary international order.

Human Rights of Migrants in the 21st Century
Edited by Elspeth Guild, Stefanie Grant and C. A. Groenendijk

Global Labour and the Migrant Premium
The Cost of Working Abroad
Edited by Tugba Basaran and Elspeth Guild

Anglo-European Intelligence Cooperation
Britain in Europe, Europe in Britain
Hager Ben Jaffel

Migration, Security, and Resistance
Global and Local Perspectives
Edited by Graham Hudson and Idil Atak

Security, Ethnography and Discourse
Transdisciplinary Encounters
Edited by Emma Mc Cluskey and Constadina Charalambous

For more information about this series, please visit: https://www.routledge.com/Routledge-Studies-in-Liberty-and-Security/book-series/RSLS

Security, Ethnography and Discourse
Transdisciplinary Encounters

Edited by Emma Mc Cluskey and
Constadina Charalambous

LONDON AND NEW YORK

First published 2022
by Routledge
4 Park Square, Milton Park, Abingdon, Oxon OX14 4RN

and by Routledge
605 Third Avenue, New York, NY 10158

Routledge is an imprint of the Taylor & Francis Group, an informa business

© 2022 selection and editorial matter, Emma Mc Cluskey and Constadina Charalambous; individual chapters, the contributors

The right of Emma Mc Cluskey and Constadina Charalambous to be identified as the authors of the editorial material, and of the authors for their individual chapters, has been asserted in accordance with sections 77 and 78 of the Copyright, Designs and Patents Act 1988.

All rights reserved. No part of this book may be reprinted or reproduced or utilised in any form or by any electronic, mechanical, or other means, now known or hereafter invented, including photocopying and recording, or in any information storage or retrieval system, without permission in writing from the publishers.

Trademark notice: Product or corporate names may be trademarks or registered trademarks, and are used only for identification and explanation without intent to infringe.

British Library Cataloguing-in-Publication Data
A catalogue record for this book is available from the British Library

Library of Congress Cataloguing-in-Publication Data
A catalog record has been requested for this book

ISBN: 978-0-367-53201-7 (hbk)
ISBN: 978-0-367-53203-1 (pbk)
ISBN: 978-1-003-08090-9 (ebk)

DOI: 10.4324/9781003080909

Typeset in Times New Roman
by MPS Limited, Dehradun

Contents

List of figures vii
List of tables viii
List of contributors ix
Acknowledgements xi

Introduction 1
EMMA MC CLUSKEY AND CONSTADINA CHARALAMBOUS

1 Researching (in)security as a lived experience: Setting the foundations for transdisciplinary dialogue 13
EMMA MC CLUSKEY, BEN RAMPTON, AND CONSTADINA CHARALAMBOUS

PART I
Conflict, (in)security and everyday peace 35

2 Everyday peace disruption in deeply divided societies: Is it really peace? 37
ROGER MAC GINTY

3 A linguistic ethnography of peace-building through language education in Cyprus 52
CONSTADINA CHARALAMBOUS, PANAYIOTA CHARALAMBOUS, AND BEN RAMPTON

4 Silence as practices of (in)security in the post-Yugoslav region 78
RENATA SUMMA AND MILAN PUH

5 Breaking taboos: The making of xenophobia as
   acceptable in Sweden   100
   EMMA MC CLUSKEY

PART II
Managing suspicion and surveillance in everyday life   117

6 Embodying the US security state: Surveilling intimate
   spaces to counter violent extremism   119
   NICOLE NGUYEN

7 Goffman and the everyday experience of surveillance   143
   BEN RAMPTON AND LOUISE ELEY

8 Auditor design and accountability in encounters between citizens and the police   170
   RODNEY H. JONES

   Afterword: Reflexive encounters when speaking across
   bounded knowledges   199
   REBEKKA FRIEDMAN

   Index   203

Figures

2.1	Key concepts of everyday peace	40
2.2	Types of social practice that constitute everyday peace	43
7.1	Focused and unfocused interaction	146
7.2	Oncoming pedestrian turning head right to look down side road	152
7.3	The scene recorded by the video-glasses at the moment when Inge is turning her head down the side-street and stops humming	152
7.4	Preparing to place a sticker covertly	155
8.1	Excerpt 1: Camera as addressee 1	178
8.2	Excerpt 2: Camera as addressee 2	179
8.3	Excerpt 3: Driver as overhearer	180
8.4	Excerpt 4: 'I'll keep recording…it's my right'	181
8.5	Excerpt 5: Non-accommodation	182
8.6	Excerpt 6: Powerade	183
8.7	Excerpt 7: 'Seems like a strange law'	184
8.8	Excerpt 8: 'I've never said that to you'	186

Tables

1.1	Comparing sociolinguistic studies of superdiversity and IPS studying the international	15
3.1	Data collection	56
7.1	Comparison of how Adnan and James anticipate the act of stickering leading to remedial interchanges	157
8.1	Excerpt 9: 'I've got this on camera'	189
8.2	Excerpt 10: 'I'm being perceived as a threat'	190
8.3	Excerpt 11: 'My hands are visible'	190
8.4	Excerpt 12: 'My brother is being put in handcuffs'	191
8.5	Excerpt 13: 'You see this'	192

Contributors

Constadina Charalambous is Assistant Professor of Language Education & Literacy at the European University Cyprus. Her work focuses on the interplay between language and larger socio-political ideologies including processes of (in) security, and is published in international journals and in a co-authored monograph ('Peace Education in a Conflict-affected society,' CUP 2016).

Panayiota Charalambous holds a PhD in Education (King's College London) and currently works as a language teacher in Greek-Cypriot secondary education. She has worked as adjunct lecturer in the postgraduate programme of the Open University of Cyprus and is a co-author of the book Peace Education in a Conflict-Troubled Society (CUP2016)

Louise Eley holds a PhD in Sociolinguistics (King's College London) and contributes to teaching in linguistics at King's College London. Drawing on linguistic ethnography and interactional sociolinguistics, her research has explored linguistic diversity and the production, regulation, placement and reception of signage in public places.

Rebekka Friedman is Senior Lecturer in International Relations in the Department of War Studies at King's College London. Her research and teaching focuses on transitional justice, peace-building, memory, reintegration, reconciliation and gender. She has conducted field research in Sri Lanka, Peru and Sierra Leone.

Rodney H. Jones is Professor of Sociolinguistics at the University of Reading. His research interests include surveillance, language and digital media, and health communication. He has published twelve books and over eighty journal articles and book chapters. Among his recent publications *Discourse and Digital Practices* (Routledge, 2015), *Spoken Discourse* (Bloomsbury, 2016). *Language and Media* (Routledge, 2020), and *Viral Discourse* (Cambridge University Press, 2021).

Roger Mac Ginty is Professor at the School of Government and International Affairs, and Director of the Durham Global Security Institute, both at Durham University. He is co-founder of the Everyday Peace Indicators, and co-editor of journal *Peacebuilding*.

Emma Mc Cluskey is a Lecturer in Criminology at University of Westminster, UK. Her research explores the relations between security, mobility, surveillance and democracy. She is author of *From Righteousness to Far Right: An Anthropological Rethinking of Critical Security Studies*.

Nicole Nguyen is Associate Professor of social foundations of education at the University of Illinois-Chicago. She is author of Suspect Communities: Anti-Muslim Racism and the Domestic War on Terror (2019) and A Curriculum of Fear: Homeland Security in US Public Schools (2016).

Milan Puh is Professor of Language Teaching at the University of Sao Paulo, working with interdisciplinary research between History, Education, Linguistics and Cultural Studies, with a special focus on immigrant communities. Published four books dedicated to Croatian immigration and thirty papers and chapters on a variety of topics.

Ben Rampton is Professor of Sociolinguistics at King's College London. His interests cover urban multilingualism; youth, ethnicity and social class; conflict and (in)securitisation; and language education policy and practice. He was founding convener of the Linguistic Ethnography Forum, and directed the King's ESRC Interdisciplinary Social Science Doctoral Training Centre from 2011–2014.

Renata Summa holds a PhD in International Relations from the Pontifical Catholic University of Rio de Janeiro and is currently a post-doctoral researcher at the same institute. She is the author of "Everyday borders, boundaries and post-conflict societies" (Palgrave, 2021).

Acknowledgements

Our thanks to the many people who contributed to the work presented in this book. These transdisciplinary encounters originated in the Language, (In)security and Everyday Practice network centred in King's College London, comprising of Constadina Charalambous, Panayiota Charalambous, Louise Eley, Kamran Khan, Ben Rampton, Lavanya Sankaran (sociolinguistics) and Didier Bigo, Vivienne Jabri, Rebekka Friedman, Emma Mc Cluskey and Maria O'Reilly (International Relations). Our conversations which informed the conception of this book and formed our understanding of and approach towards the topics presented here, were made possible thanks to the generous financial support of The British Academy (*SG160630*), King's College London, Faculty of Social Science & Public Policy Research Fund and the Cyprus Research & Innovation Foundation (EXCELLENCE/0918/0275). We are grateful to both the series editors and the team at Routledge for their encouragement and patience, as well as to the two anonymous reviewers whose suggestions helped focus and improve the book immensely.

Introduction

Emma Mc Cluskey and Constadina Charalambous

It has become almost banal to say that unease is now permeating everyday life in ways that it didn't previously. Various counter-terrorism and counter-radicalisation programmes have made schools, nurseries, hospitals and community centres sites of (in)security. Closed Circuit Television (CCTV) and bulk collection of electronic data by state agencies and private companies have become more diffuse, technocratic and routine. Securitarian and nationalist rhetorics have multiplied and intensified and discourses considered taboo only a few years ago have now become common parlance. It would be though inaccurate to frame these phenomena as linear or as infiltrating our everyday lives without any struggle, contradiction, contestation or appropriation. Indeed, the 'everyday' adds new dimensions in researching (in)security and has received increased attention lately. But despite all the overarching structures – social, economic, political, institutional, etc. – everyday life is often reduced in some way; either romanticised as struggles for emancipation, or seen through the contingency of 'mess', which cannot be effectively abstracted without losing much of its living texture.

In general, debates over how 'international' and 'local' categories manifest themselves and intersect in everyday practice vis-à-vis security, violence and conflict have multiplied in recent decades across the social sciences. Many of these analyses have examined transversal practices and technologies of various security actors, official and unofficial, in promulgating a state of unease and normalising exclusion or xenophobia (Bigo, 2006; Huysmans, 2014; Neal, 2019; Ragazzi, 2017; Ochs, 2011; Mc Cluskey, 2019). Other strands of scholarship have looked at local ownership, resistance and appropriation of post-conflict peacebuilding and the role of 'ordinary' people in what can be seen as *de*-escalation and *de*-securitisation and 'everyday peace' (Mac Ginty, 2010; Mac Ginty, 2014; Mac Ginty & Richmond, 2013; Friedman, 2015; Charalambous et al., 2018, Zembylas et al., 2016).

Bringing together these strands of research in *Security, Ethnography and Discourse: Transdisciplinary Encounters*, we go beyond dichotomies such as 'local' and 'international' and instead approach everyday (in)securitisation through ethnographic and interactional lenses. In doing so, the book aims to

DOI: 10.4324/9781003080909-101

develop an approach that is both original and productive, bringing (in)security into the study of everyday interactions and social relations, and redirecting the focus in International Relations research (IR) from public speech acts, official documents, security professionals and technologies, to ethnographic and close-up interactional approaches of how (in)security is enacted and experienced in everyday practices and spaces.

More specifically, the perspective underlying this edited volume is that our understanding of daily practices in communities, workplaces, schools and clinics, now needs to encompass the diffusion of fear and unease of large-scale violence, suspicion and surveillance *as well as* the ways this unease is evaded, subverted or indeed re-enforced in such settings. The concept of '(in) security' is useful in that it encapsulates all of these processes, as will be discussed in Chapter 1. This term points both to the institutional practices of actors with different degrees of authority and influence in the production of security/insecurity, and to the lived experiences of people affected by these securitisations. It captures the fundamentally contested nature of both security and insecurity, showing how what constitutes security for some, could precisely be seen as insecurity for somebody else (Bigo, 2006; Bigo & Mc Cluskey, 2017).

Security, Ethnography and Discourse: Transdisciplinary Encounters problematises the notions of 'everyday life' and 'everyday practices' in relation to widespread anxiety and violence and re-centres analyses of (in)security around human beings and their day-to-day practices. Our point of departure is precisely the empirical 'capturing' of these everyday processes, practices and sets of relations in order to begin to make sense of them within the current socio-political changes and (re)configurations. The chapters of this volume thus put forward a theoretical contribution which sees theory more as a means of advancing 'thick descriptions' (Geertz, 1973), advancing a type of practical reflexivity as an epistemic and collaborative process. Human beings, their interactions and their social worlds are the core of our analysis; theoretical claims are empirically grounded, and struggle, contradiction, contestation and appropriation are front and centre. To that end, this volume moves into trans- and de-disciplinarisation of studies of (in) security as a lived experience, bringing in rich empirical work from various case studies.

The volume itself emerged from a collaboration between researchers in international relations and in sociolinguistics. Abandoning traditional focuses on the 'macro' and 'micro,' these two disciplinary trajectories can cohere in an ontology that treats 'international,' 'society' and 'state' as powerful symbolic representations (and performatives), and sees the practices of actors as always engaged "in a multitude of games of different scales at the same moment, even if they may not be aware of it" (Bigo, 2017: 38; Blommaert & Rampton, 2011). Over the last three years, the complementarity of the different types of analytic expertise developed within each tradition has been explored in the

Language, (In)security & Everyday Practice collaboration[1] (see Chapter 1 this volume), and this edited volume is one of its outcomes.

De-disciplinarizing ethnography: From 'critical methods' to transdisciplinary encounters in the study of (in)security

Ethnographic methods have been popular as a means of advancing knowledge production on international politics for some decades. Pioneered by feminist and postcolonial scholars within International Relations, such works have drawn attention to the significance of practices which are often written off as apolitical or irrelevant. In more recent years, anthropologies of international 'problems' have also paid critical attention to spaces of security, borders, migration and counter-terrorism, objectivising the social relations, subjectivities and human encounters associated with such phenomena (notably Maguire et al., 2014; Tazzioli, 2019; Maghalaes, 2018; Ben Jaffel, 2019).

The work on 'critical methods' around (in)security saw the evolution of a more sophisticated understanding of the role of ethnological methods in the field of International Relations. Moving away from naïve conceptualisations of empirical methods as 'tools' in IR's 'disciplinary toolkit' (Jackson, 2008), to a much more dynamic conceptualisation of methods as political and a new site in which to critique IR claims (see especially Aradau & Huysmans, 2014, Law & Urry, 2004), the investing of criticality in methods and methodology has cultivated a new generation of scholars who see method in more experimental ways (Aradau et al., 2014).

The discussions around critical methods have undoubtedly generated more innovative interplay between theory, methods and practice, still; the investment of criticality in methods has nonetheless had a side effect of reifying methods and methodology, particularly in their codifications within different handbooks and manuals (see Salter & Mutlu, 2013). The fetishization of ethnography as a 'boots-on-the-ground' method has been also pointed out by researchers working within the anthropology of security for what they argue is a superficial importing of ethnography from its home discipline (Anthropology of Security Network, 2014). Similar critiques have also taken place in other disciplines, including sociolinguistics, particularly about ethnography being reduced to 'method,' which obscures broader aspects associated with ethnography as epistemology or as perspective (Blommaert, 2005, 2018).

Sociolinguistics has a rich history of using ethnography and ethnographic methods, combining them with 'close-up' interactional analysis. In particular, Linguistic Ethnography, which has been established in the UK and Europe (drawing on the longer tradition of US Linguistic Anthropology) maintains that close attention to language and interaction can offer insights on how social and political structures can be enacted in everyday life, provided that the communicative contexts and meaning making apparatuses are ethnographically examined and understood (see Chapter 1 this volume for extended discussion and references). In contrast to more traditional

Linguistic Anthropology, Linguistic Ethnography works more as a discursive space rather than a disciplinary paradigm and therefore can be used beyond the field of Anthropology. Indeed, in the UK it was established as part of Applied Linguistics (Rampton, 2007). What differentiates it, is that instead of trying to do a 'full-fledged' traditional ethnography as required in the anthropological paradigm, it adopts an *ethnographic perspective*, that is, it adopts the ontology and epistemology of ethnographic knowledge, together with ethnographic methods and sensitivities and uses them to look at various issues of concern in the everyday life. As Blommaert (2007: 684) argues, ethnography 'would best be seen as a general theoretical outlook,' which entails certain ontological and epistemological presuppositions:

> in an ethnographic perspective one should never have to argue for the fact that social events are contextualised, connected with other events, meaningful in a more-than-unique way, and functional to those who perform the practices that construct the event. One should not have to argue for the situated nature of any knowledge of such practices, and consequently, for the importance of subjectivity in ethnography... And one should not have to argue, consequently, for the fact that ethnographic knowledge is interpretive and hypothetical and escapes any attempt at positivist circumscription. (ibid.)

This book does not intended to be a book on methods and methodology, nor add to the emerging body of literature in 'anthropology of security.' On the contrary, this book aims to engage with (linguistic) ethnography as a mode of knowledge and knowing for better understanding (in)securitisation practices and the ways they have been routinized and become part of everyday life. In other words, beyond narrow-gauge discussions of methodology, we wish to engage with ethnographic and interactional methods in the context of a transdisciplinary collaboration, which mobilise ethnography in various ways and with different disciplinary baggage, but nonetheless engage with the themes of anxiety, fear, unease and (in)/de-security in everyday life and intimate relations. Although not all contributors in this volume claim to use Linguistic Ethnography, they all adopt an ethnographic perspective in how they approach (in)security as a situated lived experience which is enacted, enforced, evaded, silenced, or transformed, and always linked to wider ideologies of Security, Peace & Conflict.

(In)security as emergent, contingent, unexpected

In their 'networked manifesto,' the c.a.s.e collective (2006) spoke of the dangers of what they called the 'security trap'; the way in which scholars can unwillingly participate in the securitisation of new issues when analysing them solely through the lenses and frames of 'security.' Likewise, Montesinos Coleman and Rosenow (2016) have argued that at play with critical scholarship, security is an unrecognised ontological investment in 'security', which acts to set limits to what we can call into question.

In a similar vein, although the anthropology of security has admittedly produced excellent ethnographic accounts, these seem to be confined in people's everyday lived experiences within security apparatuses and specific security '-scapes,' for example within airports, heavily policed disadvantaged neighbourhoods or migrant camps (Maguire, 2019). These studies have been excellent in bringing to light all the ways in which new configurations of knowledge and power can manifest through a security framework, however, they have tended to operate with a spatial understanding of security; security apparatuses are pre-defined and demarcated. As these 'security scapes' are already pre-constituted, there is not much room for emergence, contingency or transformation of what 'counts' as security (see Chapter 1 for an extended discussion and references).

What is precisely novel in our collaboration, is that notions like security, surveillance, counter-terrorism, peace, reconciliation, silence, visibility, accountability and xenophobia were not imposed on the data a priori, but are shown to emerge in interactions; their meaning is negotiated and dynamic. This is a product of the *organic* nature of our transdisciplinary encounter and our attempt to transcend and bridge the various lacunae in our respective fields, in order to understand the lived experiences and social relations of the participants in our research studies.

Placing ontological primacy on liveable lives enabled the authors in this book to see (in)security as part of social reality, and to forge transversal links between language education and *peace education as a de-securitising practice* for example (Chapter 3). It also enabled us to trace the emergence of (in)security in *unexpected* places, and to approach it as entangled within much wider sets of power relations, which wouldn't immediately seem related (humanitarian logic, care, commerce etc) – i.e. Chs. 5 and 6. Rather than looking at predefined 'security scapes' the chapters in this book bring to light how (in)security processes have penetrated everyday spaces not traditionally thought and examined as part of a security apparatus, and practices sometimes seemingly far removed from more obvious spaces of (in)security.

Overview of the chapters

Drawing on IR, Peace and Conflict Studies, Sociolinguistics, Education, Anthropology and other relevant (sub)disciplines, the chapters of this volume address core themes associated with (in)security – post-conflict peacebuilding, refugee settlement, nationalism, surveillance and sousveillance – and examine them *outside* the bureaucratic and technocratic frames in which they are most often considered. The chapters present seven empirical studies that bring ethnographic and/or close-up interactional lenses to practices of (in)security in schools, refugee centres, care homes, city streets and road sides. Drawing on fieldwork and data from Cyprus, Croatia, Bosnia-Herzegovina, Sweden, Germany and the US, they explore what the notion of a threat, boundary or limit means and how it is manifested in people's lived experiences.

Although drawing on different disciplines, all chapters in this volume focus on similar practices of managing unease in everyday life as a result of (in)securitising discourses and process that relate to different social phenomena: migration, radicalisation, conflict, racism, xenophobia and surveillance. These seemingly different processes and different social contexts tend to be traditionally approached from different disciplinary lenses that allow for a different focus, interpretation and theorisation. But if we 'zoom' down to the level of lived experiences we can see similar practices of trying to navigate a precarious territory, and in some chapters, despite dealing with different social issues, the analysis turns to Goffman, for example, for a vocabulary that can conceptualise the interactional management of unease, insecurity, and surveillance (see for example Chs. 3, 7 & 8).

For the purposes of this book, the empirical chapters are divided in two broad themes:

1   Conflict, (in)security and everyday peace
2   Managing suspicion and surveillance in everyday life

Before moving on to the empirical chapters, Chapter 1 (by Emma Mc Cluskey, Ben Rampton and Constadina Charalambous) sets the necessary theoretical foundations that guided this transdisciplinary collaboration, and inform and connect the different chapters of this volume. It outlines the tenets of Linguistic Ethnography and the International Political Sociology (IPS) approach to (in)security and draws parallels as well as potential points of friction and incompatibilities. Analysing specific practices, strategies of justification and the ways in which these security practices empower certain groups or individuals and reproduce dominant forms of knowledge, IPS works pragmatically across disciplinary traditions, de-mystifying and de-exceptionalising the notion of security. Within sociolinguistics, *linguistic ethnography* investigates the crucial role that communication plays in the production and legitimation of social relations, and opens up 'the everyday' with concepts capable of spotlighting multi-scalar structuration in the quick of lived experience (inference, indexicality, adjacency, genre, text trajectory). The ground shared by IPS and linguistic ethnography covers substantive processes (migration, globalisation, diversity, (in)security, inequality, governmentality), as well as reference points in social theory (Foucault, Bourdieu, Garfinkel, Goffman). Although, historically, IPS and sociolinguistics/linguistic ethnography may have differed very considerably, both in the priority given to either politics or communication, as well as in the kinds of people and institutions they have studied (elites, diplomatic and military processes and organisations Vs ordinary people in civil society), the chapters that follow, explore and point towards the complementary contribution that these differences in expertise can now make to understanding some of the most pressing issues of our time.

The first section of this book, 'Conflict, (in)security, and everyday peace,' focuses on how people of different statuses deal with emerging or existing discourses of othering and hate in their everyday life, capturing the dynamics and contingency of practices of coexistence and conflict in societies permeated with politicised heterogeneity.

Chapter 2, 'Everyday Peace Disruption in deeply-divided societies: Is it really peace?' by Roger Mac Ginty, further unpacks the influential notion of 'everyday peace' and the ways it is practiced in deeply divided societies. Drawing on empirical material from the Everyday Peace Indicators project, and other fieldwork conducted by Mac Ginty and colleagues, the chapter argues that everyday peace is comprised of sociality, solidarity and reciprocity. Expanding these ideas, it illustrates how everyday peace is enacted and embodied at the very local level through micro-processes of politeness, avoidance, dissembling, etc.

The notion of everyday peace informs the discussion of other chapters in this first section as well, and within the interdisciplinary dialogue it is transferred in fields and contexts other than the one conceived and intended for. This process enriches the notion of everyday peace and points both to its theoretical potentials, as well as to some limitations.

Using the notion of everyday peace and drawing further on research on Peace & Conflict Studies (PCS) as well as on Sociolinguistics and Language Education, Constadina Charalambous, Panayiota Charalambous and Ben Rampton's chapter "A linguistic ethnography of peace-building through language education in Cyprus," presents the results of a linguistic ethnographic study on learning the language of a (former) enemy. Considering the legacy of war in Cyprus, they look at language classes of Turkish in Greek-Cypriot schools examining their potential for reconciliation and desecuritisation, arguing that participation in these classes served as a tentative first step in dealing with the controversy of the conflict. At the same time, the authors demonstrate how the lens of linguistic ethnography brings out the situated structuration of everyday practices that PCS currently sees as fluid, and challenges the assumption that discursive coping practices and 'everyday civilities' are in some way an exclusively vernacular preserve.

In Chapter 4, "Silence as practices of (in)security in post-Yugoslav region," Renata Summa and Milan Puh analyse the role of silence in post-conflict societies, scaling it up from interaction to issues of representation, violence and coexistence. Drawing on fieldwork carried in two contested cities – Mostar, in Bosnia and Herzegovina, and Vukovar, in Croatia– the chapter investigates how language education becomes intertwined with practices of (in)security, and analyses segregated and reunified schools in Mostar and the attempt to establish an intercultural school in Vukovar, in order to grasp the multiple forms silence takes in the everyday life of these cities. It argues that silence(s) is an important part of everyday practices of (in)securitisation which can enable and disable coexistence, producing interdicts but also occasionally becoming an important feature of everyday peace.

Chapter 5, "Breaking Taboos: The Making of Xenophobia as Acceptable in Sweden" by Emma Mc Cluskey moves to a (seemingly) 'peaceful' context and traces the emergence of othering and de-humanising discourses and practices, as the residents of a Swedish village were asked to coexist with refugees. This chapter examines the ways in which 'security' justifications permeated the micro-practices of peaceful coexistence and civility around a refugee settlement in Sweden during the so-called refugee 'crisis,' engaging with discourses of humanitarianism, hospitality and generosity in everyday life. It draws on extended fieldwork in a refugee centre in southern Sweden (a country labelled a 'humanitarian superpower' for its welcoming policy towards Syrians), and shows how limits were placed on solidarity, freedom of movement and the right to claim asylum, due to the gradual normalisation of the refugees as undesirable and undeserving. Disrupting ideas of the rise of securitarian politics as permeation of a specific ideology or worldview, the chapter shows that it was instead through microphysics and micro-practices that the de-humanisation of the refugees took place; what was not so long ago deemed taboo gradually became ordinary parlance amongst large swathes of people.

Moving from practices promoting or disrupting coexistence to issues of surveillance as lived experience, Section 2, deals with 'Managing suspicion and surveillance in everyday life.' The three chapters in this section focus on different aspects of surveillance – on the actors of surveillance (Ch. 6); on those being surveilled (Ch. 7), and on how the practices of watching and being watched can be negotiated in interaction (Ch. 8) – showing how the meaning of surveillance and the roles and practices involved are not fixed but rather dynamic.

In Chapter 6, "Embodying the US Security State: Surveilling Intimate Spaces to Counter Violent Extremism," Nicole Nguyen discusses the implications of (in)securitisation processes and antiterrorism initiatives on health provisions in the US, focusing in particular on the Countering Violent Extremism (CVE) initiative that called on social service providers like teachers and mental health professionals to identify, report, and work with individuals vulnerable to terrorist radicalisation and recruitment. Drawing from a two-year interpretive qualitative research study, the chapter argues that this perceptively liberal antiterrorism initiative has in fact increased insecurity by intensifying racial profiling, social exclusion, and surveillance in Muslim and other marginalised communities. At the same time, it also shows shows that even though surveillance has moved into personal and intimate spaces, (in)securitisation policies such as the CVE are not abstract discourses but are embodied and thus interpreted and enacted differently by different participants in different contexts, often in ways that transform and subvert them on the ground.

Introduction 9

In Chapter 7, 'Goffman and the everyday experience of surveillance,' Ben Rampton & Louise Eley go in even greater detail in unpacking the notion of surveillance and investigate the everyday interactional practice and experience of being surveilled. Using Goffman's account of the interaction order, and particularly the notions of 'un/non/crypto –focused' engagement they show how people arrange and organise their everyday practices (gestures, gaze, discourse, activities and bodies) in different contexts (e.g. walking on the street, stickering or gate crossing in airports) in relation to human or technological surveillors. The chapter highlights how different senses of potential threat and illegality enter the experience of surveillance, gradually building a rudimentary model. Although the paper considers only a small fraction of contemporary surveillance, it shows Goffman's value as an analytic resource that can hold large-scale generalisations about 'the surveillance society' to account, allowing us to see agentive responses to surveillance that are too subtle to be captured by notions like 'subversion' and 'resistance.' It also helps us understand the normalisation of institutional surveillance and the different configurations that the experience can involve.

In the final chapter, "Auditor Design and Accountability in Encounters between Citizens and the Police," Rodney Jones, follows the same line, also using Goffman, but focusing more specifically on sousveillance and the use of cell phone cameras in interactions with police. Although it is widely assumed that the presence of cell phones has led to emerging forms of 'sousveillance' which have an effect on the behaviour of police officers, making them more accountable, Jones, by analysing YouTube videos of police stops in the US with both White and African American drivers, reveals that 'legal rights' and 'technological means' are not sufficient. He discusses the use of video in police encounters as an embodied interactional practice and accordingly, account-ability as something that is negotiated and constructed in interactions via different means (technological instruments, body posture, discourse etc). Based on the context and the relationships created, participants negotiate the 'right to look' and, at the same time, the rights of visibility and sayability. He analyses strategically designed verbal and non-verbal communication, including the use of camera in order to manage accountability, and shows how the use of cameras can alter the audience of the interaction, bringing in potential future auditors and changing the epistemic positioning of the encounter, as well as its role and meaning. Still the analysis is not restricted in the here and now, instead, in his words, interactions 'are built upon a foundation of social relationships that inevitably involve historically sedimented forms of inequality and sets of expectations about who has the right to look and who has the right to be seen in different kinds of circumstances, and it is often these regimes of power and visibility that are responsible for how particular interactions came to occur in the first place.' So, although focusing on the moment-by-moment management of power and visibility, he shows that interaction with the police and the 'right to look' is a result of a range of complex discursive strategies that both drivers and officers engage in at the intersection of historically overdetermined narratives and positions of power.

Traversing boundaries, productivising dissonance

Working across disciplines, of course, does not come without problems. In fact, it took us a long time to shape and align our perspective and learn each others' 'language,' concepts, assumptions, and implicit moral 'baggage' of each other's fields. Things considered common sense in one field might be revolutionary or problematic for another. And after all these years, there are still incompatibilities or different readings of concepts. Transcending or overcoming this dissonance entirely is not something we have been able to do, but neither is it something that we desire to do.

Thus, as a result of the transdisciplinary encounter, the readers of this book will see ideas such as 'desecuritization' and 'everyday peace,' or 'suspicion,' 'hospitality' and 'care' mobilised together, despite them traditionally belonging to different strands of academic work, with contrasting normative assumptions. This may appear discordant to some readers. However, it is important to point out that this is not a 'pic n mix' or patchwork strategy, and that this conceptual apparatus has been operationalized with great reflexivity, conscious of how incompatibilities can emerge when we speak across (sub)disciplines. Indeed, this dissonance is something that we have come to consider as productive and it forms the ongoing basis for further intellectual collaboration across fragmented fields of knowledge. The transversal lines we have created have been opened by creating dialogue through the fragments, and will always thus be experimental, partial and somewhat unstable. Speaking across and between disciplines also allows us to linger on how these concepts are transformed and appropriated when they travel and circulate, drawing attention to emergent interests, disinterests or indifference on some issues, and not others. For example, the way *de-securitisation* is used in Chapter 3 for the analysis of Turkish language classes has shifted from how the concept is used in Security Studies. Nonetheless, in this (re)appropriation across boundaries, the concept does the work in linking processes and practices observed in the field with wider social and political reconfigurations, whilst creating broader questions and unsettling the implicit normative assumptions around its initial usage.

The second section on suspicion and surveillance, including Chapters 6, 7 and 8, also unsettles disciplinary boundaries to speak about the heterogeneity of surveillance as a lived experience. In Chapter 6, for example, suspicion and surveillance are shown to be entangled in practices with seemingly contradictory aims, such as such as 'care' and 'social work;' however, in-depth ethnographic study traces a direct pathway from social work to the materialisation of distrust and xenophobia. Finally, as we move through the studies on surveillance in Chapters 7 and 8, an ethnomethological lens is shown to forge different paths through debates on visibility, accountability

Introduction 11

and what 'counts' as surveillance, intervening in both traditional studies on surveillance, as well as in pressing problems of contemporary politics.

The art of writing throughout these chapters is also plural, creative and heterogenous with some chapters taking the form of a narrative or storytelling as a way to navigate the theory-practice relation, and others weaving theoretical framings through excerpts of empirical data. In showcasing these multiple forms, we valorise in academic writing the polycentricity, polyphony and transversality that emerge as main assumptions in the theoretical texts on which we base this transdisciplinary encounter (further analysed in Chapter 1). Though limited and exploratory, these chapters read together help us understand and study how security concerns and a sense of a threat are constituted in social relations and enacted in everyday spaces, in new and original ways.

Note

1 Supported *inter alia* by the British Academy; www.kcl.ac.uk/liep

References

Anthropology of Security Network (2014). EASA Anthropology of Security Network: About Us. Available at https://anthro-security.net/?page_id=2 [Accessed 22/02/2021]

Aradau, C., & Huysmans, J. (2014). Critical methods in International Relations: The politics of techniques, devices and acts. *European Journal of International Relations* 20(3), 596–619.

Aradau, C., Huysmans, J., Neal, A., & Voelkner, N. (Eds.). (2014). *Critical Security Methods: New frameworks for analysis.* London: Routledge.

Ben Jaffel H. (2019). *Anglo-European Intelligence Cooperation: Britain in Europe, Europe in Britain.* London: Routledge.

Bigo, D. (2006). Globalised (in)security: The field and the Ban-opticon. In N. Sakai & J. Solomon (eds) *Translation, Biopolitics, Colonial Difference.* Hong Kong: Hong Kong University Press.

Bigo, D. (2017). International political sociology: Rethinking the international through dynamics of power. In T. Basaran, D. Bigo, E.-P. Guiettet & R.B.J. Walker (eds) *International Political Sociology: Transversal Lines.* London: Routledge. 24–48.

Bigo, D. and E. Mc Cluskey (2017). What Is a PARIS Approach to (In) securitization? Political Anthropological Research for International Sociology. *The Oxford Handbook of International Security.*

Blommaert, J. (2005). *Discourse: A Critical Introduction.* Cambridge: Cambridge University Press.

Blommaert, J. (2007). On scope and depth in linguistic ethnography. *Journal of Sociolinguistics* 11(5), 682–688.

Blommaert, J. & B. Rampton (2011). Language & superdiversity. *Diversities* 13/2:1–21.

Blommaert, J. (2018). *Dialogues with Ethnography: Notes on classics, and how I read them.* Bristol: Multilingual Matters.

Charalambous, C., P. Charalambous, K. Khan & B. Rampton (2018). Security and language policy. In J. Tollefson & M. Pérez-Milans (eds) *The Oxford Handbook of Language Policy & Planning*. Oxford: OUP.

Collective, C. A. S. E. (2006). Critical approaches to security in Europe: A networked manifesto. *Security dialogue 37*(4), 443–487.

Friedman, R. (2015). Restorative Justice in Sierra Leone: Promises and Limitations. In *Evaluating Transitional Justice* (pp. 55–76). Palgrave Macmillan, London.

Geertz, C. (1973). *The Interpretation of Cultures: Selected essays*, Basic books.

Huysmans, J. (2014). *Security Unbound: Enacting Democratic Limits*, London: Routledge.

Jackson, P. T. (2008). Can Ethnographic Techniques Tell Us Distinctive Things About World Politics? *International Political Sociology 2*(1): 91–93.

Law, J. and J. Urry (2004). Enacting the social. *Economy and Society 33*(3): 390–410.

Mac Ginty, R. (2010). Hybrid peace: The interaction between top-down and bottom-up peace. *Security Dialogue 41*(4), 391–412.

Mac Ginty, R. (2014). Everyday peace: Bottom-up and local agency in conflict-affected societies. *Security Dialogue 45*(6), 548–564.

Mac Ginty, R., & Richmond, O. P. (2013). The local turn in peace building: A critical agenda for peace. *Third World Quarterly 34*(5), 763–783.

Magalhães, B. (2018). Obviously without foundation: Discretion and the identification of clearly abusive asylum applicants. *Security Dialogue 49*(5), 382–399.

Maguire, M., C. Frois, et al. (2014). *Anthropology of Security: Perspectives from the Frontline of Policing, Counter-terrorism and Border Control*. London: Pluto Press.

Maguire, M. (2019). *Spaces of Security: ethnographies of securityscapes, surveillance, and control*. NYU Press.

Montesinos Coleman, L., & Rosenow, D. (2016). Security (studies) and the limits of critique: Why we should think through struggle. *Critical Studies on Security 4*(2), 202–220.

Mc Cluskey, E. (2019). *From Righteousness To Far Right: An anthropological rethinking of critical security studies* (Vol. 2). Kingston: McGill-Queen's Press-MQUP.

Neal, A. W. (2019) *Security as Politics: Beyond the State of Exception*. Edinburgh: Edinburgh Unviersity Press.

Ochs, J. (2011). *Security and suspicion: An ethnography of everyday life in Israel*, University of Pennsylvania Press.

Ragazzi, F. (2017) 'Countering Terrorism and Radicalisation: Securitising Social Policy?', *Critical Social Policy* 37(2): 163–179.

Rampton, B. (2007). Neo-Hymesian linguistic ethnography in the United Kingdom. *Journal of Sociolinguistics* 11/5, 584–607.

Salter, M. B., & Mutlu, C. E. (Eds.). (2013). *Research Methods in Critical Security Studies: An introduction*. Routledge.

Tazzioli, M. (2019). *The Making Of Migration: The biopolitics of mobility at Europe's borders*. Sage.

Zembylas, M., Charalambous, C., & Charalambous, P. (2016). *Peace Education in a Conflict-Affected Society*. Cambridge University Press.

1 Researching (in)security as a lived experience: Setting the foundations for transdisciplinary dialogue

Emma Mc Cluskey, Ben Rampton, and Constadina Charalambous

This chapter sets out the collaboration that led to the transdisciplinary dialogue presented in this book. In a sense, this first chapter also acts as a sort of "how to" guide in doing transdisciplinary research, by documenting our own intellectual journeys, the challenges and the barriers we had to transcend, and the opportunities it created for theory and research practice. Indeed, we all begin with our own disciplinary training and baggage, and the sheer force of disciplinary habitus is not one which is easy to transcend, nor do we wish to. Our four-year project was just one attempt at building a transversal site for studying security, ethnography and discourse - in the vein of Bourdieu's "collective intellectual" or Latour's "methodological laboratory."

The chapter begins with a sketch of the origins of the *Language, (In)security & Everyday Practice* group (LIEP)[1] and the common interests and assumptions that bring its contributors together. But there are still a lot of important (and hopefully enriching) differences, so the text then offers two separate perspectives on our collaborative interest in everyday (in)securitisation: The first from International Political Sociology (IPS) and the second from linguistic ethnography. The final part of the chapter revisits the discussion in light of these differences, and reflects upon what it means to do transdisciplinary work around (in)security as a lived experience.

Language, (in)security and everyday practice: Speaking across disciplines

This volume builds on complementary developments in International Relations (IR) and sociolinguistics. In critical IR, recent years have seen a growing interest in the everyday, the vernacular, the local and the banal, extending beyond IR's traditional focus on the state and supra-state processes, exceptionality, and elite and authoritative actors (see Mc Cluskey, 2017). Meanwhile in sociolinguistics, the study of language and everyday communicative practice in changing social conditions is now starting to address the increasing (in)securitisation of ordinary life, incorporating this within its traditional interest in the relationship of language to class, ethnicity, gender, generation etc., in communities, schools, workplaces, clinics and so forth (Charalambous, 2017).

DOI: 10.4324/9781003080909-1

These two trajectories are now converging on (in)securitising discourses and institutions, on the practices of actors with different degrees of authority and influence, and on the lived experiences of people affected by official understandings. The LIEP network was set up to explore whether and how these two developments could be mutually enriching, generating perspectives on everyday (in)securitisation that they couldn't produce on their own.

The conversation started in 2014, and it was consolidated in 2016 with grants from the British Academy and King's College London for activities that have included two international colloquia, a short advanced interdisciplinary methods course, and two bibliographies (cited above). Our common interests were clear at a meeting of the *International Consortium on Language and Superdiversity* (www.incolas.eu), which situated language and communication in new conditions of transnationalism emerging from geopolitical transfigurations, in new technologies, and in the increased and diversified mobility of people across borders. The common ground not only covered substantive processes (migration, globalisation, diversity, (in)security, inequality, governmentality) but also reference points in social theory (Foucault, Bourdieu, Garfinkel, Goffman, etc.), and a shared appreciation of ethnography and anthropology as modalities of knowledge and knowing. In fact, we can bring out a number of areas of congruence through the comparison of a small selection of texts addressing language & superdiversity[2] on the one hand, and on the other, "the international" in IPS[3] – see Table 1.1.

That said, there are still a lot of obvious differences.[4] Discourse and politics may feature in both, but in sociolinguistics the former is absolutely central and the latter somewhat subsidiary, while in IR these emphases are reversed. Historically, they have also differed in the kinds of people and institutions they study: In one, elites and political, diplomatic and military processes and organisations; in the other, ordinary people in civil society, with violence and coercion hardly figuring. So they are coming from different directions to their meeting, bringing repertoires to the account of (in)security and everyday practice that are far from equal in their size and elaboration. Even so, both sides recognise that expertise always comes with blind spots and biases that can be illuminated by non-expert interlocutors, and that it is worth exploring the emerging effects – unison, polyphony or din – when our orchestrations of questions, theories, methods and data interact. So we should now turn to the two traditions most centrally involved in the encounter to hear what each brings to the table, starting with IPS and the approach it brings to the study of (in)security.

(In)security, the international and the transversal

The study of security has broadened significantly since the end of the Cold War and again post 9–11, both in the field of International Relations and beyond. Dominated for much of the twentieth century by a Cold War bipolarity, examining "security" in International Relations involved reading

Table 1.1 Comparing sociolinguistic studies of superdiversity and IPS studying the international

	Sociolinguistic studies of superdiversity	IPS approach of "the international"
Moving away from a view of society as orderly, organised in clear categories, and innovating to account for new processes	• "Rather than working with homogeneity, stability and boundedness as the starting assumptions, mobility, mixing, political dynamics and historical embedding are now central concerns in the study of languages, language groups and communication" (Blommaert & Rampton, 2011: 24) • "work on ideologies of language … denaturalises the idea that there are distinct languages, and that a proper language is bounded, pure and composed of structured sounds, grammar and vocabulary designed for referring to things" (ibid)	• an understanding of the international as merely a "level" above the "national" is rejected, moving away from the "territorial state" as the basic unit of analysis in international relations • there is a rejection of the traditional views of politics as organised "via an interstate system regulating power between territorial states … connected formally as a system of states via diplomatic agreements" (Bigo 2017: 27)
Keywords pointing to complex interconnections, not just the relations between clearly defined objects of analysis	• superdiversity • simultaneity • complexity • mixing/crossing/hybridisation • poly/pluri-lingualism • intersection • entanglement	• transversal • interconnections • hybridisation • multipositioning • dispersion/disjuncture • heterogeneity
Focusing on practices, processes and relations rather than communities	• "'Speech community' has been superseded by a more empirically anchored and differentiating vocabulary which includes 'communities of practice,' 'institutions' and 'networks' as the often mobile and flexible sites and links in which representations of group emerge, move and circulate." (Blommaert & Rampton, 2011: 25)	• "international, society, state exist as powerful symbolic representations, and performatives when they are called upon, but they are, in practice, a reconstruction of the fragmented and heterogeneous circulation of plural forms of power in a myriad of different fields, reduced to a specific range of 'levels' that try to synthetise and reduce the

(Continued)

16 Emma Mc Cluskey et al.

Table 1.1 (Continued)

	Sociolinguistic studies of superdiversity	IPS approach of "the international"
Attending both to centripetal and centrifugal forces	• "It is vital to remember just how far normativity (or 'ought-ness') reaches into semiosis and communication … There is considerable scope for variation in the norms that individuals orient to … normative expectations circulate through social networks that range very considerably in scale … All this necessarily complicates any claims we might want to make about the play of structure and agency … innovation on one dimension may be framed by stability at others …" (Blommaert & Rampton, 2011: 37) • Instead of language study's traditional assumptions of common ground and the prospects for achieving intersubjectivity, "non-shared knowledge grows in its potential significance for communicative processes" (ibid. p. 29)	complexity of the scales at work as well as the dynamics of passage between them" (Bigo 2017: 26) • a focus on change and struggle, the proliferation of borders, trajectories and relations stretching across transversal lines • "awareness of the many possible futures linked with an acceleration and a multiplication of lines and dots that are heterogeneous, and do not constitute geometrical figures distributing easily an inside and an outside" (Bigo 2017: 30) • "practices of actors are always simultaneously deployed in fields that have different dynamics. It is not their individual enactment which is important, but the set of relations and process in which they participate. Actors are plural and are always engaged in a multitude of games of different scales at the same moment, even if they may not be aware of it." (Bigo 2017: 36)
Historicity rejecting ahistorical notions, studying practices situated in time and space	• "Every aspect of the synchronically observable practice […] is historically loaded, so to speak, it drags with it its histories of use, abuse and evaluation. Thus, whenever we ethnographically investigate a synchronic	• "fields of power have boundaries moulded by their trajectories and very specific histories that cannot be resumed into major synthetic categories, such as economics, politics, communication, culture" (Bigo, 2017: 25)"This

(Continued)

Table 1.1 (Continued)

	Sociolinguistic studies of superdiversity	IPS approach of "the international"
	social act, we have to see it as the repository of a process of genesis, development, transformation. If we see it like this, we will see it in its sociocultural fullness, because we can then begin to understand the shared, conventional aspects of it, and see it as a moment of social and cultural transmission." (Blommaert & Rampton, 2011: 37)	requires also studying the practices in 'situation' both spatially and temporally, in order to avoid building transhistorical categories as 'the international community,' 'the state' or 'the governed' which results in speaking of them as if these categories were a person with intentions" (Bigo 2017: 31–32)

the canonical texts of realism and liberalism, and thinking in terms of security dilemmas, balance of power and geopolitics. Based on a particular reading of eighteenth century social contract theorists – Hobbes, Rousseau and Locke – the most dominant theory, theoretical "realism," considered human nature to be static and universal, a continuous struggle to gain more power at the expense of others and hence to render oneself more "secure" (most notably Jervis, 1978 and Mearsheimer, 1990). In this reading, security therefore also becomes universal, and securing oneself or one's collective group against dangerous or threatening others becomes the aim of communities if one wants to ensure survival.

The end of the Cold War however saw these theories largely deemed inadequate for understanding the new security landscape which was beginning to emerge. Barry Buzan's *People, States and Fear* was first to draw attention to the contradictions and inadequacies latent within the concept of "national security," and it argued that the logic of anarchy, which confirms the traditional context of security, imposes the condition that the state is automatically the referent object, that dynamics are relational and that competitive relations between states are thus both inevitable and inescapable (Buzan et al., 1998). Buzan's calls for International Security Studies to be moved away from the narrow domain of Strategic Studies were met with approval within a research group in Copenhagen, where the influential concept of "securitisation" was born. According to securitisation theory, an issue becomes securitised by virtue of a pronouncement by a securitising actor, enabling the issue to be moved from the ordinary day-to-day realm of democratic politics to the realm of exceptional politics and emergency measures (Buzan et al., 1998).

Around the same time and in continuous dialogue with researchers in Copenhagen, a more sociologically inclined critique of the way in which "security" was being analysed in the leading US journals emerged amongst researchers in the Francophone world. This had already led to the creation of the journal *Cultures et Conflits* in 1989 in Paris, in which sociologists, historians, anthropologists, and political scientists came together to put forward an alternative vision of the post-bipolar world (Bigo & Hermant, 1990). In addition to these constructivist moves, questions of culture and identity were seen to be significant for understandings of security, expanding the remit of security to conflict studies, nationalism studies and social and political theory (Burgess, 2010). The publication of the 2006 "case collective" – *Critical Approaches to Security in Europe: A Networked Manifesto* by scholars working within questions of security – was a watershed moment in articulating the cross fertilisation and disjunctures between these different strands and branches of scholarship.

Rather than focusing on the differences between various "schools" of thought, however, Bigo and Mc Cluskey (2017) have called for a more careful and closer inspection of the project of de-essentialising security, common to both approaches at the time. Indeed, a close reading of the 2006 case collective shows that what emanated from this collaboration was the desire to build an IPS that could unshackle studies on security from their disciplinary prisons. Its aim was to free IR scholars from the premises of a US political science, to emancipate sociologists from methodological nationalism, and to untether political theorists from abstraction and a history of ideas, re-rooting them back into contemporary problems (Bigo & Walker, 2007).

An IPS reading of security demonstrates that "security" cannot in fact be divided into different disciplinary objects and cannot therefore be subsumed by one theory of securitisation. The myriad of paradoxes, contradictions and heterogeneities contained in the notion of "security" reveals a panoply of different forms of disciplinary knowledge. Trying to locate a unifying principle or meta-narrative around "security" is always only, therefore, a search for a dominant position, which erases and invisibilises struggles, disputes and controversies. Bigo (2016) has gone further on this point, demonstrating that insecurity too cannot be reified or essentialised. Instead of two opposing sides, for Bigo, the relation between security and insecurity can only be conceived as a mobius strip – a metaphor which emphasises that one can never be certain what constitutes the content of security and not insecurity. What one person labels security, another can just as easily call coercion, violence, fear or indeed solidarity, privacy or freedom. For this reason, and to emphasise the consubstantiality of security and insecurity, it makes sense to speak only of (in) securitising practices and processes. In this sociological approach, analyses are thus oriented towards objectivising the logics of security which arise through the definitional struggles over (in)securitisation by diverse security professionals and experts (Balzacq et al., 2010).

A great deal of discussion within IPS, through looking at the practices of security professionals, focused on freedom of movement, mobility, migration and borders and how these practices are governed through a security framing and through practices of (in)securitisation (Côté-Boucher et al., 2014; Davidshofer et al., 2016). IPS scholars have also been successful in showing the way in which security logics and practices have encroached further on different spheres of social life. This study of seemingly more insignificant practices has gained momentum in work on "diffusing insecurities" (Huysmans, 2014). This process of diffusion characterises the shift which took place in global governance in the post-Cold-War period, moving from ideas of security as answering "threats" to notions of security as risk management, engendering the dispersal of security practices across a multiplicity of institutions far from high politics and statecraft. Different logics of risk, and the social and political implications of these rationalisations, have been examined mostly in relation to technologies of surveillance and big data (see Aradau et al., 2008; Amoore & De Goede, 2008; Aradau & Blanke, 2017), but also in various counter-radicalisation programmes with the specific aim of preventing people from becoming so-called "radicalised" (Ragazzi, 2017; Ragazzi et al., 2018; Heath-Kelly, 2013; Nguyen, this volume).

In studying everyday routines of bureaucrats, IPS scholars have also demonstrated the way in which security logics have permeated neighbouring fields. Beerli (2018), for example, has shown how the humanitarian space has witnessed the bureaucratisation and professionalisation of security in contemporary times. Similarly, within the fields of global health (Lakoff & Collier, 2008) and climate change (Dalby, 2013), logics of emergency, preparedness and prevention have focused on the implications of anticipatory logics and the way in which this has challenged traditional geopolitical assumptions. Beyond IPS, IR scholarship attempting to conceptualise the everyday lived experiences of subjects of security has been relatively limited. There are a few exceptions, notably those who use the terminology of "vernacular (in)security" to examine citizens' perceptions of threats at an "everyday level," juxtaposing this type of lay knowledge with that of elites (Vaughan Williams & Stevens, 2016).

A lively branch of anthropological scholarship, the "Critical anthropology of security" has, however, begun to engage more critically with the ways in which security practices operate at a local scale, demonstrating how new configurations of knowledge and power can manifest through a security framework (Goldstein et al., 2010; Maguire et al., 2014; Green & Zurawski, 2015). Scholars who have contributed towards this project use the term "securityscape" as a procreative formulation for conceiving security as "a hard-to-define spatio-temporal configuration that includes the affective and imaginary as well as the infrastructural and concrete" (Maguire, 2019: 12). These studies have been successful in firmly placing ethnography as central to the analysis of lived experiences of (in)security in various spatialized zones, be it migrant camps, airports or heavily policed neighbourhoods (Maguire, 2019; Maguire et al., 2014; Low, 2011).

In illuminating how practices of security operate in day-to-day life, these ethnographies have shown how the proliferation of security entities and practices by no means results in more security or safety, often in fact producing exactly the opposite (much akin to Bigo's "mobius strip"). For example, Juliana Ochs' ethnography of the second intifada in Jerusalem vividly captures how everyday security practices produce states of civilian alertness that maintain – rather than alleviate – feelings of insecurity, suspicion and violence. Similarly, Setha Low's (2003) research on gated communities in the United States encapsulates how residents felt constrained, both symbolically and materially, inside a structure which perpetuates their unease.

It is fair to say, however, that to date, there has only been rather limited dialogue and cross fertilisation between these different strands of scholarship, Anthropology of Security and IPS (see notably Bigo, 2014b). There is perhaps a danger again of retrenching disciplinary positions in the current publish or perish culture, with the incessant production of bounded knowledge often rewarded as expertise. One attempt at transcending fragmentation by discipline is the recent project and journal *Political Anthropological Research on International Social Sciences* (PARISS), which has argued for disrupting forms of bounded knowledge and makes the case for encouraging transversal social inquires, supporting flows rather than academic enclosures (see PARISS collective, 2020). It is precisely in this spirit of transdisciplinary collaboration in which we began our International Relations and sociolinguistics collaboration in 2015, with the focus on language, (in)security and everyday practice.

Let's now move to sociolinguistics and linguistic ethnography.

Linguistic ethnography

Linguistics is a huge field, and there are still somewhat structuralist schools within it where, as in traditional IR (Bigo, 2014b, 191), the "art of writing and its excellence is represented by a thin book." But battles around the emergence of sociolinguistics as a heterodox alternative took place in the 1970s, and since then, the field has flourished, using linguistics in the empirical study of communicative processes in a very wide range of domestic, recreational and institutional sites. In recent years, as Charalambous (2017) details, this has extended to processes that concern IR and IPS, with work emerging on asylum,[5] insecuritisation,[6] peace and conflict[7] and surveillance.[8] In relation to the educational domain in particular, there is increasing work on the impact of growing securitisation,[9] the positioning of undocumented migrants[10] and the effect of legacies of conflict.[11] These are all issues where sociolinguistics can gain a very great deal from IPS and the kind of interdisciplinary discussion supported within the Language (In)security & Everyday Practice group.

Within the broad field of sociolinguistics, LIEP researchers pursue linguistic ethnography (LE), which is linked to north American linguistic anthropology and is strongly influenced by Dell Hymes. In the 1960s, Hymes led a call for a de-colonising anthropology to "bring it all back home" to the study of US institutions and communities, and he criticised anthropology and the social sciences more generally for taking communication for granted, treating language simply as a transparent window on the social and cultural processes beyond it (1969). Instead, he insisted that language is organised in different genres, styles and ways of speaking that deserve to be studied in their own right, and he used the phrase "speech economy" to refer to the organisation of communicative resources and practices in different networks and institutions. More specifically, the idea of "speech economy" asserts (i) that some forms of communication are highly valued-&-rewarded while others get stigmatised or ignored; (ii) expertise and access to influential and prestigious styles and ways of speaking/writing is unevenly distributed across any population; and therefore, (iii) language and discourse play a central role in the production and legitimation of social relations, which can be extended, of course, to peace, conflict and (in)security.

As well as being widely accepted in north American linguistic anthropology, this agenda has been gathering momentum in British and European linguistic ethnography, and it informs LE's two fundamental tenets (Rampton, 2007; Rampton et al., 2015; Hymes, [1976] 1996, 87), which hold that:

i   the contexts for communication should be investigated rather than assumed. Meaning takes shape within specific social relations, interactional histories and institutional regimes, produced and construed by agents with expectations and repertoires that have to be grasped ethnographically;
ii analysis of the internal organisation of verbal (and other kinds of semiotic) data is essential to understanding its significance and position in the world. Meaning is far more than just the "expression of ideas," and biography, identifications, stance and nuance are extensively signalled in the semiotic, textual and linguistic fine-grain.

When social scientists turn from theory and abstraction to the empirical data of everyday life, they often conceive of this as "messy" or "fluid." This is also often the starting point for linguistic ethnographers, but as LE's second tenet implies, one of the central challenges is to move past first impressions of "messiness" and uncover the intricately structured orchestration with which people continuously produce themselves and the lives of others. The challenge of modelling these micro-structuration processes is sufficient in itself for some traditions (e.g. Conversation Analysis, at least in its first generation). But others try to trace and explain the connections between "small-scale interactions" and "large-scale sociological effects" (Jacquemet, 2011: 475), addressing John Gumperz's call for a "dynamic view of social environments where history, economic forces and interactive processes ... combine to create or to eliminate social distinctions" (1982: 29).

To understand how the fine-grain of communicative interaction plays in the politics of everyday life, how it contributes to the ratification or refusal of identities, institutions, ideologies etc., including relations of (in)security, linguistic ethnography draws on four sets of resources:

a   *linguistics & discourse analysis* provide a provisional view of the communicative affordances of the linguistic resources that participants draw on in communication ("provisional" because contextual contingencies always affect the meaning of a word or sentence, potentially undermining its conventional significance);
b   *Goffman* and *conversation analysis* provide frameworks and procedures for investigating situated encounters. More specifically, they help us to see:
    • the ongoing, sequential construction of "local architectures of intersubjectivity" as one speaker follows another in sequences of turns at talk, building up (what looks like) a common line of understanding
    • the rituals and moral accountabilities permeating the use of semiotic forms and strategies, and the ways in which people handle the relationship between the normal and exceptional
    • the shifting spatio-temporal distribution of attention and involvement in situations of physical co-presence – the ways in which people attend to the different people and things around them with different degrees of intensity
c   *ethnography* provides
    • a sense of the stability, status and socio-symbolic resonance that linguistic forms, rhetorical strategies and semiotic materials have in different social networks beyond the encounter-on-hand
    • an idea of how and where a practice, genre or encounter fits into longer and broader biographies, institutions and histories
    • a sense of the personal and cultural experiences, perspectives and ideologies that participants bring to interactions, and take away from them
d   *other public and academic discourses* provide purpose and relevance for the analysis (which can of course include critical IR and PCS), as well as a broader picture of the environment where the study is sited.[12]

To increase the interdisciplinary intelligibility of this quest, sociolinguists can point to the fact that figures like Bourdieu and Giddens knew a lot about this kind of linguistics. Indeed, they can turn to Foucault's governmentality and microphysics of power, claiming to possess an empirical apparatus that really can "track force relations at the molecular level, as they flow through a multitude of human technologies, in all the practices, arenas and spaces where programmes for the administration of others intersect with techniques for the administration of ourselves" (Rose, 1999: 3–5; Foucault, 1978/2003: 229–245; Rampton et al., 2015; Borba, 2015).

Of course claims of this kind require justification, and here we can only sketch some tried-&-tested concepts that lead in this direction,[13] positioning linguistics as a set of sensitising micro-ethnographic resources that can build an account of the multiple frames and processes coming together in any communicative activity. It would take a full study to show properly what this kind of conceptual *instrumentarium* can do and the chapters in this volume provide some examples of how we can use these resources for the study of processes, relations and interactions affected by security concerns (for example Rampton & Eley's use of Goffman to study surveillance through an interactional perspective, and Charalambous et al.'s use of ethnography and interactional discourse analysis to investigate the concept of everyday peace). But for the purposes of this chapter, we will illustrate four basic concepts by referring to Section 2 of Jan Blommaert's (2005) account of interviews in the Belgian asylum procedure. In his paper "Bourdieu the ethnographer: The ethnographic grounding of habitus and voice,"[14] Blommaert combines ethnography and interactional discourse analysis in a detailed description of how the talk between official and asylum-seeker produces a rejection of the latter's application, and in what follows we will use examples from this work to illustrate some basic sociolinguistic concepts. We will also make references in footnotes to how these concepts have been mobilised throughout the different chapters.

The first concept is *inferencing* – the interpretive work that individuals perform when they construe the significance of an utterance, an action or an object by matching it against their expectations of what's coming up, against their personal experience or what they've heard or read, against their perceptions of the material setting and so forth.[15] Words, phrases and sentences always denote more than just their literal meaning or dictionary definition, and in this sense they're always *indexical*, which means that they project and evoke images, ideologies and associations that are interpreted through the filter of the participants' experience and expectations as well.[16] There is no communication independent of our more general assumptions about the world, and so we can say that ideology is right at the heart of the most instantaneous and routine sense-making. In the paper on Belgian asylum interviews, Blommaert focuses on the interpretations of the officials listening to the applicants' narratives. There are of course many ways of hearing and appreciating stories, but in this setting, "the applicant's claim is 'framed' in terms of … plausibility criteria" and it is these that guide the interviewer's inferences about the story. These inferences produce "on-the-spot decisions about which parts of the performed narrative 'belong' to the range of factuality and which parts are redundant" (2005: 231–2), and these then have an impact on how the overall narrative is perceived and evaluated.

Second, scaling up to people actually exchanging utterances, there is the principle of *adjacency* – what someone says in a conversation is normally constrained by what's just been said, and in turn, it sets up a rather narrow range of options for the next speaker.[17] So if you ask someone a question, you're positioning them to produce either an answer or a disclaimer (sorry I don't know); make invitation and they'll need to accept or decline; complain and you're pushing for an apology or a rebuttal. Of course it gets more complicated than that, but even so, we can see how this speaks to Foucault's claim that "a relationship of power ... is a mode of action which ... acts upon the actions of others: An action upon an action, on existing actions or on those which may arise in the present or future" (1982: 220). In the asylum paper, Blommaert cites interactional exchanges in which the officials respond to the applicants' accounts and utterances with "supportive and collaborative expressions of conversational understanding" (2005: 232). But as we have seen, they listen with a particular set of assessment criteria in mind, and in fact their questions, comments and feedback steer asylum applicants towards the elaboration of some parts of their narrative and not others, tangibly co-constructing the accounts in doing so.

Third, scaling up a little further, we can focus on communicative *genres*, which are sets of conventionalised expectations about recognisably distinctive types of activity – a story-telling, an argument, a sales transaction, a committee meeting, etc.[18] These generic expectations include a sense of the goals and possible tasks on hand, the roles and relationships typically involved, the ways the activity is organised, and the kinds of resources suited to carrying it out. Genres provide guidelines for how to act from one moment to the next, but they're also the building blocks of institutions – think of lessons, detentions and assemblies in a school, or consultations and ward rounds in a hospital. At the same time, when people interact together, there is plenty of scope for failures in coordination. Knowledge and expertise in different genres is very unevenly spread among individuals and across social groups, and properly genred performance is a central concern in socialisation throughout the lifespan, whether this involves learning to "behave nicely at the dinner table" or to "carry out an appraisal interview." There is obviously also a lot of political dispute about genres. In Blommaert's study, the interview itself is one genre in play, orienting the participants to who should do what, when, how and why, but the analysis focuses more closely on the specific (sub)genre/type of narrative promoted within the asylum procedure: "the authorities appear to use a particular rational, linear, detailed and 'factually' coherent narrative as a model for the applicants' performance. Such models are implicitly sketched in guidelines for interviewers" (2005: 229), and this feeds through into on-the-spot inferencing and the development of the talk in the ways outlined above.

Lastly, there are *text trajectories,* involving the mobility of material signs and textual objects.[19] The focus here is on the networks that signs and texts travel through, the ways that they do and don't get changed as they get taken up in different settings, and the different types of here-&-now activity that all this entails: on the one hand, '*en*textualisation', selecting material from everything that's going on in a particular situation and turning it into textual 'projectiles' which have some hope of travelling into subsequent settings; on the other, '*re*contextualisation,' making sense of textual objects that have come through into the situated present.[20] All this can be applied, for example, to the description of political voice. In the first instance, we might define '*voice*' as an individual's communicative power and effectiveness within the here-&-now of specific events. But beyond this, the crucial issue is whether and how their contribution is remembered and/or recorded and subsequently reproduced in other arenas, travelling through networks and circuits that may vary in their scale – in their spatial scope, temporal durability and social reach. In the asylum paper, Blommaert describes entextualisation happening when "the answers of the applicant are immediately converted into summaries, in Dutch or French, word-processed on a computer-generated standard form, often already incorporating legal-categorizing terminology" (2005: 230). This is selective, and "what gets thrown out ... are things that are hard to understand interactionally ... Names of people, objects and places, but also particular anecdotes and longish, detailed subnarratives on the situation in the home country are common victims of such erasures" (p. 232). These interactional procedures are themselves geared to the next step of the procedure, the bureaucratic text trajectory (p. 231), and this amounts to the "insertion of the story in a discursive regime over which the applicant has no control. The applicant has effectively lost his or her voice in the process" (p. 232). His or her "story no longer develops on the basis of situated understandings alone, but becomes a 'case' ascribed to a particular individual" (p. 231). [21]

Processes of the kind sketched here are usually all going on at the same time – people make inferences, steering and steered by their interlocutors' adjacent actions, guided by generic expectations, alert to a material text's origins and prospects, as Blommaert's case study illustrates. To understand how communicative interaction contributes to the ratification or refusal of identities, institutions, ideologies, etc., we need to investigate the interplay of these processes, and as in any ethnographic project, this presents the analyst with difficult choices about focus and emphasis. Nevertheless, as Blommaert insists, this provides a *systemic* account, showing how "larger patterns are deployed and played out during concrete steps in the [asylum] procedure," "on-the-spot" from one moment to the next (2005: 229). A great many asylum applications are rejected, but this isn't unintelligibly messy and it isn't just the outcome of "misunderstandings between applicant and interviewer" (p. 229). Although he could have aligned his account with governmentality, Blommaert invokes "habitus" to characterise the routinized institutional performance of the official interviewers, unpacking the "black box" left by Bourdieu. In Blommaert's concluding formulation: "[t]here is no abstract institutional machinery involved here, no faceless technical apparatus testing and clinically observing. What we see is *conversational involvement* enacted in such a way that it enables institutional judgement to proceed afterwards on the basis of a particular, genred and regimented version of the story" (2005: 233).

With this sketch of the descriptive and theoretical scope of ethnographic sociolinguistics in place, it is worth turning briefly to sociolinguistic approaches to the "everyday."

In the 1970s, a formative period for contemporary sociolinguistics, everyday speech was championed as a defining interest, counter-posed to the standard languages promoted in literacy and education. In this context, "everyday" equated with vernacular, and it meant "non-standard', "non-elite," "non-prestigious," referring to people, groups and environments where mainstream symbolic, cultural and material resources were (relatively) limited. At roughly the same time, in a more interactionist line of work influenced by figures like Goffman and Garfinkel, the "everyday" referred to a socio-cognitive perception or attitude – an orientation to the "normal" in acts, events or people, perceiving them as routine and conventional rather than exceptional (terrifying, amazing, exciting, etc.). The normal and exceptional were, though, seen as mutually defining (≈ Bigo's Möbius strip?), and there has been considerable interest in the ways in which our socio-cognitive orientation to routine can be at least temporarily de-stabilised, as in Garfinkel's (1967) breaching experiments. Indeed, in Goffman's work (e.g. 1971, 1974), there is a very elaborate account of the actions and interpretative frames with which people try to produce, manage and respond to non-normal activity and events, whether these involve threats and offences, play, games and art, new arrivals or departures, etc.[22]

These two traditions and meanings – everyday-as-vernacular (⇔ resources) and everyday-as-normal (⇔ socio-cognitive orientation) – shouldn't be conflated, and they can each be an important independent focus for analysis within the same site. We get conduct that is regarded as normal/conventional in elite environments, just as we find acts treated as exceptional in vernacular domains. Rather than tying the everyday to one or other of these meanings (or both), it makes more sense to equate the everyday with a third sense, "lived experience," which actually encompasses the other two. The everyday-as-lived-experience happens to everyone everywhere, inside as well as outside elites, regardless of their resources, and having your sense of normality disturbed by exceptional events is part of life for most people. Lived experience is also often seen as the central concern in ethnography, setting it apart from research that gives overwhelming or exclusive priority to theory and abstraction. Linguistic ethnography can be seen as a specialisation within this, treating the everyday as situated communicative practice, whatever its environment or orientation. There are traditions in which these different senses of "everyday" are merged – De Certeau (1984), for example, talks as if situated practice only occurred among non-elite people (an idea flatly contradicted by Bigo's research on everyday practice among security professionals). But differentiating them is likely to produce an account of insecuritisation-as-an-intensifying-apprehension-of-vulnerability, situated in communicative practice across a range of social domains, that is descriptively richer and more theoretically generative. Or at least, that's the aspiration.

Working at the interface: Language, reflexivity and lived experience

The historical trajectories, internal struggles and external links sketched in the accounts of IPS and linguistic ethnography in Sections 2 and 3 have produced a potentially fertile intellectual space for collaboration on the pressing issue of (in)securitisation. These trajectories converge in an ontological commitment to the everyday as lived experience, where language, semiosis, discourse and communicative practice play a constitutive part, and their epistemological alignment with ethnography also brings empirical discipline to the question of reflexivity, making it rather more than the self-flagellation to which researchers sometimes fall prey.[23] Reflection on the assumptions, biases and baggage that one brings to the field is an indispensable first step, but with micro-ethnographic analysis, we can trace the ways in which the research encounter is itself shaped by the researcher's positionality. A white British woman studying Palestinian refugees in Morocco, for example, carries a multiplicity of subjectivities and could be a foreign mercenary, an expert, an object of sexual harassment, a mother, a fellow scholar or fellow member of a cosmopolitan elite. But with an attentive ethnographic ear, we can follow the shifts between these possibilities, as well as the activation of positional relations that hadn't been unanticipated.

As importantly, this type of reflexivity extends to how we interact and collaborate with each other. As scholars we are always positioned and always constrained, to some extent, by the common sense of our research communities and disciplines. A practical, epistemic reflexivity recognises this and objectivises it. That's why working as a collective to overcome disciplinary boundaries is important – we can only rely on others to point out our assumptions, our doxas and all the various bits of baggage we've brought along with us. Nobody can "be reflexive" on their own. So this volume is very much part of our collective reflexive endeavour, and it is inevitably somewhat open-ended and heteroglossic. In a similar vein to Fassin's (2017) idea of "Public Ethnography," encounters with various "publics," and the misunderstandings and alternative interpretations that these produce, are as much a part of our transdisciplinary venture as conducting fieldwork and analysing data.

And what actually happens when we try to bring these different traditions closer in particular studies and arguments? Without downplaying the differences and potential incompatibilities in the emphases, interests and objects of analysis that characterise IPS and LE, what lines of enquiry emerge from their interaction, and what can this actually contribute to an understanding of (in)securitisation? The following chapters present some of the

28 *Emma Mc Cluskey et al.*

research which has been growing in the dialogic space flagged by LIEP, attempting to transcend strict disciplinary boundaries in the effort to produce better accounts of (in)securitisation as lived experience affected by war and peacebuilding, nationalism, extremism, racism and surveillance.

Notes

1 The core contributors to this have been Constadina Charalambous, Panayiota Charalambous, Louise Eley, Kamran Khan, Ben Rampton, Lavanya Sankaran (sociolinguistics) and Didier Bigo, Vivienne Jabri, Rebekka Friedman, Emma Mc Cluskey and Maria O'Reilly (IR).
2 Blommaert & Rampton, 2011; Arnaut, 2012; Karrebæk & Charalambous, 2018; Blommaert & Rampton, 2011.
3 Bigo, 2006, 2017; Bigo & Mc Cluskey, 2017.
4 Indeed, as the commonalities in Table 1.1 are shared with a lot of other traditions in contemporary social science, neither can we claim that in their similarities they are uniquely matched.
5 E.g. Maryns & Blommaert, 2001; Maryns, 2006
6 E.g. Khan, 2017.
7 E.g. Footit & Kelly (eds.) 2012; Liddicoat, 2008.
8 E.g. Garcia Sanchez, 2014; Rampton et al., 2015; Jones, 2017.
9 E.g. Zakharia & Bishop, 2013.
10 E.g. Gallo, 2014.
11 E.g. Charalambous et al., 2018.
12 Training in linguistic ethnography is available at the annual five-day summer school in *Ethnography Language & Communication* at King's, and there are overviews in e.g. Rampton et al., 2015 and Tusting (ed.) ftc.
13 Rampton and Charalambous, 2015 (2014: section 2) for an elaboration of each of these. For introductions to a much larger array of concepts relevant to this approach, see Duranti, 2001 and Ahearn, 2012.
14 For further sociolinguistic work on refugee and asylum procedures, see e.g. Blommaert, 2009; Maryns, 2006; Jacquemet 2005, 2011.
15 See Gumperz, 2001.
16 See Hanks, 2001; in this volume see Chapter 3 on the indexical associations of the Turkish language in the Greek-Cypriot context.
17 In this volume see Chapters 7 and 8 for practical examples of how principles of adjacency function in relations of surveillance.
18 Hanks, 1987; Bauman, 2001.
19 Blommaert, 2005; Kell, 2015; Maybin, 2017; Bauman & Briggs, 1990; Silverstein & Urban, 1996; Agha & Wortham, 2005.
20 In Chapter 6, Nguyen shows how the ECE policy was recontextualised in different settings.
21 In Chapter 4, Summa and Puh show through their empirical work in Bosnia Herzegovina and Croatia, ways of conceiving silence as *not* the absence of voice.
22 In Chapter 3, Goffman's notion of technical redoing is used to describe the interactional processes through which the participants navigated the discourses associated with Turkish language by treating it as mostly a classroom exercise.
23 Cf. Bourdieu & Wacquant, 1989: 19: "To proclaim 'I am a bourgeois intellectual, I am a slimy rat!' is devoid of any meaning. But to say 'I am an assistant-professor at Grenoble and I am speaking to a Parisian professor' is to force oneself to ask whether it is not the relation between these two positions that is speaking through my mouth."

References

Agha, A. & Wortham, S. (eds) 2005. Discourse across speech events. *Special Issue of Journal of Linguistic Anthropology. 15/1*.

Ahearn, L. (2012). *Living Language: An Introduction to Linguistic Anthropology*. Malden MA: Wiley-Blackwell.

Amoore, L. & M. De Goede (2008). *Risk and the War on Terror*. Routledge.

Aradau, C. (2004). Security and the democratic scene: Desecuritization and emancipation. *Journal of International Relations and Development* 7(4), 388–413.

Aradau, C. & T. Blanke (2017). "Politics of prediction: Security and the time/space of governmentality in the age of big data." *European Journal of Social Theory* 20(3): 373–391.

Aradau, C., L. Lobo-Guerrero, et al. (2008). *Security, Technologies of Risk, and the Political: Guest Editors' Introduction*. Los Angeles, CA: Sage Publications Sage CA.

Arnaut, K. (2012) Super-diversity: elements of an emerging perspective. *Diversities 14*.

Balzacq, T., T. Basaran, et al. (2010). Security practices. *International Studies Encyclopedia online 18*.

Basaran, T., D. Bigo, et al. (2016). Transversal lines. *International Political Sociology: Transversal Lines 1*.

Bauman, R. & Briggs, C. (1990). Poetics and performance as critical perspectives on language and social life. *Annual Review of Anthropology 19*: 59–88.

Bauman, R. (2001). Genre. In A. Duranti (ed.) *Key Terms in Language & Culture* (pp. 79–82). Oxford: Blackwell.

Beerli, M. J. (2018). Saving the saviors: Security practices and professional struggles in the humanitarian space. *International Political Sociology* 12(1): 70–87.

Bigo, D. (2014). The (in) securitization practices of the three universes of EU border control: Military/Navy–border guards/police–database analysts. *Security Dialogue* 45(3): 209–225.

Bigo, D. (2014b). Afterword: Security – Encounters, misunderstanding and possible collaborations. In Maguire, M., C. Frois, et al. (2014). *Anthropology of Security: Perspectives from the Frontline of Policing, Counter-terrorism and Border Control* (pp. 189–205). London: Pluto Press.

Bigo, D. (2006). Globalised (in)security: The field and the Ban-opticon. In N. Sakai & J. Solomon (eds) *Translation, Biopolitics, Colonial Difference*. Hong Kong: Hong Kong University Press.

Bigo, D. (2016). The Moebius strip of national and world security. Available at: http://explosivepolitics. com/ blog/ the- mobius- strip- of- national- and- world- security. [Accessed 20/4/2020].

Bigo, D. (2017). International political sociology: Rethinking the international through dynamics of power. In T. Basaran, D. Bigo, E.-P. Guiettet & R.B.J. Walker (eds) *International Political Sociology: Transversal Lines* (pp. 24–48). London: Routledge.

Bigo, D. & Hermant, D.. (1990). La prolongation des conflits: introduction. *Cultures et Conflits*, 1(1): 2– 15.

Bigo, D. & Mc Cluskey, E. (2017). What Is a PARIS Approach to (In) securitization? Political Anthropological Research for International Sociology. *The Oxford Handbook of International Security*.

Bigo, D. & Walker, R. B. (2007). Political sociology and the problem of the international. *Millennium* 35(3): 725–739.

Blommaert, J. & Rampton, B. (2011). Language & superdiversity. *Diversities 13/2*: 1–21
Blommaert, J. (2005). *Discourse: A Critical Introduction*. Cambridge: Cambridge University Press.
Blommaert, J. (2005b). Bourdieu the ethnographer: The ethnographic grounding of habitus and voice. *The Translator. 11/2*: 219–236. Also at academia.edu.
Blommaert, J. (2009). Language, asylum and the national order. *Current Anthropology. 50/4*: 415–425.
Borba, R. (2017) 'The semiotic politics of affect in the Brazilian political crisis', in *Working Papers in Urban Language & Literacies #228*, 1–19.
Borba, R. (2015). How an individual becomes a subject: Discourse, interaction & subjectification at a Brazilian gender identity clinic. *Working Papers in Urban Language & Literacies 163*. At academia.edu.
Bourdieu, P. & Wacquant, L. (1989). For a socio-analysis of intellectuals: On Homo Academicus *Berkeley Journal of Sociology 34*: 1–29.
Burgess, J. P. (Ed). (2010). *Handbook of new security studies*. London: Routledge.
Buzan, B. , Wæver, O. , & De Wilde, J. (1998). *Security: A new framework for analysis*. Lynne Rienner Publishers.
Charalambous, C., Charalambous, P., Khan, K. & Rampton, B. (2018). Security and language policy. In J. Tollefson & M. Pérez-Milans (eds) *The Oxford Handbook of Language Policy & Planning* (pp. 633–653). Oxford: OUP. Also in *Working Papers in Urban Language & Literacies* # 177 (2015) at academia.edu.
Charalambous, P. (2017). *Sociolinguistics and security: A bibliography*. At www.kcl.ac.uk/liep
Côté-Boucher, K., F. Infantino, et al. (2014). Border security as practice: An agenda for research. *Security Dialogue 45*(3): 195–208.
Dalby, S. (2013). Biopolitics and climate security in the Anthropocene. *Geoforum 49*: 184–192.
Davidshofer, S., J. Jeandesboz, et al. (2016). Technology and security practices: Situating the technological imperative.
De Certeau, M. (1984) *The Practice of Everyday Life* (trans. S.F. Rendall) (Berkley and Los Angeles (CA), London: University of California Press).
De Certeau, M. (1984). *The Practice of Everyday Life*. Berkeley: University of California Press.
Duranti, A. (ed) (2001). *Key Terms in Language & Culture*. Oxford: Blackwell.
Fassin, D. (ed) (2017). *If Truth be Told: The Politics of Public Ethnography*. Durham NC: Duke University Press.
Footitt, H., & Kelly, M. (Eds). (2012). *Languages at war: Policies and practices of language contacts in conflict*. Palgrave Macmillan.
Foucault, M. (1980/2003) 'Questions of method', in P. Rabinow and N. Rose (eds) *The Essential Foucault: Selections from Essential Works of Foucault 1954–1984* (pp. 246–258) (New York: The New Press).
Foucault, M. (1978/2003). Governmentality. In P. Rabinow and N. Rose (eds) *The Essential Foucault: Selections from Essential Works of Foucault 1954–1984* (pp. 229–245). New York: The New Press.
Foucault, M. (1980/2003). Questions of method. In P. Rabinow and N. Rose (eds) *The Essential Foucault: Selections from Essential Works of Foucault 1954–1984* (pp. 246–258). New York: The New Press.

Gallo, S. (2014). The Effects of Gendered Immigration Enforcement on Middle Childhood and Schooling. *American Educational Research Journal. 51*, No. 3, pp. 473–504.

Garcia Sanchez, I. M. (2014). *Language and Muslim Immigrant Childhoods: The Politics of Belonging*. Malden, MA, Wiley-Blackwell.

Garfinkel, H. (1967) *Studies in Ethnomethodology*. Oxford: Blackwell.

Geertz, C. (1973). *The Interpretation of Cultures: Selected essays*. Basic Books.

Goffman, E. (1971) *Relations in Public: Microstudies of the Public Order*. New York: Harper & Row.

Goffman, E. 1974. *Frame Analysis*. Harmondsworth: Penguin

Goldstein, D. M., Albro, R., et al. (2010). Toward a critical anthropology of security. *Current Anthropology 51*(4): 000-000.

Green, N. & Zurawski, N. (2015) Surveillance and Ethnography: Researching Surveillance as Everyday Life, in *Surveillance & Society 13/1*: 27–43.

Gumperz, J. (1982). *Discourse Strategies*. Cambridge: CUP.

Gumperz, J. (2001). Inference. In A. Duranti (ed) *Key Terms in Language & Culture*. Oxford: Blackwell. 126–128.

Hanks, W. (1987). Discourse genres as a theory of practice. *American Ethnologist. 14/4*: 668–692.

Hanks, W. (2001). Indexicality. In A. Duranti (ed) *Key Terms in Language & Culture*. Oxford: Blackwell. 119–121.

Heath-Kelly, C. (2013). Counter-terrorism and the counterfactual: Producing the 'radicalisation'discourse and the UK PREVENT strategy. *The British Journal of Politics and International Relations, 15*(3), 394–415.

Huysmans, J. (2014). *Security Unbound: Enacting Democratic Limits*. London: Routledge.

Hymes, D. (1969). The use of anthropology: Critical, political, personal. In D. Hymes (ed) *Reinventing Anthropology* (pp. 3–82). Ann Arbor: University of Michigan Press.

Hymes, D.(1996). *Ethnography; Linguistics, Narrative Inequality: Toward an Understanding of Voice*. London: Taylor and Francis.

Jacquemet, M. (2005a). The registration interview: Restricting refugees' narrative performances. In M. Baynham & A. De Fina (eds) *Dislocations/Relocations: Narratives of Displacement* (pp. 197–220). Manchester: St Jerome.

Jacquemet, M. (2011). Crosstalk 2.0: Asylum and communicative breakdown. In Auer & Roberts (eds) 475–498.

Jervis, R. (1978). Cooperation under the security dilemma. *World Politics: A Quarterly Journal of International Relations*, 167–214.

Jones, R. (2017). Surveillant landscapes. *Linguistic Landscape 3/2*: 150–187.

Karrebæk, M. & C. Charalambous (2018). Superdiversity and linguistic ethnography: Researching people and language in motion. *Working Papers in Urban Language & Literacies # 212*. At academia.edu.

Kell, C. (2015). Ariadne's thread: Literacy, scale and meaning making across space and time. In C. Stroud & M. Prinsloo (eds) *Language, Literacy & Diversity: Moving Words* (pp. 72–91). London: Routledge. Also in *Working Papers in Urban Language & Literacies # 118* (2013) at academia.edu.

Khan, K. (2017). Citizenship, securitisation and suspicion in UK ESOL policy. In K. Arnaut, M. Karrebæk, M. Spotti & J. Blommaert (eds) *Engaging Superdiversity* (pp. 303–320). Bristol: Multilingual Matters.

Kitis, E. D. & T. M. Milani (2015) The performativity of the body: Turbulent spaces in Greece, in *Linguistic Landscape* 1/3: 268–290.

Lakoff, A. & Collier, S. J. (2008). *Biosecurity interventions: global health & security in question*, Columbia University Press.

Leonardsson, H., & Rudd, G. (2015). The 'local turn'in peacebuilding: A literature review of effective and emancipatory local peacebuilding. *Third World Quarterly* 36(5), 825–839.

Liddicoat, A. (2008). Language planning and questions of national security: An overview of planning approaches. *Current Issues in Language Planning* 9(2), 129–153.

Low, S. M. (2003). *Behind the gates: the new American dream--searching for security in America*. New York: Routledge.

Low, S. M. (2011). Claiming space for an engaged anthropology: spatial inequality and social exclusion. *American anthropologist* 113(3), 389–407.

Lyon, D. (2009). Surveillance, power and everyday life. In C. Avgerou, R. Mansell, D. Quah & R. Silverstone (eds) *The Oxford Handbook of Information and Communication Technologies*. Oxford: OUP.

Mac Ginty, R. (2010). Hybrid peace: The interaction between top-down and bottom-up peace. *Security Dialogue* 41(4), 391–412.

Mac Ginty, R. (2014). Everyday peace: Bottom-up and local agency in conflict-affected societies. *Security Dialogue* 45(6), 548–564.

Mac Ginty, R., & Richmond, O. P. (2013). The local turn in peace building: A critical agenda for peace. *Third World Quarterly* 34(5), 763–783.

Maguire, M., C. Frois, et al. (2014). *Anthropology of Security: Perspectives from the Frontline of Policing, Counter-terrorism and Border Control*. London: Pluto Press.

Maguire, M. (2019). *Spaces of security: ethnographies of securityscapes, surveillance, and control*. New York: NYU Press.

Maryns, K. & Blommaert, J. (2001). Stylistic and thematic shifting as a narrative resource: Assessing asylum seekers' repertoires. *Multilingua 20-1*/61–84.

Maryns, K. (2006). *The Asylum Speaker: Language in the Belgian Asylum Procedure*. Manchester: St Jerome.

Maybin, J. (2017). Textual trajectories: Theoretical roots and institutional consequences. *Text & Talk 37/4*:415–435.

Mearsheimer, J. J. (1990). Back to the future: Instability in Europe after the Cold War. *International Security* 15(1), 5–56.

Mc Cluskey, E. (2017). *Everyday (in)security: A bibliography*. At www.kcl.ac.uk/liep.

PARISS collective (2020). The Art of Writing Social Sciences: Disrupting the Current Politics of Style. *Political Anthropological Research on International Social Sciences (PARISS)* 1(1), 9–38.

Pennycook, A. (2010) *Language as a Local Practice*. Abingdon: Routledge.

Ragazzi, F. (2017) Countering Terrorism and Radicalisation: Securitising Social Policy?. *Critical Social Policy* 37(2): 163–179.

Ragazzi, F., Davidshofer, S., Perret, S., & Tawfik, A. (2018). Les effets de la lutte contre le terrorisme et la radicalisation sur les populations musulmanes en France. *Paris, Rapport du Centre d'étude sur les conflits*.

Rampton, B. (2007). Neo-Hymesian linguistic ethnography in the United Kingdom. *Journal of Sociolinguistics* 11/5: 584–607.

Rampton, B. (2016). Foucault, Gumperz and governmentality: Interaction, power and subjectivity in the twenty-first century. In N. Coupland (ed) *Sociolinguistics:*

Theoretical Debates (pp. 303–328). Cambridge: CUP. Also in *Working Papers in Urban Language & Literacies* # 136 on academia.edu.

Rampton, B. & Charalambous, C. (2015). Breaking Classroom Silences in London & Nicosia. *Working Papers in Urban Language and Literacies*, Paper 116. At academia.edu.

Rampton, B. & Charalambous, C. (2016). Breaking Classroom Silences: A View From Linguistic Ethnography. *Language and Intercultural Communication 16*(1), 4–21.

Rampton, B., Maybin, J. & Roberts, C. (2015). Theory and method in linguistic ethnography. In J. Snell, S. Shaw & F. Copland (eds) *Linguistic Ethnography: Interdisciplinary Explorations* (pp. 14–50). Palgrave Advances Series. A version is also available at: *Working Papers in Urban Language and Literacies.* 125 (2014).

Rampton, B., Maybin, J. & Roberts, C. (2015). Theory and method in linguistic ethnography. In J. Snell, S. Shaw & F. Copland (eds) 2015. *Linguistic Ethnography: Interdisciplinary Explorations* (pp. 14–50). Basingstoke: Palgrave Macmillan. (also 2014 in *Working Papers in Urban Language & Literacies* # 125 on academia.edu).

Rose, N. (1999). *The Power of Freedom*. Cambridge: CUP.

Scollon, R. & Scollon, S.W. (2003) *Discourses in Place: Language in the Material World* (London: Routledge).

Silverstein, M. & Urban, G. (eds) (1996). *Natural Histories of Discourse.* Chicago: University of Chicago Press.

Vaughan-Williams, Nick & Daniel Stevens (2016). Vernacular theories of everyday (in) security: The disruptive potential of non-elite knowledge. *Security Dialogue* 47(1), 40–58.

Zakharia, Z. & Bishop, L. M. (2013). Towards positive peace through bilingual community education: language efforts of Arabic-speaking communities in New York. In O. Garcia, Z. Zakharia & B. Otcu. *Bilingual community education and multilingualism: beyond heritage languages in a global city.* 169–189.

Zembylas, M., Charalambous, C., & Charalambous, P. (2016). *Peace education in a conflict-affected society.* Cambridge University Press.

Part I
Conflict, (in)security and everyday peace

2 Everyday peace disruption in deeply divided societies: Is it really peace?

Roger Mac Ginty

Introduction

A criticism made of the notion and practice of everyday peace is that it does not constitute peace. Consider the following example: An Israeli Jew and a Palestinian might have cordial relations. They might work together, have immense respect for each other, and their friendship might extend to their families. Their relations are social and humane. A critic of the notion of everyday peace might dismiss this hyper-local example of good relations across a politico-identity fissure as being irrelevant in the face of overwhelming structural division. While the inter-personal friendship might be commendable, for a critic it pales into insignificance when set against a backdrop of power relations between a powerful state (Israel) and Palestinians who are stateless and disadvantaged in many ways. This chapter has sympathy with this view, but it wishes to make the point that everyday peace deserves serious consideration as a form of peace. Sometimes, political and security contexts are so dire that even minimalist pro-peace and pro-social acts and stances can be regarded as a form of peace.

Everyday peace is understood as a form of tactical agency used by individuals and groups of individuals as they navigate through life. It is comprised of a form of social awareness and emotional intelligence that inform actions, stances, speech-acts and communicative practices (Mac Ginty, 2014). It is bottom-up in the sense that it operates at the lowest-level of society (the individual, family, friendship group, work colleagues) but, as it operates on a social sphere, it has possible ramifications for the wider society. This last point is crucial for the essential purpose of the chapter in illustrating that everyday peace should be taken seriously as a form of peace. Everyday peace operates in all societies, but its importance is particularly acute in deeply-divided societies in which different identity groupings might live in close proximity. The risk of indirect violence spilling into direct violence might be ever present and so everyday de-escalation and conflict management tactics are important. Quite simply, everyday peace activities of avoidance or dissembling might mean that an individual from a minority group who works in a majority group area gets home safely each evening.

DOI: 10.4324/9781003080909-2

Everyday peace operates at the inter and intra-group levels, and much rests on the ability of individuals to read social situations and act accordingly. It takes the form of multiple actions and stances (for example, tactical silence, pretending not to notice something designed to give offence, or dressing in inconspicuous ways (Mac Ginty, 2014)) that firstly do not escalate a conflict, and secondly might contribute to the de-escalation of the conflict. In many respects, everyday peace is a logic or mode of thinking (Brewer, 2018).

This mode of thinking might be fleeting or inconsistent. An individual can engage in an everyday peace act in the morning and fail to repeat it for the rest of the day. In many ways, everyday peace can be seen as negative peace, or passive. Non-escalation of conflict is not the same as encouraging peace and so can be interpreted as condoning, or even reinforcing, the structural drivers of conflict. This chapter, however, makes the argument that everyday peace has the potential to disrupt the logic and narrative of violent conflict. Therefore, it deserves to be taken seriously as a form of peace.

For example, everyday peace may take the form of neighbours from different identity groups maintaining a friendship despite wider political tensions. Or it may be acts of civility in the micro-interactions between a former child soldier and villagers in northern Uganda. It could take the form of momentary displays of humanity and compassion within a wider context of war. It can be seemingly inconsequential actions, communications and stances that can be non-escalatory and help puncture the logic of division and exclusion.

The chapter begins with a conceptual unpacking of everyday peace that builds on the above definition. It provides examples of various communicative/interactional practices and stances that constitute everyday peace, and makes the point that everyday peace often draws on three concepts: Sociality, reciprocity and solidarity. The chapter then briefly introduces the concept of conflict disruption and the ability of everyday peace, in certain circumstances, to disrupt the logic and narrative of conflict. This paves the way for a last substantive section that considers the potential of everyday peace to be considered a form of peace.

Before proceeding, it is worth making a note on the perspectives utilised in this chapter. While multiple disciplines and sub-disciplines have approached the notion of the everyday, and of everyday peace, this chapter is written from the perspective of Peace and Conflict Studies. This is something of a mongrel sub-discipline that has drawn from multiple disciplines but is probably most heavily influenced by International Relations and Politics (Krause, 2019). As such, and despite decades of critical scholarship that has been aware of the importance of post-colonial and post-structuralist lenses, Peace and Conflict Studies has to work hard to transcend a legacy that regards the state and formal political institutions as the primary unit of analysis (Baron, 2014; Sabaratnam, 2011). A focus on the everyday and relational practices, that is on individuals and groups of individuals going about their daily business, is something of a subversive perspective. Potentially, it bypasses formal political units to foreground people. As a result, the chapter is informed by sociological, anthropological and feminist perspectives that are aware of the social and relational aspects of peace and conflict. It is also worth noting the ethnocentric bias that attend Peace and Conflict Studies and very many academic endeavours. The focus of many studies is on conflicts that are based in the Global South. Yet the political economies that shape most of academia mean that conflicts in the Global South are often studied *from* the Global North. Academic institutions and publishing houses based in Europe, North America, Australia and a few other places on the planet dominate formal studies and published outputs. Local expertise and experiences are often ignored, relegated, or shoehorned into formats that suit the academic gaze from the Global North. A quick perusal of the bibliography of this chapter will reveal that it is not free from this positionality defect.

While the academic endeavour to unpack the everyday suffers from epistemological colonialism, it is worth noting that the chapter is based on reflections arising from the Everyday Peace Indicators programme (Everyday Peace Indicators 2020). This programme, which has operated in multiple conflict-affected locations, asks community members to identify indicators of peace, conflict and change from communities themselves. In other words, rather than academics from the Global North imposing indicators on communities, communities are encouraged to identify their own indicators from their everyday experiences. Thus indicators of everyday peace (for example, allowing children to walk to school, or not being harassed by security officials) are often highly-localised and spoken of in the vernacular. A major finding from the projects that comprise the Everyday Peace Indicators programme (everydaypeaceindicators.org) is that people tend to narrate, embody and enact peace and security in very local and hyper-local ways (Firchow, 2019). The home and the immediate vicinity of the home, key routes to school, work and shops, and friendship and familial networks constitute the main sites of concern. These sites and networks are usually personal, familial or connected to one's immediate political economy, and underscore the social and connected nature of how everyday peace operates. But this also presents us with a challenge: How do we connect the local and hyper-local to wider contexts and structures? The local and the hyper-local are nested within, and contribute to, wider levels, networks and structures. We need analyses that are mindful of the hyper-local, the local, the national, the international, the transnational and all levels in between. The multi-scalar nature of peace and conflict is best seen as a system (De Coning, 2018) or complex circuit (Mac Ginty, 2019) in which the local informs the wider structure, as well as being shaped by the structure.

It should be noted that there is no attempt to pretend that community-sourcing indicators redresses the imbalance in academia and the structural exclusion of those in the Global South who actually experience conflict. It may though add a different perspective and remind us that those who are not situated in the everyday of conflict will be unlikely to have a full understanding of the context.

Unpacking the concept of everyday peace

Everyday peace is dynamic, social, and context dependent (Berents, 2015; Berents & Ten Have, 2017). As a result, the concept and practice is resistant to overly neat definitions and conceptualisations. On the basis of evidence from the Everyday Peace Indicators programme, and reading of mainly sociological literature, this author locates the motivations behind everyday peace in three human stances and consequent actions: Sociality, reciprocity and solidarity. The three can be thought of as operating along a continuum, with sociality involving limited emotional investment and action and solidarity involving significant amounts of involvement. Sociality by a member of one group towards a member of another group might develop into reciprocity and solidarity. In this schemata, the continuum of sociality, reciprocity and solidarity might map onto, respectively, weak, medium and strong varieties of everyday peace (see Figure 2.1.).

As will be discussed later, everyday peace might scale-up and scale-out from small acts and stances to ones that are more significant and might establish new norms. There is no guarantee, of course, that everyday peace acts and stances take root. They may be one-off isolated incidents with little wider consequence. Yet, the possibility that everyday peace can become normalised and have a demonstration effect is worth investigating. Here the concept of socialisation, or a positive version of societalization (Alexander, 2018), comes into play whereby actions and stances are adopted by community members, perhaps through demonstration, example and eventually familiarity.

Sociality is simply a recognition among individuals and groups of individuals that we are human and have shared characteristics and aspirations (and possibly rights) (Enfield, 2013; Tomasello, 2020). In this view, a shared humanity is the glue that produces society and liberates our species from atomised co-existence to something more shared, convivial and relational. It may manifest itself in empathy with others. This empathy might cross the main fissure in a deeply-divided society. For example, a member of the majority Bamar community in Myanmar might see scenes of displacement of Rohingye on the Myanmar/Bangladesh border and might feel a basic sympathy. Scenes of displaced children might resonate with the Bamar viewer because they have children or grandchildren of a similar age. This sociality may stop at a feeling of sympathy, a momentary reflection on similarities between members of the in-group and the out-group. But it may take root and develop in a change of stance, a willingness to speak out or

Sociality	Reciprocity	Solidarity
Weak Everyday Peace	Medium Everyday Peace	Strong Everyday Peace

Figure 2.1 Key concepts of everyday peace.

even engage in some humanitarian action in aid of the out-group. Such an act, which goes beyond mere sociality, would be transgressive of the in-group norm and may leave the individual open to criticism, or worse, from fellow group members who might see the Rohingye as somehow inferior to themselves. Sociality in this example requires a perspective to look beyond identity-related divisions and instead see points of commonality. Many actors in deeply-divided societies work hard to emphasise division and the uniqueness of identity groups, thus sociality can be transgressive and may require bravery.

Archbishop Desmond Tutu tells a story about sociality from his childhood in apartheid South Africa:

> But I believe the most defining moment of my life occurred when I was about nine years old, outside the Blind Institute in Roodepoort where my mother was a domestic worker. We were standing on the stoep when this tall white man in a black cassock, and a hat, swept by. I did not know that it was Trevor Huddleston. He doffed his hat in greeting my mother.
>
> I was relatively stunned at the time, but only later came to realise the extent to which it had blown my mind that a white man would doff his hat to my mother. It was something I could never have imagined. The impossible was possible. (Tutu, 2013)

Trevor Huddleston, later an archbishop, was a founder of the Anti-Apartheid Movement (McGrandle, 2004). The simple gesture of doffing his hat transcended racial boundaries and signalled that he could see an underlying shared humanity beyond the politically-charged identity of race.

Reciprocity can be summarised as extending a favour (for example, an action or opinion) in the hope or expectation that others will match this favour in return (Simpson et al., 2018). It should be seen as more than a simple trading relationship, although it may begin this way. Advanced forms of reciprocity can be systemic and constitute statements on the type of society we want to inhabit. Thus, for example, if a driver on a narrow country lane pulls in to let another driver pass the exchange is about more than the interaction between the two drivers. It is unlikely that the drivers will meet at precisely the same point on their return journeys and the second driver will feel obligated to let his or her benefactor through. Instead, by pulling over to let oncoming traffic through, drivers are making a statement about acceptable and unacceptable norms. In a deeply-divided society where relations between communities might be tense, the importance of inter-group reciprocity is amplified. It is a way of signalling trust and may develop into a virtuous cycle with the reciprocal actions between individuals from different groups developing into something more broadly based. A common message in deeply-divided societies revolves around the untrustworthy nature of the outgroup and its members. Reciprocity, for example between Christian and Muslim traders in northern Nigeria, is a way of disproving a prejudice that might be widely held.

Solidarity is the toughest of the inter-group everyday peace stances to achieve. Definitions of solidarity often regard it as more than standing with the out-group, a difficult enough action given the depth of mistrust in many conflict-affected contexts (Komter, 2005; Turner, 2001). Instead, for solidarity to become manifest and move beyond declarations it must take material form. Thus, for example, members of a majority group might accompany members of a minority group to offer them protection. Such an act occurred in 2011 in Egypt when Muslims acted as 'human shields' to protect Coptic church services at a time of increased sectarian violence (Alexander, 2011). As a public act, solidarity may expose participants to criticism (or worse) from those who feel that outgroup members pursue an illegitimate cause and so to stand with them is a betrayal of the ingroup cause.

The extent to which individuals and groups of individuals can display sociality, reciprocity and solidarity, and particularly do so in public, will be context dependent. Importantly, we should not expect consistency across different contexts and situations. Individuals might engage in reciprocity with one outgroup member but shun others. The extent to which individuals engage in everyday peace actions and stances is difficult to model and predict. Contextual factors, such as the security situation or a period of tolerance and calm among political leaders might embolden those at the hyper-local level to engage in everyday peace activities. The immediate micro and communicative context will be important: The time of day, the original purpose of the interaction, and who else is present all come into view. At the same time, however, some individuals, through force of personality, might feel emboldened to engage in everyday peace activities or stances regardless of the wider political or security situation. An individual might feel strongly that people should be treated the same regardless of their identity or affiliations. Thus, for example, a Christian bus driver in Ambon province in Indonesia might extend the same level of courtesy to all passengers regardless of their faith. The bus driver might have a confidence that allows him or her to transcend social norms that might involve a coolness to outgroup members. This type of everyday peace, comprised of simple courtesy and non-discrimination, might not be formally taught. Here it is important to note that issues of personality and micro-context meld with societal norms, themselves often (co-)produced by structures. As a result, it is useful to think of everyday peace operating within a multi-scalar system with multiple 'moving parts', power relations, and lines of (mis-)communication. The civility between the bus driver and passengers mentioned above might be mandated by law, bus company policy, and indeed the religious instruction that the bus driver experienced as a child. All of these comprise social norms and, to a large extent, the expression of structures of power. All of these might inform the bus driver's behaviour, but their own moral compass and personality also matter too.

Types of everyday peace activity

Avoidance
- contentious topics of conversation
- offensive displays
- high-risk people and places
- escapism into subcultures
- not drawing attention to oneself
- live in the present

Ambiguity
- concealing signifiers of identity
- non-observance or 'not seeing'
- dissembling in speech and actions

Ritualized politeness
- system of manners

Telling
- ethnically informed identification and social ordering

Blame deferring
- shifting blame to outsiders to appear more socially acceptable

Figure 2.2 Types of social practice that constitute everyday peace.

In terms of activities and stance, earlier work by the author gave examples of the types of actions and stances that constitute everyday peace (Mac Ginty, 2014). See Figure 2.2.

The ability of individuals or groups of individuals to engage in these activities tended to depend on the nature and stage of the conflict. These actions and stances may be embedded into the social behaviour of individuals and groups of individuals and thus allow a society to be more liveable. In a sense, everyday peace can be regarded as the first and last peace. It might be the first peace in that small acts of intergroup tolerance and conciliation might follow a violent conflict and signal that intergroup relations are improving. It might be the last peace in that intergroup social bonds may remain as a wider context slips towards conflict. For example, as inter-ethnic fissures widen in a country and the political and security situation worsens, intergroup friendships and social links may persist. This might provide enough social glue, or bridging social capital (Leonard, 2004), to prevent a complete rupture. Small acts of kindness or instances of civic mindedness that cross the main fissure of society might be enough to puncture the notion that a conflict is totalising and that groups are homogenous and united in their bitterness to each other.

Before moving on to discuss conflict disruption, it may be worth adding a note of caution in relation to everyday peace. Alongside pro-peace and pro-social activities, there is also everyday sectarianism, identity politics, exclusion, and violence. So the everyday is not a domain to be romanticised. Instead, it can be a site of contestation, and often contradictory behaviour. Indeed, pockets and moments of everyday peace can be contained within wider dynamics. Thus it can be appropriate to use a vocabulary of resistance, subversion, and persistence when discussing everyday peace.

Conflict disruption

It is argued here that everyday peace can, in certain circumstances, disrupt conflict and thus have a significant multiplier effect. An act of inter-group friendship between individuals might be meaningful, but only between those who are directly involved. But can we think of such an act factoring up or out and having a more significant impact? Many everyday peace acts and stances occur at the hyper-local level of individual-to-individual interactions. Civility between individuals is important and can have a major and positive effect on those directly concerned. For example, good interpersonal relations between a Shia and a Sunni in Beirut may not only be good for their wellbeing but it also means that these individuals are unlikely to engage in escalatory behaviour. But can we think of everyday peace acts and stances having a wider impact, and being implicated in community, society, and relational networks?

Here it is useful to introduce the concept of conflict disruption. A conflict can be thought of as a system (perhaps like a market) in which various factors come together to fuel and sustain it (on conflict as a market see: De Waal, 2015). Systemic notions of conflict help us understand why some conflicts are so longstanding and have intergenerational qualities (De Coning, 2016, 2018). In order to staunch the conflict, or dramatically lower its costs, the conflict will need to be disrupted. Importantly, the term being used is 'disrupted' rather than 'interrupted.' An interruption can be thought of as a pause, perhaps a ceasefire, in which the conflict stops but is ready to restart without any qualitative difference upon resumption. Conflict disruption is of a different order. In this scenario, the conflict will be disrupted and will be compelled to change. Again the notion of a 'conflict market' is useful. The business world provides multiple examples of new companies and technologies that disrupt established business models and force an industry to engage in major change. Low-cost no-frills airlines, for example, forced so-called 'legacy carriers' to cut their own costs and launch competitor spin-off companies. Streaming services have forced traditional television, movie and music providers to rethink what they produce and how it can be accessed. In other words, new actors, methods and technologies have the capacity to shake-up entire industries and question the assumptions upon which business as usual operated.

It is worth thinking if the Schumpeterian logic of 'creative destruction' (Louçã, 2014; Schumpeter, 1954) can apply to violent conflict and if everyday peace actions and stances could fall under the conflict disruption mantle (Goss, 2005). In this case, the 'conflict market' would be disrupted by new behaviour that would force conflict actors to recalculate their stance. For example, towards the end of World War I mutinies in the French, German and Russian armies became so widespread that the traditional military logic – that subordinates would follow orders – became unsustainable (Grinev, 2017; Peiz, 2016). These mutinies started at a very small scale. They required extraordinary bravery. Not only did soldiers, quite literally, have to put their heads over the parapet and negotiate and test 'trench ceasefires' but they had to brave accusations of treachery and cowardice from their own side (Ashworth, 1968). Such actions often occurred on the margins and away from the surveillance of superiors. But gradually, and encouraged by other meta developments such as the Russian Revolution and the change in the balance of forces brought about by the entry of the United States into the war, these highly-localised truces became more generalised. They were able to spread horizontally through imitation, word-of-mouth, hidden transcripts (Scott, 1990), one group of soldiers observing other soldiers, and the ability of small groups of soldiers to read a situation and make decisions accordingly. The collapse of military discipline made elite-directed warfare impossible. State narratives that there was unity of purpose behind the war effort were punctured by bottom-up initiatives.

Most conflict disruption does not occur on such a large-scale. Often it is highly localised and may only impact on small numbers. At the micro-level, it can operate at the level of family with, perhaps a parent or older sibling making sure that a son is not radicalised (Sutton, 2017). This might involve a mix of advice (to the extent of nagging), family surveillance, and offering alternatives in terms of employment, education or emigration (Dekel & Solomon, 2016). While this may sound trivial compared to the last example, at the level of the individual, family and community it may be quite significant. The son and family might be spared heartache and disruption that might come with the death, injury or imprisonment that might accompany radicalisation in a conflict-affected area. But the family intervention also disrupts the conflict model. It signals that at least one family is unpersuaded by the narrative of political or militant elites who believe that all sons should be radicalised or follow a particular conflict path. Moreover, the actions of a single family might serve as an exemplar to others and so the single example might have a multiplier effect.

Everyday peace can be seen as a form of power whereby the actions of individuals and communities can be scaled up and out. Through example, ideas, stances, and actions might be socialised or spread horizontally across society. It is an often immaterial form of power that operates subtly, on the margins, and perhaps gradually.

Is it really peace?

The task now facing this chapter is to discuss if everyday peace is really a form of peace. In many respects, everyday peace may be seen as a form of negative peace (Roberts, 2008). That is, it may be a form of non-escalation rather than de-escalation. In this view, everyday peace is marginal and limited in ambition. For example, individuals from opposing sides of a politico-identity divide may decide to have civil everyday relations. But this is far removed from more ambitious actions and stances that would actively engender conciliation, reconciliation or an examination of the causes of violent conflict. As a result, sceptics may be wary of extending the label 'peace' to everyday peace. They may see it as a minimalist form of peace that fails to challenge the basis of division and instead concerns itself with 'work arounds' or forms of tactical agency designed to avoid rather than confront conflict. This section accepts that there are, of course, forms of peace that are more emancipatory and fulsome than the types of everyday peace discussed here, but nonetheless everyday peace deserves the label 'peace' for three reasons.

The first reason why everyday peace deserves to be called peace is that it might be all that is possible given a context of violence and exclusion. Everyday peace, that is stances and actions that occur at the lowest levels of social organisation, are dependent on the context. Often much of the political, economic and security context will be controlled by powerful actors such as states, militias, international organisations and commercial interests - all of which will be able to mobilise significant material and immaterial power. Individuals and groups of individuals may have little power in such circumstances. What little power they do have may be highly-localised and often outwith the purview of the state or other actors. It is in these marginal and often un-surveilled spaces that individuals and groups of individuals may engage in everyday peace acts and stances. Small acts of kindness, sociality and reciprocity might occur between individuals and families who come from different identity groups. For example, tensions between Armenia and Azerbaijan have deteriorated into violence a number of times in the post-Soviet era. An Armenian and an Azerbaijani family may live side-by-side in the disputed region of Nagorno-Karabakh. The territory is majority Armenian, although it is formally in Azerbaijan. The families may have long-standing cordial relations of good neighbourliness and may be determined to maintain these during periods of political tension. To do so, however, may risk incurring the wrath of other neighbours who might take umbrage at cordial inter-group relations at a time of heightened tension. Yet the small acts of sociality, reciprocity and solidarity that characterise neighbourly relations may be important in signalling that the rupture between the communities is not total. While political leaders and many in both communities may be in an escalatory mood, the neighbours – at least – are able to maintain space for interpersonal civility.

This civility between the families may be 'toned down' during the hostilities. A very public stance may invite opprobrium from other neighbours. But it may continue surreptitiously or in a toned-down way. While the actions of the neighbours may not be confronting the bases of the conflict, they are significant in that they are transgressive to the generalised mood of escalation and inter-group hostility. They might help with the well-being of the individuals and families involved, but to the extent that these actions and stances are visible to others they signal the failure of nationalism and exclusionary strategies to be hegemonic.

This leads to the second reason why we should take care before dismissing everyday peace as a form of peace, or even dismissing it as conflict reinforcing. In some circumstances, everyday peace can factor up and factor out. Actions and stances that are hyper-local, perhaps restricted to a few individuals, can have an exemplar effect. What was once marginal and restricted to the shadows, may be copied by others to the extent that it is normalised or at least becomes more common or visible. To use an example not necessarily related to a conflict-affected society, consider public attitudes towards public displays of affection between same-sex couples in major metropolitan areas of the United Kingdom or United States. Just a few decades ago, such signs would have been unthinkable because of legislation and public attitudes. But legislation and attitudes have changed. This is not to say that bigotry has ceased or that same-sex couples do not have to care. It is, however, to point to how social attitudes are capable of changing over relatively short time frames. Activities and stances that were once regarded as taboo have become more normalised and mainstream. We can think of deeply-divided societies in which inter-group relations thaw with the passage of time and temporal distance from a conflict. Relations between individuals from different identity groups may begin cautiously but may thaw with time. A few individuals may engage in tentative inter-group social or economic relations. Others in the wider communities may observe these from afar and calculate – over time – that such relations are non-threatening and possibly to be emulated.

Given the nature of everyday peace, as actions and stances that occur at the lowest level of social organisation, it is likely to be factored out rather than factored up. In other words, the spread of everyday peace is likely to be horizontal rather than vertical. Individuals and groups may, on the basis of observed evidence and cost-benefit analysis, be imitative of one another. In something akin to a blotting paper effect, islands of pro-social and pro-peace acts and stances may spread horizontally across communities and geographies. It is also possible to conceive of a ground-up vertical spread of everyday peace whereby political and militant elites notice that communities are more minded towards conciliation and thus recalculate their positions. Certainly, states, political parties and militant groups may have to work hard to keep communities mobilised and to persuade them that group primacy matters more than other more plural ways to organise society. At times, this mobilisation may falter and become difficult to maintain. Political leaders may take their cue from communities – in effect becoming followers rather than leaders.

A third factor to bear in mind when considering if everyday peace is worthy of the label 'peace' is that everyday peace should be considered alongside other peace initiatives and contextual factors. In other words, it seems to be a tough test to expect individuals and communities to be the pathfinders towards peace in the face of authoritarian leaders, mobilised communities, and well-established narratives of division. Transgressive acts in such circumstances require bravery and the ability to choose the moment.

This might read like a plea to lower the bar for considering everyday peace to legitimately belong in the category marked 'peace.' It is. The bitterness of enmity in many conflict-affected areas means that any acts and stances that break with escalatory or exclusionary norms should be considered for their pro-social or pro-peace merits. The norms of war and conflict are often insidious and embedded within everyday cultural and social processes. Any break with this, interrupts, if not disrupts, the conflict imperative.

It could be that everyday peace communicative practices and stances work in complementary ways with other peace initiatives. Bottom-up and top-down peace initiatives might be mutually encouraging, with each edging ahead and opening up new territory. Importantly, everyday peace can give life to top-down peace. Elite-level peace accords are essentially declarations made by political elites. To become real they need to become manifest in the conflict-affected territory. One way of this happening is through the actualisation and enforcement of peace accord provisions, such as the holding of elections or the establishment of new institutions. Another way of this happening is for people, from the various conflict-affected communities, using and inhabiting the spaces and instruments established through the peace accord. Some of this might be formal or legally encouraged or enforced by a peace accord. For example, it might take the form of former combatants going through a disarmament and reintegration process. But some of this activity might be informal and highly-localised. It might take the form of a slight warming of inter-group relations in a community with an increase in inter-group civility, a lowering of guards, and a normalisation of inter-group social or commercial relations. This everyday activity turns peace from an abstraction and a noun into a verb. In one sense it is enabled by a top-down peace accord and certain behaviours and stances might be given 'permission' by the elite-level accord. But in another sense, it validates and gives life to the peace accord. More than this, it might bring the accord, or the peace as envisaged by the peace accord framers, to new pro-peace and pro-social spaces.

Concluding discussion

In an essay on sociality in urban spaces in South Asia, Hoek and Gandhi refer to 'provisional perches' or 'temporary toeholds' that people have as they seek to understand their surroundings and their place within them (Hoek & Gandhi, 2016: 72). Such perches are precarious in any society, but this is especially the case in a deeply-divided society in which structural divisions could erupt into violence. They remind us of the permanent impermanence of conflict-affected contexts, whereby there may be uncertainty – at the meta-level – over a border, a constitution, or the prevailing political dispensation (Bell & Pospisil, 2017). At the micro-level, this uncertainty may inflect multiple aspects of life: Whether it is safe to leave the house or take a particular route to work or school; whether it is advisable to be seen walking or talking with a member of the out-group; whether it is worth investing in home improvements if the neighbourhood might be prone to violence. The essential point is that individuals and groups of individuals must engage in a permanent conflict analysis and processes of social analysis and make judgments on whether the neighbourhood is and remains safe, and whether certain behaviours are sensible. This requires having a social antennae to 'read' the surroundings, an ability to filter and analyse information (and separate the credible from the not so credible), and an ability to react accordingly. Not everyone will have those skills, nor the ability to act unilaterally. Sometimes contexts are just so restraining that people are compelled to act in particular ways. But in some circumstances, individuals and groups of individuals are able to dissent, disrupt and engage in acts and stances that are pro-peace and might be transgressive to the prevailing pro-conflict norms.

It is possible to think of everyday peace as a social infrastructure or prosocial connective tissue that can maintain relations across identity fissures. The connective tissue might be, at times, tenuous or difficult to observe given societal dynamics. Indeed, it may be prudent for individuals or groups to keep their cross-community activities quiet. Yet, everyday peace is fundamentally social and relational. While we naturally see the everyday at the local and hyper-local levels, clearly these levels are nested within, and co-constitute, other levels. It becomes feasible to think systematically of local relations contributing to other sets of relations: The community, the society, the polity, etc. We are also encouraged to see beyond mere 'security-scapes' to see something more nuanced in which neat categorisations are disrupted, and our analyses centre on human experiences. Everyday peace – and multiple other experiences – are located in transversal, diverse, and diffuse environments in which terms like 'micro' and 'macro' or 'bottom-up' and 'top-down' (while useful shorthand) do not adequately capture the textured environments in which individuals and communities operate.

The essential question facing this chapter has been whether everyday peace can be legitimately considered as peace. Criticism that everyday peace is negative peace, or even conflict-reinforcing has merits. But on balance, this chapter argues that everyday peace should be considered as a form of peace. Context is all important. In situations of significant violence or deep division, everyday peace might be all that is possible. More than this, it might be that the disruption and transgression that it causes opens up space for something more significant. The 'first peace' referred to earlier might be one that has significant material and immaterial benefits in terms of saving and improving lives.

References

Alexander, Anne. 2011. Egypt's Muslims and Christians Join Hands in Protest. *BBC News*. https://www.bbc.com/news/world-middle-east-12407793 (February 10, 2021).

Alexander, Jeffrey C. 2018. The societalization of social problems: Church pedophilia, phone hacking, and the financial crisis. *American Sociological Review 83*(6): 1049–1078.

Ashworth, A. E. 1968. The sociology of trench warfare 1914–18. *The British Journal of Sociology* 19(4): 407–423.

Bachmann, K.M. 1972. *The Prey of an Eagle: A Personal Record of Familly Life Written Throughout the German Occupation of Guernsey 1940-45*. St Peter Port: The Guernsey Press.

Baron, Ilan Zvi. 2014. The continuing failure of international relations and the challenges of disciplinary boundaries. *Millennium* 43(1): 224–244.

Bell, Christine, and Jan Pospisil. 2017. Navigating inclusion in transitions from conflict: The formalised political unsettlement. *Journal of International Development* 29(5): 576–593.

Berents, Helen. 2015. An embodied everyday peace in the midst of violence. *Peacebuilding: Every Day Peace and Youth* 3(2): 1–14.

Brewer, John D. 2018. *The Sociology of Everyday Life Peacebuilding*. Basingstoke: Palgrave. https://www.bookdepository.com/Sociology-Everyday-Life-Peacebuilding-John-D-Brewer/9783030076931 (October 8, 2020).

De Coning, Cedric. 2016. From peacebuilding to sustaining peace: Implications of complexity for resilience and sustainability. *Resilience* 4(3): 166–181.

De Coning, Cedric. 2018. Adaptive peacebuilding. *International Affairs* 94(2): 301–317.

De Waal, Alex. 2015. *The Real Politics of the Horn of Africa: Money, War and the Business of Power*. Cambridge, UK: Malden, MA: Polity.

Dekel, Rachel, and Dan Solomon. 2016. The contribution of maternal care and control to adolescents' adjustment following war. *The Journal of Early Adolescence* 36(2): 198–221.

Enfield, N. J. 2013. *Relationship Thinking: Agency, Enchrony, and Human Sociality*. New York: Oxford University Press. http://ezphost.dur.ac.uk/login?url=10.1093/acprof:oso/9780199338733.001.0001 (October 8, 2020).

Everyday Peace Indicators. *Everyday Peace Indicators*. https://everydaypeaceindicators.org/ (October 8, 2020).

Firchow, Pamina. 2019. *Reclaiming Everyday Peace: Local Voices in Measurement and Evaluation After War*. Cambridge: Cambridge University Press. https://discover.durham.ac.uk/primo-explore/fulldisplay?docid=TN_cambridge_s10_1017_9781108236140&context=PC&vid=44DUR_VU4&lang=en_US&search_scope=DSCOP_ARTRES&adaptor=primo_central_multiple_fe&tab=art-res_tab&query=any,contains,firchow&offset=0 (December 7, 2020).

Goss, David. 2005. Schumpeters legacy? Interaction and emotions in the sociology of entrepreneurship. *Entrepreneurship Theory and Practice* 29(2): 205–218.

Grinev, A. 2017. October 1917: An armed revolt of the masses, a bolshevik coup, a socialist revolution, or something else? *Herald of the Russian Academy of Sciences* 87(5): 426–431.

Helen Berents and Charlotte Ten Have. 2017. Navigating violence: Fear and everyday life in Colombia and Mexico. *International Journal for Crime, Justice and Social Democracy* 6(1): 103–117.

Hoek, Lotte, and Ajay Gandhi. 2016. Provisional relations, indeterminate conditions: Non-sociological sociality in South Asia. *South Asia: Journal of South Asian Studies* 39(1): 64–72.

Komter, Aafke E. 2005. *Social Solidarity and the Gift*. Cambridge: University Press. http://ezphost.dur.ac.uk/login?url=http://lib.myilibrary.com/detail.asp?ID=43135 (October 8, 2020).

Krause, Keith. 2019. Emancipation and critique in peace and conflict research. *Journal of Global Security Studies* 4(2): 292–298.

Leonard, Madeleine. 2004. Bonding and bridging social capital: Reflections from belfast. *Sociology* 38(5): 927–944.

Louçã, Francisco. 2014. The elusive concept of innovation for schumpeter, marschak and the early econometricians. *Research Policy* 43(8): 1442–1449.

Mac Ginty, Roger. 2014. Everyday peace: Bottom-up and local agency in conflict-affected societies. *Security Dialogue* 45(6): 548–564.

Mac Ginty, Roger. 2019. Circuits, the everyday and international relations: Connecting the home to the international and transnational. *Cooperation and Conflict*.

McGrandle, Piers. 2004. *Trevor Huddleston: Turbulent Priest*. London: Continuum.

Peiz, William A. 2016. *Protest and Mutiny Confront Mass Slaughter:: Europeans in World War I*. London: Pluto Press. https://www.jstor.org/stable/j.ctt1c2crfj (October 3, 2020).

Roberts, David. 2008. Post-conflict statebuilding and state legitimacy: From negative to positive peace? *Development and Change* 39(4): 537–555.

Sabaratnam, Meera. 2011. IR in dialogue … but can we change the subjects? A typology of decolonising strategies for the study of world politics. *Millennium – Journal of International Studies* 39(3): 781–803.

Schumpeter, Joseph A. 1954. *History of Economic Analysis*. New York: OUP.

Scott, James C. 1990. *Domination and the Arts of Resistance: Hidden Transcripts*. New Haven: Yale University Press. https://ebookcentral.proquest.com/lib/durham/detail.action?docID=3420907 (June 10, 2020).

Simpson, Brent et al. 2018. The roots of reciprocity: Gratitude and reputation in generalized exchange systems. *American Sociological Review* 83(1): 88–110.

Sutton, Tara E. 2017. The lives of female gang members: A review of the literature. *Aggression and Violent Behavior* 37: 142–152.

Tomasello, M. 2020. The adaptive origins of uniquely human sociality. *Philosophical Transactions of the Royal Society B-Biological Sciences* 375(1803): 20190493.

Turner, Bryan S. 2001. *Society and Culture: Principles of Scarcity and Solidarity*. London, London; Thousand Oaks, Calif.: SAGE. http://ezphost.dur.ac.uk/login?url=https://sk.sagepub.com/books/society-and-culture (October 8, 2020).

Tutu, Desmond. 2013. The man who changed my life. *IOL*. https://www.iol.co.za/capetimes/the-man-who-changed-my-life-1533199 (October 8, 2020).

3 A linguistic ethnography of peace-building through language education in Cyprus

Constadina Charalambous,
Panayiota Charalambous, and Ben Rampton

Introduction

This chapter explores links between International Relations (IR) and Peace & Conflict Studies (PCS) on the one hand, and linguistic ethnography and sociolinguistics on the other. In doing so, it focuses on the role of language and language education in peace-building in Cyprus, a country riven by a legacy of war and separation. The chapter's authors are ethnographic sociolinguists who seek to engage with the interest in the 'everyday' that is currently emerging in Critical International Relations, Critical Security Studies and Peace & Conflict Studies (see Mc Cluskey, 2017 for a bibliography), and their goals here are threefold: to illustrate the perspective on everyday practice provided by linguistic ethnography; to start to address the role that language and language education can play in peace-building; and to reflect on whether and how our findings and methods can contribute to significant concerns in critical IR.

To achieve this, the chapter begins with a brief outline of IR's increasing interest in the everyday (next section). After that, it returns to key elements in the account of linguistic ethnography in Chapter 1 (this volume), recapping on its guiding assumptions, the resources it draws on, and the perspective on the everyday that it offers (third section). This is followed by a methodological summary of how we used linguistic ethnography in this case study (fourth section). The chapter then turns to the empirical account of Greek-Cypriots learning Turkish, the language of their (former) enemy, and this covers the affordances of language education as a space for potentially normalizing inter-ethnic relations after conflict, as well as the interactional practices involved (sections 5–7). After that, it suggests that an account of this kind can contribute to the discussion of IR concepts like 'desecuritisation' and 'everyday peace' (final).

We can begin a sketch of the developments in IR to which linguistic ethnography seems most relevant.

The local, vernacular and everyday turns in IR/PCS

In the 'local,' 'vernacular' and 'everyday' turns in IR, there seems to be burgeoning interest in widening the angle of vision in studies of (in)security,

DOI: 10.4324/9781003080909-3

peace building and transitional justice beyond top-down and state-centred processes (Bigo, 2016; Marsden et al., 2016, Gready & Robins, 2014; Mac Ginty & Richmond, 2013; Leonardsson & Rudd, 2015). According to Huysmans, "the question of the everyday is often introduced to draw attention away from elite politics and highly institutionalized security practices, towards sites of routine, individual identity and especially interaction in proximity" (2009: 197). Comparable interest can be found in studies of surveillance (Green & Zurawski, 2015: 40), diplomacy (Marsden et al., 2016: 6–7; Constantinou, 2016), and peacebuilding and reconciliation (Mac Ginty & Richmond, 2013: 764).

Despite differences in their central areas of interest, there are a number of common features in this expansion of horizons beyond political professionals and elites. There is shared interest in the diversity of actors and audiences involved (in terms of culture, class, gender, social role etc), and their different experiences, agendas and possibilities for action. This in turn requires attention to different institutional and life domains (beyond political and diplomatic offices), and the circulation of different representations of security, peace and conflict through different networks. In addition, practices and lived experiences need to be considered, and these include tensions, struggle, resistance and creativity (cf Vaughan Williams & Stevens, 2016 and Bigo, 2015, 2016 on insecurity; Marsden et al., 2016 on diplomacy and political mediation; Mac Ginty, 2010 and Mac Ginty & Richmond, 2013 on peace-building). All these need to be placed alongside the policies and political interventions designed and promoted by actors with state and/or institutional authority, and when it comes to a notion like 'peace' (a central concern in this chapter), this generates a number of terms that attempt to conceptualise the plurality of people, practices, representations, arenas and experiences involved: for example, plural 'peaces' (Leonardsson & Rudd, 2015), 'hybrid peace' (Mac Ginty, 2010; Mac Ginty & Richmond, 2013), and 'everyday peace' (Mac Ginty, 2014).

It is within this theoretical line that we approach the notion of 'peacebuilding,' aligning with critiques of liberal peace interventions. These critiques argue that "[w]hat happens at the local level is as important [as the international level] and far less understood," and emphasise the need to consider "the critical and resistant agencies that have a stake in a subaltern view of peace, how they act to uncover or engage with obstacles, with violence and with structures that maintain them" (Mac Ginty & Richmond, 2013: 764). Drawing on Mac Ginty (2010), Mac Ginty & Richmond (2013) and Leonardsson & Rudd (2015), we approach peacebuilding as a situated process that is shaped by culture, history and identity struggles that go beyond elite offices and interventions, and that requires an understanding of the needs of different actors in various everyday contexts.

Within this array of interests, there are sure to be arguments and nuances that, as non-specialists in IR, we are not able to report or assess. Even so, it is clear that the orientation emerging here is substantial enough for the 'everyday' to serve as a potentially productive bridge between IR and ethnographic sociolinguistics, and it is to the latter that we now turn.

Sociolinguistics and linguistic ethnography

In recent years in sociolinguistics and applied linguistics, there has been growing interest in issues of (in)security (e.g. Makoni, 2017; Khan, 2017), peace and conflict (e.g. Footitt & Kelly (eds) 2012; Liddicoat, 2008), asylum (Maryns & Blommaert, 2001; Maryns, 2006) and surveillance (e.g. Garcia Sanchez, 2014; Rampton, 2016; Jones, 2017) (see Charalambous, 2017 for a bibliography). This is especially evident in studies of education, addressing, *inter alia*, the impact of growing securitization (e.g. Zakharia & Bishop, 2013), the positioning of undocumented migrants (e.g. Gallo, 2014), and the effect of legacies of conflict (Charalambous et al., 2018).

This work is *linguistic* in *two* ways, often at the same time: First, it examines the social and political significance of named/different languages as symbols of group affiliation and identity (languages as ideological 'objects'); and/or second, it focuses on language as a major element in communicative practice and the ongoing negotiation of social relations that this entails, whether or not people are speaking different languages (language as a communicative 'medium'). There are huge literatures on both, but our own work owes a particular debt to the linguistic anthropology associated with figures like John Gumperz and Dell Hymes, working mainly but not exclusively in north America.

Hymes called for "a social inquiry that does not abstract from verbal particulars, and a linguistic enquiry that connects verbal particulars ... with social activities and relationships" (1976/1996: 87). This concise formulation unpacks into the axioms guiding linguistic ethnography outlined in Chapter 1 in this volume:

- the contexts for communication should be investigated rather than assumed. Meaning takes shape within specific social relations, interactional histories and institutional regimes, produced and construed by agents with expectations and repertoires that have to be grasped ethnographically;
- analysis of the internal organisation of verbal (and other kinds of semiotic) data is essential to understanding its significance and position in the world. Meaning is far more than just the 'expression of ideas,' and biography, identifications, stance and nuance are extensively signalled in the linguistic and textual fine-grain.

Putting these principles to work in the analysis that follows, our account draws on four sets of resources:

a *linguistics & discourse analysis* (providing a provisional view of the communicative affordances of the linguistic resources that participants draw on in communication);
b *Goffman* and *conversation analysis* (offering frameworks and procedures for investigating situated encounters);
c *ethnography*; and
d *other public and academic discourses* (suggesting purpose and relevance for the analysis). (See Chapter 1, for more detail).

Within the sociolinguistic framework that we will be working, it is also important to disentangle three different meanings of the term 'everyday' (again, see Chapter 1). First, 'everyday' is often used to refer to a people, groups and environments in non-elite social strata, also sometimes called 'vernacular' or 'popular,' distinguished from the standard and official. Second, 'everyday' is often associated with a socio-cognitive orientation to the 'normal' in acts, events or people, regarding them as 'ordinary' rather than exceptional. These two meanings shouldn't be conflated, and as we will show, they can each be an important independent focus for analysis – conduct can be seen as normal as well as special in the realms of the elite, just as acts can be treated as exceptional, not just ordinary, in vernacular domains. Instead, for us, aligning with the basic ideas underpinning this volume, it makes more sense to equate the everyday with 'lived experience,' which actually encompasses the other two. Lived experience is also often seen as the central concern in ethnography, setting it apart from research that gives overwhelming or exclusive priority to theory and abstraction, and linguistic ethnography can be seen as a specialisation within this, focusing on situated communicative practice, whatever the environment or orientation, elite/vernacular, normal/exceptional.

With this outline of our framework in place, we can now move to an account of the fieldwork in our study.

Methods in our case study

Our investigation of the links between Greek-Cypriots' learning Turkish and Cyprus's troubled past involved two periods of fieldwork, the first in 2006–7, close to the initial introduction of Turkish language classes (henceforth the '2006' study) and the second in 2012–13 (the '2012' research). Fieldwork was undertaken by the 1st and 2nd named authors (who both grew up and live in Cyprus and belong to Greek-speaking families affected by the conflict), and it lasted five months in 2006–7 and nine months in 2012–13 (Table 3.1). In both periods, the researchers participated as students of Turkish in one of the adult classes they were observing.

Analysis was guided by the ethnographic assumption that the significance of a form or practice depends on the interaction of a range of different dimensions of socio-cultural organization and processes (Hymes, 1996), and the resources sketched in (a)–(d) in the previous section were treated as 'sensitising'

Table 3.1 Data collection

2006 Fieldwork	2012 Fieldwork
53 hours of observation	146 hours of observation
25.5 hours of audio-recording in four classes	84 hours of audio-recording in six secondary and two adult classes (116 students, four teachers)
20 interviews with 30 students; interviews with four teachers; interviews with four ministry officials	c. 40 interviews with 77 students and 5 teachers
Document analysis (textbooks, curricula and other government texts).	document collection (textbooks, curricula and other government texts).
	93 questionnaires

frameworks that "suggest directions along which to look" rather than as sets of 'definitive' constructs that "provide prescriptions of what to see" (Blumer, 1969: 148). As we will see, attending Turkish language classes was controversial, especially at secondary school, even though there were 1138 students learning Turkish in 75 classes in the Greek-Cypriot secondary system in 2006, and 873 in 61 classes in 2012. This contentiousness leads to the two questions that guide our analysis, which will centre on the adolescent learners:[1]

- how did the practices and institutional organization of schooling manage the associations of Turkish with violent conflict?
- how far and in what ways can we say that the Turkish lessons contributed to peace-building?

Our answer will draw on other public and academic discourses in its account of government policy (point [d] in the previous section; analysed in the next section below); ethnography in its description of the symbolic connotations and ideological values linked with Turkish and the effects of its positioning at school and in student networks ([c]; the section after that), and on Goffman and interaction analysis in the portrait of what happened in class ([b]; in the 7th section).

The 'Cyprus Issue,' education and the introduction of Turkish

Since the eruption of bicommunal violence, mainly in the second half of the twentieth century, and the 1974 war, Cyprus has been *de facto* divided into officially Turkish-speaking and Greek-speaking parts, and despite on-going diplomatic negotiations, there is no formal settlement to what is called the 'Cyprus Issue.' Over this period, the Greek-Cypriot and Turkish-Cypriot communities have engaged in separate nation-building processes, and hostility has been institutionalised. In the Greek-speaking (government-controlled) part of the island where our work is based, conflict perpetuating activities can be found in different institutions (Adamides, 2013, 2020), especially in education where there is ample ethnographic evidence of textual representations and teaching and commemoration practices that instil an emotional and political stance toward the conflict that solidifies the boundaries between 'us' and the 'others' (Papadakis, 2005; Philippou & Theodorou, 2014; Spyrou, 2006; Zembylas et al., 2013, 2016). But there hasn't been recent violence and overall, the political situation has been described as an intractable but 'comfortable conflict' (Adamides & Constantinou, 2011; Adamides, 2015).

Although the Republic of Cyprus was established in 1960 as a bicommunual state, with both Greek and Turkish as official languages, education had been always a mono-communal issue without any official provision for bilingual education. But around 2003, there was intense diplomatic negotiation about entry to the EU and resolution to the Cyprus Issue. As part of this, the Turkish authorities partially lifted the restriction of movement across the buffer zone in Nicosia (after almost 30 years), and the Greek-Cypriot government responded with a package of Measures of Support to Turkish-Cypriots which, along with the offer of passports, access to health care and so forth, included the introduction of classes to teach Greek-Cypriots the Turkish language. These were set up as an optional foreign language in the modern language curriculum at secondary school, and as free afternoon classes in government adult education institutes.[2] The introduction of these classes was also accompanied by a rhetoric of reconciliation – according to ministry officials, it aimed to "bring the two communities closer" and "cultivate mutual understanding" (Charalambous, 2019; Charalambous & Rampton, 2012).

But this wasn't accompanied by a widespread and unanimous shift in public discourse or in education, and the students who attended these classes told us that had to deal with adverse reactions from peers, teachers and even family members (accusations of 'traitor' and so forth). These were more intense in the first years after the classes were introduced, but they were also reported and observed ten years later in 2013:

Extract 1   An interview in 2006 with secondary students[3]

```
1 C.C.:     have your classmates ever said anything bad
            to you because you learn Turkish?
2 Andri:    YEAH!
3 Athina:   of course!
4           ((they laugh))
5 Andri:    YEAH!
6 C.C.:     for example what do they [say
7 Andri:                             ["you are ((Cypriot
                                     accent)) Turks"
8 Christalla: ((laughs)) they call us Turks
```

> **Extract 2   Interview with secondary students in 2013**
> Myria: ok my parents didn't say anything [...] but my brother who is a soldier told me like 'I am there protecting you from the- like from these people and you go and learn Turkish?'

The motivation behind choosing Turkish as a foreign language varied amongst the students and some of the most popular reasons were: 'easy language that can give good marks,' useful in the future, employment prospects, advice from family/friends, 'my friend chose it' etc. Many students also referred to intercommunal relations but their stances also varied. A substantial proportion of these secondary students were in favour of better inter-communal relations, seeing Turkish-Cypriots as "different than Turks" and "more towards our side," "more familiar with us," "more friendly" and stating that learning Turkish was "fair" and a way of showing respect. Nevertheless, in the 2012 questionnaire, around 25% of the 93 secondary students indicated 'learning the language of the enemy' as amongst the three most important reasons for taking the Turkish lessons. In interview, learning Turkish was sometimes described as a 'precaution' against "being tricked' or "taken advantage of," and despite the fact that they were actually learning the Turkish language themselves, some students said they didn't like Turkish-speakers and didn't "want any relations with them," on some occasions even saying "I wish they were effaced" and "may they all die":

> **Extract 3   Interview with secondary students 2012**
> Costas: and even if they give us our land back, there are so many people who died because of them, these are not coming back, they cannot bring back the missing persons of so many thousands that are still waiting, (...) so there cannot be friendship between these two peoples, us and them

At first sight, then, the socio-symbolic connotations ('indexical associations') of Turkish suggest that it might be a difficult language to teach, and with sharp differences in attitude like these, it sounds as though the classes might be volatile. But even though the indexical associations of a language are normally rooted in widely circulating ideologies, they are always sensitive to the particular activities, situations and social relations in which people attend to the language (Ochs, 1996). In addition, it is vital to address the subtle and complex communicative dynamics in which policy is enacted – relayed, received, adjusted, resisted or neglected – as it circulates discursively in the institutions that it targets (cf Ball et al., 2012: 2–3). So it is worth giving more detailed consideration to the social and cultural activity that language learning involves – its institutional embedding, its position in the daily round of people's activity, the interactional genres and routines with which it is conducted. This will generate a clearer sense of language learning's affordances and limitations in peace building and reconciliation, and help to identify its distinctiveness vis-à-vis other policies and measures for building trust (interventions by international actors, other local peace education projects and so forth).

Language provision at school: (i) Institutional structures, their affordances and effects

Turkish language lessons were not the only peace-building endeavour to have been introduced to Greek-Cypriot schools. From 2008 to 2010, the left-leaning government introduced a national peace education project which invited schools to organise pedagogical activities that emphasised commonalities between the Greek- and Turkish-Cypriot communities, cultivated solidarity and understanding, and 'avoided aphorisms and negative stereotypes' – perspectives that had been hitherto missing from the hegemonic curricular discourse of 'I don't forget and I struggle,' a discourse which emphasized Greek-Cypriot victimhood and promoted antagonism through the cultivation of a militant spirit (see Zembylas et al., 2016). But this project provoked fierce public reaction, and it was widely seen as "leftist propaganda" (Charalambous et al., 2013). The uptake and implementation was low, and when the government changed, it was officially abandoned, 'I don't forget' being re-emphasized once again (Charalambous et al., 2014).

In contrast, institutional structures for the provision of language teaching allowed material traditionally associated with the other side to be introduced in ways that partially extricated Turkish from the Cyprus issue, and slotted it into the existing routines of schooling. As already noted, Turkish is in fact an official *national* language in the Republic of Cyprus (appearing in stamps, coins, signs, ID cards and so forth), but its insertion into the list of *foreign* language options available at secondary school, alongside English, French, Spanish, Italian, German and Russian, downplayed its specifically national significance, recontextualised it in an international frame beyond the local, and drew on well-regarded international discourses about the value of language learning. In the policy advocated by the EU, for example, citizens should speak their mother tongue plus two other languages, and discourses like this were appropriated in later drafts of the Turkish secondary curriculum (2010), which shifted the emphasis from Trust Building and community solidarity to European calls for intercultural dialogue and neo-liberal discourses of language as a resource for professional and economic development (see Charalambous, 2019). In addition, a large and relatively well-functioning apparatus for the administration and delivery of language teaching was already in place in schools, and this could be expanded with relative ease to accommodate Greek-Cypriot teachers proficient in Turkish.[4] As a school subject, progress in Turkish was also ratified through the existing grading system, and this allowed students to select and/or succeed in it for a multiplicity of reasons. Some students opted for Turkish as part of their commitment to reconciliation and a bi-communal future for Cyprus, but many said they chose it because they needed good grades for their matriculation or GPA and Turkish was supposed to be easy (Charalambous et al., 2017, 2018).

So when the Turkish lessons and the 2008–10 peace initiative are compared, it seems that their incorporation within the existing language teaching structures made learning Turkish more defensible, less out of the ordinary, less exceptional. But this still fell quite a long way short of entirely normalizing the activity. As an optional subject, anyone selecting Turkish had had to consider the part that the language should play in their future (even if this only stretched as far as end-of-year exams), and attending Turkish classes meant committing – and being seen to commit – to this for a significant period of time (90 minutes a week for two years). So students of Turkish had to develop justifications for their choice, which they needed to argue with their critics and accusers. The substance of their justifications varied, and on occasion, even among students who supported reconciliation, this could involve the tactical adoption of a nationalist stance:

Extract 4 Interview 2006
```
C.C.:    are there any people who oppose to that? either
         classmates of yours or…-
Monica:  there are many people who think that Turks and
         especially Turkish language cannot be good …
         and they swear at them and they don't want to
         see them although … I can't understand it be-
         cause they are so racists … and although for
         example an English-Cypriot … why should they
         like an English-Cypriot but not a Turkish-
         Cypriot let's say? It's the same thing! This
         thing I cannot understand! And I don't think
         it's right, I tell them that.
```

Extract 5 Interview 2013
```
Gabriela:  one day […] Mrs S. came, a historian
           ((laughs)) her nation is high up there
           let's say, ((laughs)) and she tells me 'why
```

> did you choose Turkish?' and she is also my
> teacher, I was scared, I me::an
> Fotis: ((laughs))
> Gabriela: eh I tell her 'Miss, whether we like it or not
> Turkish-Cypriots are there and we have to
> learn it too at- and I have an uncle who is in
> the- a military officer and he tells me, to
> combat the enemy you have to know his culture,
> everything, you have to know everything'
> Petros: you have to learn the language of the enemy
> Christina: hey what mark did she give you?
> Gabriela: eighteen ((out of 20))

In fact, even though there was very little political discussion in the lessons themselves (as we shall see), and even though the discursive shift among secondary students was subtle rather than spectacular, there is a case for saying that taking the Turkish classes itself succeeded in *denaturalising* the anti-Turkish nationalist perspective.

In 19 of the 21 interviews in 2012, we asked students whether they thought that "choosing or not choosing Turkish" was influenced by political beliefs. In their answers, nobody focused on the *positive* choice of Turkish as something driven by political considerations, even though they might, for example, have associated it with leftist politics (as often happened with the 2008–10 peace education initiative mentioned above). Instead, students all concentrated on political reasons for *not* opting for Turkish, and in nine of the interviews,[5] they talked about nationalist students, several also referring explicitly to ultra-right ELAM party supporters:

> **Extract 6 Interview 2012**
> P.C.: ok, now that you mention politics, would you say
> that one's political beliefs can influence his/
> her decision to choose or not choose Turkish?
> Students: ((in chorus)) yes, surely, yes yes
> Georgia: me for example, I have friends who are sup-
> porters of ELAM let's say and they wouldn't
> choose Turkish for sure, while myself I have
> a different view on politics, erm yes, I'm
> more open-minded on some things

> **Extract 7   Interview 2012**
> P.C: e::rm would you say that one's political positions and ideas can influence his/her decision to choose or not choose Turkish?
> Christi: yes! ((laughs)) yes! ok, there are some who are let's say very passionate with this, let's say 'they are our enemies,' this and that 'I don't want to choose their language, or to go to the occupied areas and if I see them I'll swear at them' something like that, and that's why most people don't choose it

Borrowing from Bourdieu (1977: 164–171), we can say that in these responses, nationalism was no longer a seamless part of the educational mainstream, and that Turkophobia had lost its unquestioned authority. Although there certainly were strong and numerous expressions of nationalism, the potentially very heterodox practice of learning Turkish was now part of the ground from which these students all spoke, and as a result, nationalism was downgraded from 'doxic' truth to *ortho*doxy, moving from something on which everyone would of course agree, to becoming a noticeably partisan counter-protestation against the language learning option that these particular students had chosen. So even though it was heavily promoted elsewhere in the Hellenocentric curriculum, nationalist hatred of Turks was no longer taken for granted as a matter of political commonsense among these Turkish language learners.

In addition, of course, the identity of 'pupil' and the practices of schooling aren't confined within the gates of school. They are also regularly carried home and enacted from time to time with parents and siblings. In this way, a lot of students reported conversations about the Turkish language and the Turkish lessons with members of their family – choosing which language to opt for, checking homework, talking about tests and exams, relating anecdotes of classroom experiences etc. Turkish certainly wasn't always welcome:

> "my mum simply doesn't like it and she told me not to speak it at home but she is ok with me learning it" (Corina; Interview 2012)

> "erm ok because they lived through the war and they had a hard time, there's no chance that they'll want to hear the Turkish language at home, ok" (Froso; Interview 2012)

Peace-building through language education 63

But for others, learning Turkish was an enjoyable activity worth sharing:

Extract 8   Interview 2013
Maria: erm I speak it at home with my parents and I
         like it
P.C.: what do you mean you speak with your parents?
Maria: eh these things, "hello" "how are you," I like it
P.C.: ah because you said earlier that both your parents
       learn Turkish right?
Maria: yes, and it's very nice, it's fun, I enjoy it

Extract 9   Interview 2013
Areti: I can- like I talk to my mum, to my mum let's say,
        when she tells me something, {I tell her}
        Turkish words that she can easily learn like
        'good morning' 'how are you' 'what's your name'

Extract 10   Interview 2013
P.C.: erm, do you use it anywhere?
Marina: yes, all the time!
P.C.: really? where?
Marina: with my siblings, my cousins, we are learning
         foreign languages and we are exchanging
Despo: me with my brother, because he knows, sometimes
        he sits and we spend time together talking and
        learning it
P.C.: ah really?
Despo: yes, also new words and things like that

Extract 11   Interview 2013
Despo: my brother had it {the lessons} last year and
        told me (...) he is a soldier now but he told me, he
        says 'you should take Turkish, it's both easy
        and nice'

In this way, linguistic forms, objects and activities associated with Turkish were carried outside the predominantly Hellocentric and rather Turkophobic school environment, brought home and recontextualised in domestic relationships that could be more receptive, thereby potentially shifting the language's indexical associations.

So although learning Turkish was much more controversial than learning French or Italian, its insertion into the structural fabric of secondary modern language provision made it more stable and more easily justified than the 2008–10 peace education project, and unlike the latter, it also survived the change to a more nationalist government in 2012.[6] Turning to more general questions of interpretation, we can't claim that learning Turkish was part of the everyday if the 'everyday' is interpreted as a vernacular domain counter-posed to the standard or elite, since schooling is itself an official institution managed by state (at least in this study). But we can say that the everyday as 'ordinary' and 'unexceptional' was an important concern in the effortful processes of normalisation we have described, not as a cultural profile that Turkish had actually already achieved as a subject at school, but as a goal both in the institutional enactment of language policy and in the self-justifications of its stakeholders.

In the account so far, we have focused on institutional organisation and the possibilities for engaging with Turkish that this generated, and methodologically we have drawn on ethnography and document analysis (Section 3 points [c] and [d]). But we have said very little about what actually happened *inside* Turkish language classroom, and in now turning to this, we will draw more fully on frameworks for the analysis of interactional practice (Section 3, point [b]), where the normative tension between the ordinary and exceptional can also be seen in play.

Language provision at school: (ii) Activity in lessons

On a few occasions in our dataset, Turkish lessons did allow for serious political discussions. The extract below, for example, took place in a small class where there was an explicit political consensus on inter-communal relations and the teacher described the students as 'exceptional' and 'adult-like.' In the extract, one of the students starts a critique of dominant ideologies in state education that the teacher picks up and elaborates:

Extract 12   During a Turkish language lesson in a secondary school in 2013, after watching a documentary about Istanbul
```
Gabriela: yes, let's say in school they never told me- or
          last year when we learnt about Islam in history
P.C.:     what did you learn about Islam
Gabriela: eh ok more about the Koran but the references
          we made to Turkish contemporary history or
          even to today, they only tell us the negative
          sides.
```

```
Renos: yes
Gabriela: they don't tell us - you know... eh:: that
         {Turkey} is more modern
Petros: yeah! racism
TEACHER: yes because in the cities there are Turks who
         are more European, because there are girls
         like you with jeans and short tight T-shirts
```

But this was very rare, and it was much more likely that any positive reference to Turkey, Turks or Turkish Cypriots would provoke protest (see Charalambous, 2013 for detailed analysis of one such episode). Talking about the other four classes that she taught, the same teacher commented:

Extract 11   On not provoking the students

Stella (f; 40s), Greek-Cypriot teacher of Turkish in interview with Panayiota (2012)

```
Stella: I tried once to say that Turkey is beautiful,
        and Istanbul, and they tried to tell me that I
        am defending Turkey in class, we have to be
        very careful about what we say so that students
        don't go out and say that we are doing propa-
        ganda in favour of Turkey and that we say the
        Turks are good and they do this and that, we
        have to be very careful and stay in matters of
        the language
```

Analysis of classroom interaction confirmed that for the most part in both 2006 and 2012, teachers were indeed "very careful and stay[ed] in matters of language." There was a strong tendency to avoid any talk about Turkish people, Turkish-Cypriots or Turkish-speaking culture, and the language was presented in most classrooms as a neutral linguistic system consisting of grammatical rules and maths-like formulae (see Charalambous 2012, 2013, 2014 and Charalambous et al., 2017 for an overview). There is in fact a long line of teaching that treats language as a formal code, enacted in traditional lesson genres that consist of explanations from the teacher, tests, exercises, translations and so forth (rather than project work, interaction with material from the real world of the 'target culture,' or simulated encounters with target language speakers). But it wasn't because the teachers were just 'old-fashioned' that they taught Turkish in this way. Like Stella, they were aware that they were presenting a very narrow view of Turkish, and they said that they were doing this deliberately because of the ideological controversy around the language.

At this point, the socio-cognitive boundary between the ordinary and the exceptional moves back into focus, although here it is an interactional concern and Goffman's work becomes directly relevant.[7] One way to make threatening or contentious material safe is by 'keying' it, framing it so that everyone involved knows that its use is not to be treated naively or taken 'straight' (1974: Ch. 3). Goffman identifies several general keys, and these include 'make believe,' which includes playful mimicry, dramatic scriptings and activity "done with the knowledge that nothing practical will come of the doing" (1974: 48–56), and 'contests' (games and sports) in which "the rules... supply restrictions of degree and mode of aggression" (1974: 56,57; Rampton & Charalambous 2012: 489–493; Rampton et al., 2019: Section 7). But he also talks about 'technical redoing,' in which novices are given "the experience in performing under conditions in which (it is felt) no actual engagement with the world is allowed, events having been 'decoupled' from their usual embedment in consequentiality" (p. 59). Technical redoings are activities which are [i] "performed out of their usual context, [ii] for utilitarian purposes openly different from those of the original performance, [iii] the understanding being that the original outcome of the activity will not occur" (p. 59; numerals added). Goffman cites stage rehearsals, exhibitions and pedagogic demonstrations as examples of technical redoing (1974: 58ff) and it also matches the Turkish lessons, in which the language was extracted from its socio-cultural context ([i] above) and turned into something you needed to pass exams rather than communicate with ([ii]), thereby accommodating students who never wanted to talk to a Turkish speaker ([iii]). And just as technical redoing also allows "all sorts of perspectives and ... motivational relevances" (p. 64), these culturally sterilised lessons could accommodate students who saw Turkish as a potential weapon alongside those who hoped for better inter-ethnic relations in the future.

In fact, students themselves sometimes touched up controversial political issues, though here too they keyed them as non-serious in a way that avoided argument and allowed the normal business of the lesson to continue. For example, Extract 14 involved two close friends in 2012, one who was usually pro-reconciliation (Filippos), and the other who held ultranationalist views (Nikos). The teacher was trying to show the class how the names of countries, nationalities and languages are formed in Turkish, and a few minutes earlier, Nikos had reacted upon hearing the use of 'Istanbul' instead of 'Constantinople' (the city's name in Greek). Just before the episode in Extract 14, the teacher has noticed that the class is starting to lose concentration. He invites one girl to come and sit at a desk in the front, and then he turns to Nikos and tries to 'wake him up' with a 'hello/good morning' in Turkish. Nikos responds but fails to carry the exchange through correctly (lines 2–4); the teacher flags up an error (line 5); and Filippos intervenes with a comment in the next turn that attributes the mistake to his friend's irredentist politics (lines 6–7):

Extract 14[8]

1. TEACHER: merhaba (*(Hello)*)
2. Nikos: merhaba (*(Hello)*)
3. TEACHER: nasilsin? (*(how are you?)*)
4. Nikos: nasilsin? (*(how are you?)*)
5. TEACHER: Is that how you answer this question?
6. Filippos: Nikos is thinking of other stuff sir,
7. he is thinking of how to get Constantinople back
8. (*(the lesson carries on)*)

In lines 6 & 7, Filippos' pushes Nikos' politics into the spotlight, implying that he is too preoccupied with nationalist issues to participate successfully in class. Juxtaposing a longstanding territorial dispute to a banal classroom greeting routine like this, he produces an abrupt but substantial shift of topic and scale that sounds somewhat anomalous. When this is also contextualised within their well-known friendship and the practical impossibility of actually knowing exactly what Nikos is thinking at just this point, the remark comes across as playful, and the business of the lesson carries on as usual.

In 2006, Dimos and Kyriakos were also good friends with very different views on the Cyprus issue (Dimos was active in the leftist youth organisation EDON), and in Extract 15, politics was also slipped into the class in a humorous key, on this occasion partly outside the main flow of classroom activity. In a lesson that was rather unusual in its inclusion of cultural material, the students were supposed to sing along to a Turkish song,[9] but one of them was wearing a radio-microphone which picked up some quieter 'subordinate communication' (Goffman, 1981: 133):[10]

Extract 15 Turkish language lesson, secondary school 2006 (see Charalambous, 2012)

1. Dimos: (*(talking to the mic)*) we are against Greece and 'Enosis'[11] (*(Unification)*)
2. we are just 'Cypriots united shall never be defeated'![12]
3. Kyriakos: Cyprus Turkey 'Enosis'
4. Dimos: (*(laughs)*)
   (*(they join the rest of the class in singing)*)

Addressing the researcher through the radio-mic, the boys are playing with political slogans, inserting elements of their own. When Dimos claims that "we are against Greece and 'Enosis'" (line 1), he can't actually speak for Kyriakos, but in line 2, the political substance of the claim is subordinated to verbal play in the substitution of 'Cypriots' for 'the people/el pueblo' in the famous chant "the people united shall never be defeated." Kyriakos then intensifies the improvisation in line 3, using the comically self-contradictory "Cyprus Turkey Enosis" to articulate a political position that neither of them embrace. In this way, their knowledge and sensitivity to the Cyprus issue penetrates the sanitised neutrality of the classroom, but it is kept to the side of the main activity in class, while the humorous elaboration and exchange of slogans cloaks their own personal stances in comic anomaly (for further discussion and analysis see Charalambous, 2012).

At this point, we can summarise our answer to the two questions motivating the analysis.

a *How was the controversial potential of Turkish handled in the provision and practice of teaching and learning in Greek-Cypriot secondary schools?* We have described how government policy inserted Turkish in a pre-existing option slot in the foreign language curriculum, where it was sustained and somewhat normalised by the structures and routines of language study, which also sent it into family homes in homework books, learnt phrases and so forth. The lessons put Turkish language materials in front of adolescents with very different political views, but the teachers neutralised the risk of conflagration by focusing on language as a grammatical code, while the students only acknowledged the politics lightly, in non-serious exchanges and asides.

b *How far and in what ways can we say that the Turkish lessons contributed to peace-building?* This was only an intra- rather than an inter-group arena, with no Turkish-Cypriots present, but even so, it provided a different way of relating to 'things Turkish.' In contrast to other school subjects which consolidated the lines between 'us' and 'them' (Zembylas et al., 2014, 2016), these lessons provided very little scope for the articulation of traditional discourses of hostility. Instead, participation in these classes can be seen as a first step, a first 'lesson' in how to deal with the controversy of the conflict, how to respect other views, how not to overstep the boundaries, how to justify yourself as an individual choosing the Turkish option. Nationalist Turkophobia appeared to have lost its unquestioned authority, and of course just in terms of learning the language itself, the lessons could also bear fruit in the future, with students going on to study Turkish at university, meeting Turkish-speakers, using the language at work etc.

Overall, though, claims for reconciliatory benefits of learning Turkish at secondary school are safer focusing on "the modest goals of coexistence and tolerance" than on "a more expansive concept of peace," as Mac Ginty puts it in his discussion of 'everyday peace' (2014: 549; also Chapter 2 this volume). Indeed, 'everyday peace' is one of the concepts within IR that appears to fit the scene we have described, at least in part, and it is to these that we should now turn.

Greek-Cypriots studying Turkish: 'De-securitisation' and 'everyday peace'?

How far and in what ways does our case study connect with recent or contemporary work in IR, and what could linguistic ethnography add? Two topics seem relevant, one more obviously linked to the account of policy and institutional organisation in Section 6 ('de-securisation'), and the other to the descriptions of interaction in Section 7 ('everyday peace').

The notion of de-securitization is linked to the theory of securitization, which itself refers to the discursive and institutional processes in which 'existential threats' to the state and other bodies are identified, and groups or issues are moved out from the realm of ordinary politics into the realm of exceptional measures, where normal political rights and procedures are suspended (Buzan & Waever, 2003; Emmers, 2013). De-securitisation reverses this process, and according to Aradau, it entails a "democratic challenge to the non-democratic politics of securitization [that] has to be inscribed institutionally and needs to create a different relation from the one of enmity, a relation which is not rooted in the exclusionary logic of security" (2004: 400). In securitization, "the speed introduced by security does away with the possibility of scrutiny as well as the expression of voice," but in de-securitization "the slowness of procedures ensures the possibility of contestation" (2004: 393). Applying this to our case-study, the Turkish language lessons institutionalised the government's reconciliatory expressions of good will in 2003; the lessons brought students with very different political attitudes together over a substantial period of time and exposed them to Turkish "in a different relation from the one of enmity"; and even though the teachers actually tried very hard to avoid "the possibility of contestation" during lessons, these classes opened a space which provoked argument and deliberation outside, disrupting nationalism's taken-for-granted status as well. So these Turkish language lessons for Greek-Cypriots can be aligned with de-securitisation, and we have invoked it in earlier work as a relatively abstract characterisation of these processes (Charalambous et al., 2017).

A second connection is to work on 'hybrid peace,' which attends to "the engagement of policy makers, peacebuilders, NGOS and donors with local civil society's potential to initiate and sustain a peaceful polity in a range of different but overlapping contextual frames" (Richmond & Tellidis, 2017: 137). Referring to the EU, the Republic of Cyprus government, local institutional structures and the situated activity of individuals, the span of our case study is loosely compatible with the horizons covered in accounts of hybrid peace (Mac Ginty, 2010: 391; Mac Ginty & Richmond, 2013). But within this, Mac Ginty's notion of 'everyday peace' has particular resonance for sociolinguists.

'Everyday peace' refers to:

> "the routinized practices used by individuals and collectives as they navigate their way through life in a deeply divided society ... It involves coping mechanisms such as the avoidance of contentious subjects in religiously or ethnically mixed company, or a constructive ambiguity whereby people conceal their identity or opinion lest they draw attention to themselves" (2014: 549; see also Chapter 2).

These practices also include 'ritualized politeness' (avoiding anything that may cause offence), 'telling' (discerning ethnic identification and social ordering), and 'blame deferring' (shifting blame to outsiders) (2014: 556), and they are produced within an alert sensitivity to the possibility of rapid conflict escalation (p. 549). So, their everyday routinization certainly isn't 'doxic' or taken-for-granted – these are coping mechanisms that "allow a façade of normality to prevail," and they involve "innovation, creativity and improvisation" (p. 555). This is consistent with our account of, for example, grammar-focused Turkish language teaching as 'technical redoing' – as a pedagogy that was carefully tuned to the risk of controversy, and that involved much more than just the unthinking reproduction of a traditional teaching style. Like us, Mac Ginty also cites Goffman. But there are two ways in which sociolinguistic research qualifies this account of everyday peace.

First, although Mac Ginty recognizes that these coping practices are "possible at some periods and impossible at others" (p. 552), he uses the term 'fluid' to characterise them (p. 549, 552). Seen from a distance, from the vantage point of state policy analysis for example, these small-scale acts might well look fluid, but fine-grained sociolinguistic analysis shows that they are actually very closely woven into the intricate structuring of social interaction. So in Extract 14, Filippos' quip about Constantinople is skilfully timed to pre-empt Nikos' response to the teacher's question, and its structural positioning as a peripheral insertion of the main business of the lesson means that it can be easily ignored and swiftly passed over. Similarly, in Extract 15, Kyriakos' "Cyprus Turkey Enosis" (line 3) achieves its comic effect by incorporating and extending the materials presented by his friend a moment before (adding 'Turkey' to Dimos' 'Enosis' and 'Cypr(iots)' in lines 1 & 2). The bigger point is that there is structuration and an element of conventionality in even the briefest utterance. It is through a plurality of co-occurring structures that we can recognise and differentiate actions as belonging to a particular type, and these structures are the frames within which we produce and construe the unceasing improvisation which is also intrinsic to interaction (Giddens, 1976; Bourdieu 1977). Going one step further, the notion of indexicality points to the systematic links between tiny linguistic forms and more general ideological structures (as attested in the story of shibboleth in the Book of Judges (Chs. 12.5 & 12.6)), and far from the free and fluid play of agency, this brings relations of power right to the heart of the most instantaneous sense-making.[13] In fact, Mac Ginty recognises that the practices associated with everyday peace "rel[y] on opportunities and context, as well as the ability of groups and individuals and groups to exploit these" (p. 550), but as sociolinguists, we would call this variation *situated* rather than fluid, in an account that sees agency inextricably tied to a multiplicity of structures, 'all the way down.'

Second, rather than seeing a contrast between 'bottom up local agency' and 'top-down actors and professionals,' we claim that 'everyday peace' practices like these are not the exclusive preserve of non-elite people interacting in non-formal environments. In our own study, for example, it certainly wouldn't be possible to equate avoidance or 'keying' practices with informal domains, since we mainly focused on official settings sponsored by the state (schools and classrooms). Indeed, the dichotomisation of formal and informal itself looks fragile when adolescents can be seen joking with friends in lessons, and there's light-hearted talk at home in Turkish imported from the classroom. It is important, in other words, to disentangle two of the senses of 'everyday' identified in Section 3: environments and people endowed with high or low ranked material, cultural and linguistic resources on the one hand, and on the other, socio-cognitive orientations to what's deemed normal and exceptional that are negotiated in interaction. So when Mac Ginty distinguishes between

> "everyday civilities produced by local people directly affected by conflict on the one hand, and the 'expert' peace-building discourse of expatriates, a discourse that's standardised and professionalised though 'best practice' and 'lessons learned'" (2014: 551),

we can agree that locals and expatriates are likely to differ in the linguistic resources they can draw on – the genres, the languages, the styles and so forth. It is also very possible that these differences themselves get politicised, and that local communicative practices are ignored or dismissed. But as Goffman's *oeuvre* makes clear, virtually everyone produces 'everyday civilities' (ritualized politeness, blame deferral etc), and even though peace-building professionals may well be pressured by their overseers to adhere to scripts and rulebooks, the subtleties of communicative interaction always exceed institutional prescriptions, and there is still room for them to produce coping practices creatively adjusted to the communicative exigencies on hand (even though their success can never be guaranteed).

Conclusion

Although we have not dwelt on it here, we are convinced that the frameworks now emerging in IR for apprehending the growing significance of insecurity and violent conflict in ordinary life have a great deal to offer to the sociolinguistics of everyday communication (Rampton & Charalambous, 2020). But in this chapter, we have looked in the other direction, addressing researchers in IR with a linguistic ethnography of Greek-Cypriot secondary school students learning Turkish, the language of the (former) enemy. As well as suggesting some of the ways in which language and language education can play a role in peace-building, we have used this material both as a practical illustration of the kind of account that ethnographic sociolinguistics can generate, and as a platform from which to engage with specific IR topics. We have also differentiated several meanings of 'everyday,' and tried to demonstrate the significance of these differences empirically. Overall, we have sought, minimally, to declare our own incursions into the domain of IR, and started making our interaction with its concepts accountable to IR experts. Beyond that, of course, it is not for us to judge whether or not the frameworks of linguistic ethnography resonate in the work on everyday International Relations, though of course we hope they do.

Notes

1 The challenge to the reconciliatory potential of these classes was substantially greater in the adolescent than in the smaller and more self-selected adult classes. Among other things, hostility to Turks and Turkish-Cypriot was very powerful at school, while in the voluntary adult institutes, all the learners gave up their own time to attend, and generally tended to bring a personal commitment to learning Turkish as a contribution to improved relations with Turkish speakers, with whom a number of students already had quite extensive contact.
2 There were actually many more sites in Cyprus where Greek-Cypriots could learn Turkish than those we describe below (these included a Turkish Studies programme at the University of Cyprus, private tuition, and inter-communal centres committed to reconciliation)
3 All transcripts are translated from Greek, unless stated otherwise
4 Although the Turkish Studies department at the University of Cyprus produced its first graduates in 1996, the first teachers to be appointed to Turkish language teaching posts in 2003 were trained at universities in the former Soviet bloc.
5 In 2 interviews the students didn't find the question relevant, and in 8 they referred to various ideological reasons.
6 However, in 2015,all MFL choices were replaced with compulsory French and English teaching in a new educational reform. At the time of the publication of this chapter, Turkish is only available to students who wish to choose an MFL-route in their studies (other routes include Humanities, Economics, Sciences, etc.)
7 Throughout his career, Goffman was interested in the tension between (what's sensed as) the ordinary and the exceptional, as well as in the actions and activities produced to handle the threats they pose each other. This stands out even in his first two books. The first was his 1959 *The Presentation of Self in Everyday Life*

but the second, just two years later, was *Asylums,* and this focused on total institutions where people are cut off from everyday life, often because they're deemed to be a threat to the community (1961:16). In subsequent work, he addressed the dynamic relationship between these two orientations both in people's behaviour in public spaces and in the details of face-to-face interaction (e.g. 1971, 1981).
8 This is taken from Panayiota's fieldnotes, rather than being audio-recorded as in the other extracts
9 The cover version of a song that was originally in Greek, as the teacher explained.
10 Goffman distinguishes several different lines of communication when people are physically co-present (1981:133). As well as the dominant communication on the main floor of the interaction, there is often subordinate communication, which can be either open/unconcealed, or collusive/surreptitious. This includes 'byplay' (communication between subset of ratified participants), 'cross-play' (communication between ratified participants and bystanders), and 'side-play' (hushed words between bystanders).
11 "Cyprus, Greece, Enosis (Unification)" had been for many years the slogan of Greek-Cypriot nationalism, and residual elements of this ideology can be encountered either in extreme Rightist discourses or in the form of nostalgic visions of what could have been an alternative reality.
12 From the leftist Chilean political anthem "El pueblo unido jamás será vencido" ['the people united will never be defeated'], known in Greek as "λαός ενωμένος ποτέ νικημένος."
13 This is vividly illustrated in, for example, Bourdieu's account of symbolic violence, in which "ways of looking, sitting, standing, keeping silent or even of speaking ('reproachful looks' or 'tones,' 'disapproving glances' and so on) are full of injunctions that are powerful and hard to resist precisely because they are silent and insidious, insistent and insinuating" (1991:51).

References

Adamides, C. (2015). A comfortable and routine conflict. In J. Ker-Lindsay (Ed.), *Resolving Cyprus: New approaches to conflict resolution* (pp. 5–15). London: IB Tauris.
Adamides, C. (2020). *Securitization and Desecuritization Processes in Protracted Conflicts.* Springer International Publishing.
Adamides, C., & Constantinou, C. M. (2012). Comfortable conflict and (il) liberal peace in cyprus. In O. Richmond, & A. Mitchell (Eds.), *Hybrid forms of peace: From everyday agency to post-liberalism* (pp. 242–259). London: Palgrave Macmillan.
Aradau, C. (2004). Security and the democratic scene: Desecuritization and emancipation. *Journal of International Relations and Development, 7*(4), 388–413.
Ball, S. J., Maguire, M., & Braun, A. (2012). *How schools do policy: Policy enactments in secondary schools* Routledge.
Balzacq, T. (2010). *Securitization theory: How security problems emerge and dissolve* Routledge.
Bar-Tal, D., Diamond, A. H., & Nasie, M. (2017). Political socialization of young children in intractable conflicts: Conception and evidence. *International Journal of Behavioral Development, 41*(3), 415–425.
Bigo, D. (2014). The (in) securitization practices of the three universes of EU border control: Military/Navy–border guards/police–database analysts. *Security Dialogue, 45*(3), 209–225.

Bigo, D. (2016). International political sociology: Rethinking the international through dynamics of power. In T. Basaran, D. Bigo, E. Guittet & R. Walker D. (Eds.), *Transversal lines* (pp. 24–48). London: Routledge.

Blumer, H. (1969). *Symbolic Interaction*. Berkeley: University of California Press.

Borba, R. 2015. How an individual becomes a subject: Discourse, interaction & subjectification at a Brazilian gender identity clinic. *Working Papers in Urban Language & Literacies* 163. At academia.edu.

Bourdieu, P. (1977). *Outline of a Theory of Practice*. Cambridge: CUP.

Buzan, B., & Waever, O. (2003). *Regions and powers: The structure of international security* Cambridge University Press.

Charalambous, C. (2012). 'Republica de Kubros': Transgression and collusion in Greek-Cypriot adolescents' classroom 'silly-talk'. *Linguistics and Education*, *23*, 334–349.

Charalambous, C. (2013). The 'burden' of emotions in language teaching: Negotiating a troubled past in 'other'-language learning classrooms. *Language and Intercultural Communication*, *13*(3), 310–329.

Charalambous, C. (2014). 'Whether you see them as friends or enemies you need to know their language': Turkish language learning in a Greek-Cypriot school. In V. Lytra (Ed.), *When Greek meets turk: Interdisciplinary perspectives on the relationship since 1923* (pp. 141–162). London: Ashgate.

Charalambous, C. (2019). Language education and 'Conflicted heritage': Implications for teaching and learning. *The Modern Language Journal*, *103*(4), 874–891.

Charalambous, C., Charalambous, P., Khan, K. & Rampton, B. (2018). Security and language policy. In J. Tollefson W., & M. Pérez-Milans (Eds.), *The Oxford handbook of language policy and planning.* (pp. 632–652). Oxford: OUP.

Charalambous, C., & Rampton, B. (2012). Other-language learning and intercultural communication in contexts of conflict. In J. Jackson (Ed.), *The Routledge Handbook of Language and Intercultural Communication* (pp. 195–210). London: Routledge. Also available as *Working Papers in Urban Language & Literacies* # 60, at academia.edu

Charalambous, C., Charalambous, P., & Zembylas, M. (2013). Doing 'Leftist propaganda' or working towards peace? Moving Greek-Cypriot peace education struggles beyond local political complexities. *Journal of Peace Education*, *10*(1), 67–87.

Charalambous, P., Charalambous, C., & Zembylas, M. (2014). Old and new policies in dialogue: Greek-Cypriot teachers' interpretations of a peace-related initiative through existing policy discourses. *British Educational Research Journal*, *40*(1) 79–101.

Charalambous, C., Zembylas, M., & Charalambous, P. (2016). Diversity and conflict: Negotiating linguistic, ethnic and emotional boundaries in Greek-Cypriot literacy classrooms. *Linguistics and Education*, *35*, 50–62.

Charalambous, P., Charalambous, C., & Rampton, B. (2017). De-securitizing Turkish: Teaching the language of a former enemy, and intercultural language education. *Applied Linguistics*, *38*(6), 800–823.

Charalambous, P. 2017. *Sociolinguistics and security: A bibliography*. At www.kcl.ac.uk/liep

Constantinou, C. (2016). Everyday Diplomacy: Mission, Spectacle and the Remaking of Diplomatic Culture. In J., Dittmer, & F. McConnell (Eds.), *Diplomatic Cultures and International Politics: Translations, Spaces and Alternatives.* (pp.23–40) Routledge.

Emmers, R. (2013). Securitization. In A. Collins (Ed.), *Contemporary security studies* (3rd ed., pp. 131–143) Oxford Univeristy Press.
Footitt, H., & Kelly, M. (Eds.). (2012). *Languages at war: Policies and practices of language contacts in conflict*. Houndmills: Springer.
Gallo, S. (2014). The effects of gendered immigration enforcement on middle childhood and schooling. *American Educational Research Journal, 51*(3), 473–504.
Garcia Sanchez, I. M. (2014). *Language and Muslim immigrant childhoods: The politics of belonging*. Malden, MA: Wiley-Blackwell.
Garfinkel, H. (1967). *Studies in Ethnomethodology*. Cambridge: Polity Press.
Giddens, A. (1976). *New Rules of Sociological Method*. London: Hutchinson.
Gillespie, M., & O'Loughlin, B. (2009). News media, threats and insecurities: An ethnographic approach. *Cambridge Review of International Affairs, 22*(4), 667–685.
Goffman, E. (1959). *The Presentation of Self in Everyday Life*. Harmondsworth: Penguin.
Goffman, E. (1961). *Asylums*. Harmondsworth: Penguin.
Goffman, E. (1971). *Relations in Public*. Harmondsworth: Penguin.
Goffman, E. (1974). *Frame Analysis*. Boston: North Eastern University Press.
Goffman, E. (1981). *Forms of Talk*. Philadelphia: University of Pennsylvania Press.
Gready, P., & Robins, S. (2014). From transitional to transformative justice: A new agenda for practice. *International Journal of Transitional Justice, 8*(3), 339–361.
Green, N. , & Zurawski, N. (2015). Surveillance and ethnography: Researching surveillance as everyday life. *Surveillance and Society, 13*(1), 27–43.
Gumperz, J. (1982). *Discourse Strategies*. Cambridge: Cambridge University Press.
Huysmans, J. (2009). Conclusion: Insecurity and the everyday. In P. Noxolo, & J. Huysmans (Eds.), *Community, citizenship, and the 'war on terror': Security and insecurity* (pp. 197–207). Basingstoke: Palgrave Macmillan.
Hymes, D. (ed)(1969) *Reinventing Anthropology*. Ann Arbor: University of Michigan Press.
Hymes, D. (1976) 1996. Report from an underdeveloped country: Toward linguistic competence in the United States. In D. Hymes 1996. *Ethnography, Linguistics, Narrative Inequality* (pp. 63–105). London: Taylor & Francis.
Hymes, D. (1996). *Ethnography; Linguistics, Narrative Inequality: Toward an Understanding of Voice*. London: Taylor and Francis.
Jarvis, L., & Lister, M. (2013). Disconnected citizenship? the impacts of anti-terrorism policy on citizenship in the UK. *Political Studies, 61*(3), 656–675.
Johnson, H. L. (2016). Narrating entanglements: Rethinking the Local/Global divide in ethnographic migration research. *International Political Sociology, 10*(4), 383–397.
Jones, R. (2017). Surveillant landscapes. *Linguistic Landscape* 3/2: 150–187.
Khan, K (2017). Citizenship, securitisation and suspicion in UK ESOL policy. In Arnaut, K., M. Karrebæk, M. Spotti & J. Blommaert (eds) *Engaging Superdiversity: Recombining Spaces, Times and Language Practices* (pp. 303–320). Bristol: Multilingual Matters. Also available as *Working Papers in Urban Language & Literacies* 130 at academia.edu
Leonardsson, H., & Rudd, G. (2015). The 'local turn'in peacebuilding: A literature review of effective and emancipatory local peacebuilding. *Third World Quarterly, 36*(5), 825–839.

Liddicoat, A. J. (2008). Language planning and questions of national security: An overview of planning approaches. *Current Issues in Language Planning*, *9*(2), 129–153.

Mac Ginty, R. (2010). Hybrid peace: The interaction between top-down and bottom-up peace. *Security Dialogue*, *41*(4), 391–412.

Mac Ginty, R. (2014). Everyday peace: Bottom-up and local agency in conflict-affected societies. *Security Dialogue*, *45*(6), 548–564.

Mac Ginty, R., & Richmond, O. P. (2013). The local turn in peace building: A critical agenda for peace. *Third World Quarterly*, *34*(5), 763–783.

Makoni, S. B. (2017). Language planning, security, police communication and multilingualism in uniform: The case of south african police services. *Language & Communication*, *57*, 48–56.

Marsden, M., Ibañez-Tirado, D., & Henig, D. (2016). Everyday diplomacy. *The Cambridge Journal of Anthropology*, *34*(2), 2–22.

Maryns, K. & J. Blommaert (2001). Stylistic and thematic shifting as a narrative resource: Assessing asylum seekers' repertoires *Multilingua* 20–1 (2001), 61–84.

Maryns, K. (2006). *The Asylum Speaker: Language in the Belgian Asylum Procedure*. Manchester: St Jerome.

Mc Cluskey, E. 2017. *Everyday (in)security: A bibliography*. At www.kcl.ac.uk/liep

O'Reilly, M., Súilleabháin, A. Ó., & Paffenholz, T. (2015). *Reimagining peacemaking: Women's roles in peace processes*. New York: International Peace Institute, 11–13.

Ochs, E. (1996). Linguistic resources for socialising humanity. In J. Gumperz & S. Levinson (eds) *Rethinking Linguistic Relativity* (pp. 438–469). Cambridge: CUP.

Papadakis, Y. (2005). *Echoes from the dead zone: Across the cyprus divide*. London: I.B. Tauris.

Papadakis, Y. (2008). Narrative, memory and history education in divided cyprus: A comparison of schoolbooks on the "history of cyprus". *History & Memory*, *20*(2), 128–148.

Philippou, S., & Theodorou, E. (2014). The 'europeanisation'of othering: Children using 'Europe'to construct 'others' in cyprus. *Race Ethnicity and Education*, *17*(2), 264–290.

Rampton, B. (2007). Linguistic ethnography and the study of identities. *Working Papers in Urban Language & Literacies* 43. At academia.edu.

Rampton, B. (2016). Foucault, Gumperz and governmentality: Interaction, power and subjectivity in the twenty-first century. In N. Coupland (ed) *Sociolinguistics: Theoretical Debates* (pp. 303–328). Cambridge: CUP. Also availabe as *Working Papers in Urban Language & Literacies* # 136 at academia.edu.

Rampton, B., Charalambous, C., & Charalambous, P. (2019). Crossing of a different kind. *Language in Society*, *48*(5), 629–655.

Rampton, B., & Charalambous, C. (2016). Breaking classroom silences: A view from linguistic ethnography. *Language and Intercultural Communication*, *16*(1), 4–21.

Rampton, B. & Charalambous, C. (2020) Sociolinguistics and everyday (in)securitization. *Journal of Sociolinguistics* 24/1:75–88.

Rampton, B, Maybin, J. & Roberts, C. (2015). Theory and method in linguistic ethnography. In J. Snell, S. Shaw & F. Copland (eds) *Linguistic Ethnography: Interdisciplinary Explorations* (pp. 14–50). Palgrave. Also available as also *Working Papers in Urban Language & Literacies* 125 at academia.edu.

Richmond, O., & Tellidis, I. (2017). The complex relationship between peace-building and terrorism approaches: towards post-terrorism and a post-liberal peace? In *Assessing the War on Terror*. (pp. 32–58). London: Routledge.

Spyrou, S. (2006). Constructing 'the turk' as an enemy: The complexity of stereotypes in children's everyday worlds. *South European Society & Politics, 11*(1), 95–110.

Tusting, K. (ed) (ftc). *The Routledge Handbook of Linguistic Ethnography*. London: Routledge.

Vaughan-Williams, N., & Stevens, D. (2016). Vernacular theories of everyday (in)security: The disruptive potential of non-elite knowledge. *Security Dialogue, 47*(1), 40–58.

Zakharia, Z., & Bishop, L. M. (2013). Towards positive peace through bilingual community education: Language efforts of arabic-speaking communities in new york. In O. García, Z. Zakharia & B. Otcu (Eds.), *Bilingual community education and multilingualism: Beyond heritage languages in a global city* (pp. 169–189). New York: Multilingual Matters.

Zembylas, M. (2010). Racialization/ethnicization of school emotional spaces: The politics of resentment. *Race Ethnicity and Education, 13*(2), 253–270.

Zembylas, M., Charalambous, C., & Charalambous, P. (2014). The schooling of emotion and memory: Analyzing emotional styles in the context of a teacher's pedagogical practices. *Teaching and Teacher Education, 44*, 69–80.

Zembylas, M., Charalambous, C., & Charalambous, P. (2016). *Peace education in a conflict-affected society* Cambridge University Press.

4 Silence as practices of (in)security in the post-Yugoslav region

Renata Summa and Milan Puh

Introduction

Security is a crucial aspect in contemporary societies, and it gains a particular outline in post-conflict societies. In such places, where memories about war are still fresh, and the consequences of conflict are highly pervasive, it seems to be a strong desire for a secure, 'normal life' (Maček, 2009; Jansen, 2015). However, this has to be achieved among parts that, not so long ago, were drawn by war to be on opposite sides and to identify (or be identified) as enemies. In this longing for safety, we notice that many aspects of the everyday become embedded in practices of (in)security. In this chapter, we analyse how practices of (in)security become part of people's everyday lives in two cities located in the post-Yugoslav region, more specifically Vukovar, in Croatia, and Mostar, in Bosnia and Herzegovina. We seek to understand how an everyday aspect of those societies – language education – becomes subject to (in)security practices.

A growing body of literature analyses everyday practices and places to understand the outcomes of a conflict and the relations between security, reconciliation, justice and peace in post-conflict societies (Mac Ginty, 2014; Forde, 2019; Gusic, 2020). Those authors argue that the everyday is a crucial site to be investigated in order to escape a top-down, structural or statist analysis of post-conflict situations, stressing the more complex, nuanced and dynamic features of an analysis based on the everyday. However, this does not necessarily mean that an everyday approach will constitute a 'bottom-up' analysis or a focus on the local or the 'micro level'. We argue that the everyday favours a transversal approach in which politics of scale such as 'top-down,' 'bottom-up' or 'micro-macro' and 'macro-micro' are destabilised. Through this approach, scales are somehow flattened, and we understand relations transversally (Summa, 2021). The everyday is, therefore, a meeting place between institutionalised, official structures and a myriad of practices conducted by people.

In the post-Yugoslav region, researchers have been discussing several aspects of the everyday life through the analysis of space and place (Forde, 2019; Summa, 2021); renaming and memorialization (Palmberger, 2017;

DOI: 10.4324/9781003080909-4

Wollentz et al., 2019); mobility (Jansen, 2015) and school segregation (Bozic, 2006; Laketa, 2019; Hromadžić, 2015a). Although the latter have already explored how formal education becomes a battlefield in post-conflict Mostar, this chapter focuses more specifically on how language education is mobilised in this 'battle' and the role that silence plays in it – e.g. silencing other groups, other languages and other ways of thinking or silencing as a tactic to coexist. Thus, we ask: What does silence do in post-conflict spaces?

We ask this question while analysing two contested cities: Mostar, in Bosnia and Herzegovina, and Vukovar, in Croatia. They are understood as contested in the sense that they are regarded as urban spaces where ethnonational aspirations to exclusive sovereignty manifests spatially into the desire to acquire more territory for one community at the expense of others (Carabelli et al., 2021, p. 117). One of the features of those two contested cities is the stigmatisation of the 'other' community, often portrayed as a threat to stability and peace and/or as guilty for deadlock situations in which those cities find themselves. Our methodology combines multiple visits to both cities between 2013 and 2017, where we carried semi-structured interviews with students, teachers and other inhabitants, together with detailed research in the media regarding the cases of planning, integration and/or segregation in/of schools.

We proceed in this chapter as follows: First, we discuss the role of language, and language education in what concerns discursive claims about (in)security in post-conflict societies, and how they entail (in)security practices in everyday life. Second, we analyse silence in the multiple ways it is used and employed in such contexts. Then, we present a contextualisation of the two cases we analyse – Mostar, in Bosnia and Herzegovina, and Vukovar, in Croatia. Finally, by presenting the findings of multiple visits to both cities, we analyse how the cases speak and contribute to understanding the relation between language education, everyday (in)security practices and silence(s).

Language and everyday practices of (in)security

On the eve of the dissolution of Yugoslavia, a popular comedy show in the region, *Toplista Nadrealista*, made a sketch that was regarded, years later, as a prediction of the future. In a country where basically all its citizens could at least understand Serbo-Croatian[1], the show mocked nationalist impulses of the time, presenting a situation where a journalist declared that 'there were now six different languages in the region' of (now former) Yugoslavia, in the place of Serbo-Croatian. Then, the show presented a clip of everyday situations where customers and acquaintances suddenly no longer understood each other and requested a dictionary or a translator to carry on the conversation. This third person would 'translate,' using the exactly same words but, since it was supposedly now in 'Serbian' or 'Bosnian,' instead of, say, Serbo-Croatian, they would finally understand what was being said.[2]f

Although the vignettes are meant to be surreal, they reflect current struggles in the region. Even though inhabitants from the ex-Yugoslavia region have no difficulties in talking and understanding each other, almost 30 years after *Toplista Nadrealista*'s episode, language is increasingly presented as a matter of state and peacebuilding in the region. Along with Yugoslavia, the Serbo-Croatian language was dissolved into Serbian, Croatian, Bosnian and, more recently, Montenegrin.[3] What we notice is that language – and, more specifically, language education - has become increasingly associated with (in)security.

Security, here, is understood as a process, a 'practice of making enemies and fear the integrative, energetic principle of politics' (Huysmans, 2014, p. 3) and, therefore, it is an intrinsic political project. We can establish a close relation between security practices and the feeling of insecurity. Where security practices are supposedly designed and/or employed to address a threat, they may also be the very source of production of a threat or the feeling of insecurity (Huysmans, 2006). This is why we adopt the term (in)security through this chapter – in line also with the approach followed in this volume (see Introduction).

In post-war societies, where the concept of 'otherness' has been associated with the idea of the 'enemy,' security practices became embedded in many aspects of everyday life. More precisely, in order to create independent states, people who once were neighbours – and everything that was associated with the 'other group,' such as food, culture, religion, scripts, accents – became targets of (in)security practices. When those groups were not presented as immediate physical threats, their very presence in a city or in a certain area represented a threat to the attempts of homogenisation driven by nationalist groups who fomented the war and who thrived since. Therefore, nowadays, the 'other' hardly represents a violent threat in the ex-Yugoslavia region (although memories of violence are still present), but it can represent a threat to the idea of an homogeneous city or state, these considered as the main guarantee of safety in official and non-official discourses.

Language has a very long and broad history throughout the multiple human experiences of societal organisations, but the idea of national language is more recent and intrinsically related to the emergence of the modern nation-state (Hobsbawm, 1996). Indeed, although language has always been an important tool to construct and maintain a polity (Kamusella, 2009 p. 8), it has been only a recent development in history that a language has to equate to a certain, bounded, territory and its people. Multiple discussions have been made about its place in modern societies (Hobsbawm, 1996; May, 2016; Shapiro, 1984). In the late 1800s, the development of national languages was considered a fundamental aspect to support political claims about both the distinction of a nation towards the other, and its internal cohesion and homogeneity. The efforts to create distinctive languages out of the Serbo-Croat to match the new, independent countries, in the 1990s and to demarcate national identities are, thus, not new. However, in a post-conflict context, what we pay attention to is how language education is intertwined with the consolidation of the idea of (internal) other(s). Language(s) became an issue of dispute in this context. It served as a cover for conflicting national aspirations and strategies that were to cause the ultimate destruction of the state of Yugoslavia (Bugarski, 2004: 12). And it is still an ongoing issue, since the production of distinct, "pure languages" (Shapiro, 1984: 198) is mobilised to promote segregation at the educational system and elsewhere in these societies.

The aspects of language we are looking at go beyond their capability of communication and comprehension. Indeed, we are interested in how language becomes an issue of dispute, and how this issue permeates the everyday of post-conflict societies. Although all languages have elements of political self-assertion, this becomes more evident when claims for political independence are enhanced by language separatism (Hobsbawm, 1996). And when those disputes structure the educational system, demarcating students from one another and promoting segregated spaces in a city, language also becomes a base for nationalist agendas. Therefore, language – and its consolidation through formal education - is an important political tool for bolstering identity. It is in this context that we understand how language becomes embedded in practices of (in)security.

Charalambous et al. (2018) and Charalambous et al. (2017) have already approached this subject, by looking at language, (in)security and everyday practice while discussing the sociolinguistic context in the UK and Cyprus (see also Chapter 3 this volume). Charalambous et al. (2018) discuss how 'enemy' and 'fear' can be active principles in language policy development. The contribution provided by the Cyprus case is particularly relevant for our analysis, since it shows 'how legacies of large-scale violent conflict can generate rather unexpected ground-level enactments of language policy' (p. 635). It reveals how language (1) played a crucial role in the historical development of identities and distinctions among Turkish Cypriots and Greek-Cypriots; (2) how it becomes an object of (in)security, when associated with the 'language of the national archenemy' and (3), how it can be (de)securitised through policies of teaching and learning the 'other language,' notably, Turkish for Greek-Cypriots. By showing how other bodies and cultures are produced as threats to the state both in Cyprus and the UK, the authors highlight how securitisation may turn some aspects of everyday life 'exceptional.'

A different approach is provided by Ochs (2013). The author investigates how the militarisation of the streets, cafes and transportation in Israel produces the seeming paradox of an everyday/exceptional life. The author argues that everyday security practices enhance the perception of insecurity, rather than mitigate it, and produce a state of fear and alertness in Israeli society. Therefore, everyday life, which is usually associated with the banal and uneventful, becomes increasingly involved and captured by exceptional practices, producing an atmosphere of perpetual insecurity.

The two cases we analyse give us an example of an exceptional everyday, even if not through extensive militarisation, physical barriers and violent threats such as in Ochs' (2013) narratives. The disputes we look at are over crucial sectors of a society, such as the educational policies. While the everyday lives in the two cities we study are no longer plunged into armed conflicts, the securitisation of other ethnonational communities is still at work.

Silence and/as security in post-conflict societies

Understanding everyday (in)security practices towards language depends not only on what is being said, but especially on what has been left unsaid or has been suppressed from the public debate. Silence is a common feature in post-conflict societies, and may happen in various situations, serving a range of different intended and unintended purposes (Eastmond and Mannergren Selimovic, 2020). In this section, we explore the link between silence and (in)security (Dingli, 2015; Rampton & Charalambous, 2016; Guillaume, 2018), but focus more specifically on the multiple forms silences may take in the lived space of post-conflict societies. Then, we discuss the relation between silences and (in)security, and how they are used in regard to language education. To promote this debate, we discuss the works of Eastmond and Mannergren Selimovic (2020), more precisely, their distinction between 'silence that enables peace' and 'silence that disables peace' and of Orlandi (2009) and her concept of 'silences and interdicts.' We also argue that silence can be a crucial feature of everyday peace (Mac Ginty, 2014; also Chapter 2), where unwritten rules establish what can be discussed where and by whom, and it is 'highly context-, location- and time-specific, and relies on well-honed interpersonal skills' (Ibidem p. 554).

Silence has been associated, in International Relations, with corporeal and epistemic violence (Dingli, 2015). Feminist perspectives highlight the everyday efforts by groups at the centre to keep (silenced) marginal groups silent and at the margin of the political debate (Enloe, 1996). On a different, but related note, scholars have called attention to the epistemic silence in the discipline towards the racial question (Krishna, 2001). Highly influenced by the linguistic turn, security studies have given centrality to language and associated speech to action, implicitly relegating silence to inaction. Guillaume (2018), however, shows that things can be done with silence, and he introduces the notion of 'silence-as-doing,' highlighting that silence is more than an absence. Important here is the idea that silence carries an ambiguity that makes different meanings possible. It could be a form of violence, as previously discussed, a choice of not engaging with a specific matter, or even a form of resistance. This corroborates the idea of silence as an important feature of 'everyday peace' (Mac Ginty, 2014), which is very context-dependent and a possible tool to navigate one's passage through post-conflict societies.

Let's now look at how silence has been used as a tactic in post-conflict ex-Yugoslavia. Eastmond & Mannergren Selimovic (2012, 2020), Kolind (2008) and Stefansson (2010) have exposed situations in different locations in the region where dwellers silenced sensitive topics – especially regarding what happened during the war. Kolind (2008), in his research about a small, ethnonational 'mixed' town in Herzegovina, concludes that the "parties have to develop some kind of 'working consensus' or unspoken agreement about social interaction". He recalls the story of a 'Muslim woman who told me (him) that she never discussed politics with her Croat colleagues. They only talked deliberately about cooking and children' (p. 78). Silence, here, works as a 'possibility of living together,' or being 'civil' especially in places shared by different ethnonational groups or in situations where one finds him/herself as a minority (Eastmond & Mannergren Selimovic, 2012).

Stefansson (2010) also explores the role of silence as a way to live together. Although the literature that approaches transitional justice in post-conflict contexts usually understands silence as something oppressive and related to impunity (Connerton, 2011), Stefansson highlights silence as a way of rebuilding the pre-war social fabric. He suggests that reconciliation does not occur only through outspoken empathy, but also through silencing controversial topics.

Those authors who think silence as a productive tactic stand in contrast to more classical approaches in peace and transitional justice literature that highlight the importance of bringing the truth to the surface and speaking out about injustices and crimes. According to this approach, silence is associated with impunity, and provides a less fertile ground to blossom a peaceful and just society. Silence is thus perceived as the opposite of speech, action and empowerment and even politics. It is considered as 'lacking' and possibly demining. Jansen (2015), however, argues that, in the everyday, people (in his case, dwellers of the Sarajevo neighbourhood of Dobrinja) made the shared concern with 'normal lives less through action and more through non-verbal communication: "It was in rants and laments, in sighs and silences, that 'normal lives,' and (…) state-craft took centre stage" (p. 16).

Eastmond and Mannergren Selimovic (2020) provide an analytical framework which explores silences in their different meanings, instead of fixing one single interpretation to them. They classify different forms of silences as those that 'disable peace' and 'enable peace.' In the first category, they rank the denial and revisionist approach towards the Srebrenica's genocide by some (Bosnian-)Serbian leaders and citizens and so on. Usually, they are the kind of silence that drives to impunity of war crimes or crimes committed by the State, while establishing an official (often negationist) narrative to the events. On the other hand, they discuss silence as a tactic to make peace durable. These are particularly present in societies that have experienced interethnic or interreligious violence and that are trying to return to 'normality' and live together after such events. Here we notice an attempt to avoid recalling painful memories in public, of trying not to discuss historical events or 'politics,' of silencing as a way to disapproving past or present attitudes and even as a way of showing respect to those victims of violence.

We corroborate with Eastmond and Mannergren Selimovic's (2020) point on the multiplicity of meanings silence may acquire, and the need to analyse different forms of silence within their context. Also, we pay attention to the dynamic relationship between silencing and speaking out and between disabling and enabling silences (Ibidem). Therefore, we share the idea that silence is not a phenomenon of secondary importance and or a 'residue' of language. Moreover, as Orlandi (2009) states, the words are made of silence and silence is full of meaning. 'Silence is not merely a complement to language. It has its own significance.' (Orlandi, 2009, p. 23).

During fieldwork in Vukovar and Mostar, we could observe those different kinds of silence operating in everyday life: the revisionism of crimes committed during the wars (both World War II and the 1990s wars), the renaming of streets, the abandonment of monuments to just 'not talking about the war'; silences are a strong presence – and not an absence – in everyday life. We want to stress here the relation between silence and language education, a relation that is still under-explored.

The fluctuation between the act of silencing and saying is of utmost importance, as it is where the interdictions function. Orlandi (2009) explains how interdictions function as operators that cut or prevent all saying. And furthermore, in order to be able to say something, one must decide what to say and what not, and here the idea of a discursive cut is fundamental. Discourse analysis in this way helps us to see that if it were possible to say everything, nothing would be said, since there would be no differentiation between one speech and another. We can say that history and the society intervene here to the extent that what is available (and what is not) for discourse making depends on what is expected or permitted to say in a situation and moment. An individual learns over time what their own group, community or society deems fit to be said, and if he or she breaks 'the rules,' they learn the consequences. The learning process is one made of different discourses that are embedded in speaking about almost anything in the world, and our way of dealing with the silence and the interdictions are a result of everyday experiences. When something is defined as a threat, it may not always be overtly said or communicated, but it can make itself present in the silence that one receives or the unwillingness or refusal of people to speak about it. This is not just a personal decision, but one of societal importance as the way one speaks or acts can be perceived as a risk or threat by others. Therefore silence and the interdictions of speech are of great importance if we are to understand better how everyday life functions in post-conflict societies.

Contextualising language and silence in two contested cities

Vukovar has a complex history of heterogeneous contacts between ethnic groups, especially between Croats and Serbs. It lies on the border between

Croatia and Serbia, geographically in eastern Croatia. After 1991, Vukovar became the frozen fragment of the war in ex-Yugoslavia, since the so-called post-war period is still full of (non-armed) conflicts. Nowadays, what seems to prevail is that it is no longer a multinational city and there are many attempts to forget this shared past and silence minorities. During Puh's field trips between 2013 and 2016, which were made initially to understand how the local language policy functions in cities with a present Ukrainian community in Croatia and Brazil, many interlocutors reported the lack of coexistence among different ethnonational groups in their everyday convivial life. According to them, the lack of coexistence turned the multicultural city into an abstraction rather than into a place of encounter. When asked about the practices and events of other groups other than their own, our interlocutors would reply with vague responses: 'well, people say that they (*the other group*) have x or y in that place' or 'I hear that they meet in x place, but I'm not sure' or 'I don't really know, probably they do something, but who is to know,' accompanied by a uneasiness to speak and creating an awkward silence in order to ensure that the topic would be changed. There were many of these situations occurring during the observations and interviews realised within the four-year period, much more so in Croatia than in Brazil, a phenomenon that caught the researchers' attention. Not only it became an issue while trying to comprehend the local linguistic policy that was created and enacted by the Croatian Ukrainian immigrant community, but also required the development of special ethnographic strategies in order for the research to be possible. We can sum them up as situational and interactional strategies; thinking things through and carefully before the interviews and field observations; avoiding certain topics that would create overt commentaries; and using additional types of sources to triangulate the data: Official documents and media texts. The interactional strategies were used in moments where the uncomfortable situation could not be foreseen, reinforcing the idea that the anonymity would be guaranteed and that things could be said 'off the record.'

As for Vukovar, despite its past, it is now used discursively by the Croatian institutions as a symbol of war destruction but also resilience (it even has its own day to 'celebrate' – 18th of November), following the entry of the Serbian and/or Yugoslav forces in the city on November 18th in 1991 after the three month resistance by the local Croatian forces. Thus, the city represented the first step towards the liberation of the Serbian people and/or the subjugation of the Croatian people, depending on the perspective and the interpretation of History. The relationship between neighbours and communities disappeared or changed significantly after the war with urban, economic and industrial destruction, eliminating congregation points and severing social and family ties until they caused almost total separation. This dissolution of the social fabric created a psychological void, which was filled with other stories, values, attitudes and conceptions, as stated by Čorkalo (2008).

However, the city did not become ethnically homogenous as other places in Croatia and the region. In the 2011 national census, the percentage of Croats in Vukovar was 57,37% and of Serbs 34,87%, while 7,76% were from other ethnicities/nationalities. Reconciliation, nevertheless, seems far to be reached. The predominant political discourse is that it is expected that the 'other' side assumes its crimes and pays accordingly, which is translated in a state of tension in everyday life. Official politicians bring up the war and ethnic tensions almost on a daily basis, not allowing the silence to take over itself, but also interdicting that certain discourses of conciliation are brought up. This resonates with the educational system, with separate classes for Croatian and Serbian children who study on different curricula, with almost no interaction among them. Changes are met with resistance, as in the case of a proposal to put in place bilingual signs in Croatian and Serbian with Latin and Cyrillic scripts, as we will explain later.

The situation in Mostar is not so different from Vukovar. Although Bosnia and Herzegovina has constituted itself as a multinational state, home of three constituent peoples – Bosniaks (or Muslims), Serbs and Croats – there are nowadays few municipalities in the country which are not actually dominated by one of the three ethnonational groups. With over 100,000 inhabitants, Mostar has been historically known as a multi-ethnic and multicultural city, home of Croats, Bosniaks and Serbs, with none of them being a majority. It is important to note that, during Tito's Yugoslavia, the language spoken in the city was only one: The 'Serbo-Croatian' or 'Croatian-Serb.'

The 1990s war hit Mostar severely, shifting the social fabric of the city – which was *de facto* and *de jure* divided into East Mostar (mostly inhabited by Bosniaks) and West Mostar (mostly inhabited by Croats). The Serb community almost completely fled during the conflict. At this point, the war front went through the centre of the city, cutting neighbourhoods and the relation among former neighbours, while transforming Mostar into a contested city – a similar development to what we saw in Vukovar.

After the conflict, Mostar emerged as one of the few cities that do not have an expressive ethnonational majority in BiH as the result of war-induced migrations, deaths, and demographic shifts across the country. Instead, it houses two communities (Bosniak and Croat), roughly equal in size, that are both contending the city's territory. Accordingly, there are nowadays two official languages in the educational system: Croatian and Bosnian.

In what follows, we look at both Vukovar's and Mostar's educational systems to understand how language(s) represents an issue of security for the cities and their inhabitants. We analyse how language education becomes a factor of segregation, stigmatisation or maintenance of the privileges of a certain group, and also how language education might also represent a possibility of dialogue in these two cities. Finally, we look at silences and interdicts, both in how they might be detrimental to coexistence and in how they might provide a possibility of living together.

Mostar: A segregated and 'reunified' school system

The emergence of three official languages in the place of Serbo-Croat was both concomitant to and had consequences to the education system in Bosnia and Herzegovina and Mostar, more specifically. The educational system was affected by the war and split among the different sides of the conflict, becoming a tool for nationalists to both enhance and consolidate divisions in the everyday of the city. As Hromadžić (2015a) argues, "children began to be educated according to the 'tripartite pattern,' which was based on the area in which people lived and the ethnicity to which they belonged". Among other consequences, war thus left Mostar with this segregated 'infrastructure' legacy. Moreover, from 1992 onwards, the country has adopted three separated curricula: a Serbian, a Croatian and a Bosniak (Kreso, 2008: 357).

Language plays a decisive role here: Since there are three official recognised languages in the country, education on the students' mother tongue must be assured. In our visits to the city, this aspect was highlighted by some of our informants, who argued that either they or other people they knew would prefer to send their children to school in their 'own language,' bringing also the aspect of how history and religion are taught in different curricula.

According to the 2018 OSCE report 'Authorities commonly re-named schools to honour persons or events from the conflict and displayed nationalist insignia or religious symbols. The teaching process was also conducted based on curricula and textbooks that were ethnically coloured, including the victimisation of one constituent people and the exclusion or even villainization of the other constituent peoples.' Immediately after the war, many parents refused to send their children to local schools with students 'from the other side.' The international community responded to this by formulating the controversial practice of 'two schools under one roof' – i.e. bringing together in a single building two schools corresponding to two different communities, two different curricula, two different groups of teachers and, sometimes, even two different entrances or shifts. What was supposed to be a temporary solution for the lack of infrastructure after the war is still an ongoing practice in 56 schools (OSCE, 2018) throughout the country. Moreover, while the 'two schools under one roof' was understood as a first step towards the full integration of schools – and, thus, cherished at first by the international community as a step towards removing the the educational field from the security sphere – it has, through all those 25 years, been ruled as a breach to multiple national and international conventions[4].

As such, this educational practice has been portrayed from a solution to a threat to the well-being of the students, to the integration of the different communities and even to the future of BiH itself. The international community and some groups of parents are certain to affirm that the two school under one roof segregate children and instil division and the notion of differences: 'In post-conflict BiH, this fosters mistrust, impedes reconciliation and is a long-term threat to stability and economic prosperity' (OSCE, 2018: 10) and '(segregation) emphasised differences and encouraged mutual ignorance and, perhaps more important, mutual suspicion' (Bush and Saltarelli, 2000: 15). The lack of coexistence and dialogue among the youth, therefore, is seen as detrimental to a sustainable peace.

The New York Times, in its article 'In a divided Bosnia, Segregated School Persists' (2018), argues that 'since the end of the war, the hard-line nationalists (…) have turned the school into a battlefield,' while showing many examples of students who have demanded through multiple initiatives to unify schools. The article presents a distinction between nationalist politicians from both sides, who would like to silence any attempt to reunify schools, and students, who work against the interdiction to attend school together and, at the same time, break with the logics of war.[5]f

The segregation in the educational system, however, is far from being eradicated from local educational practices, as it could be observed during multiple fieldwork visits between 2014 and 2017 by Summa, who investigated how ethnonational boundaries are enacted, contested and displaced in post-Dayton BiH. During several stays in the city, Summa conducted 20 interviews with students from private and public high schools, one school director, journalists and 'ordinary citizens' from different ages, gender, economic and ethnonational backgrounds. Most of them deplored the educational system and the silences that are being instilled in BiH's youth, while sometimes also mocking the linguistic argument to justify it: 'Nobody in my school speaks pure Croatian … we all speak this mixture of everything (Croatian, Serbian and some Turkish words, as she explained earlier). I seriously doubt that even our professors speak Croatian …' – according to a high school student who attended the Croatian curricula.[6]

The argument on which the maintenance of school segregation in BiH relies carries in its core the principle that each ethnonational community has the right to be taught in its own language. This is why it is so important to understand political engineering to foster and deepen the demarcation and division of national languages in the region. The existence and maintenance of three different curricula opens the gateway to multiple practices of segregation. Indeed, in the ex-Yugoslavia region, 'linguistic human rights discourse, despite its conscious goal of preventing discrimination, has actually helped legitimise ethnic divisions' (Pupavac, 2006). Moreover, it forces children and their parents to identify with one or other ethnonational community, and it is particularly damaging to children who were born from so-called 'mixed marriages' (Hromadžić, 2015a).

Mostar stands out as an important city to study this phenomenon. The city hosts a 'two schools under one roof' and another school which has been 'reunited.' The Secondary School of Machinery and Traffic and the Secondary School of Traffic share the same building, have a common entrance and a joint teachers room. However, the first one teaches the curricula in Bosnian language and the second, in Croatian language. Although they share a school yard, which could facilitate the socialisation and integration among students, students go to school in different shifts. On the other hand, there is the Mostar Gymnasium. The sizable Austro-Hungarian building dating from 1893 has hosted one of the most popular High Schools in Yugoslavia. It was almost completely destroyed during the war when only one wing of the ground floor was left functioning. During nearly ten years, thereafter, only students following the Croatian Curriculum of Mostar Gymnasium could use that building.

While the Gymnasium was one of the first schools to be integrated in BiH (in February 2004) after years of heated negotiations, demonstrations and the investment of an important amount of money (Hromadžić, 2011), the integration of the opposite group is yet to be proved. The reunification of Mostar Gymnasium was cherished by many who opposed the 'two school under one roof model' as an example that would be followed by other schools and a proof that students did not need to be segregated. However, this landslide effect did not take place. Moreover, even if the school is unified, Bosniak and Croat students still attend different classes in two different curricula. Official places for mixing inside the school exist, however, as Hromadžić (2011) explains, 'mixing' does not happen there.

The Christian Science Monitor (2007)[7] highlights the attempts of Croatian nationalists to seize Mostar Gymnasium by naming it after a Catholic priest after the war and fiercely opposing the reunification of the school: "(Opposition) was particularly strong from Croats, who emerged from the war clinging to a threatened sense of national identity and who insisted on speaking their 'own' language, even though the differences in language used by Bosniaks, Croats, and Serbs are barely distinguishable". This attempt to rename the Gymnasium can be interpreted as a discursive practice of silencing this multicultural past of the school while interdicting Bosniak students to attend it. As Palmberger (2017) argues, renaming is a practice of inscribing one's group claim upon that landscape or institution. The article stresses this dispute by stating that 'there was some fierce resistance initially, even the proposed name of the reunified school was subject to months of political debate.'

The Bosnian television show 'Perspektiva' (2015) brought together high-school students from both the segregated and unified schools in Mostar to discuss their impressions of their everyday life and the reminiscences of war in their city. Although many students said they got along with students from other ethnonational group, what stood out was the declaration of some students who had never crossed to the 'other side' of the city (meaning, the side mostly populated by the other ethnonational group) and others reporting fear to cross. The show may be perceived as a portrait of the consequences of two decades of segregated education in the young generations who were not even born at the time of the war and the continuous nationalist politics that foster division among the constitutive groups from BiH. Moreover, it stood out as an attempt to break the silence among students from different communities in

Mostar and make them talk to each other, exposing their fears, hopes and the things they had in common. It provided a rare opportunity for dialogue broadcasted in national television, and was portrayed as a general attempt to break with silence and interdictions.

However, silence also emerged in research data as a strategy to live together. Some of our interlocutors stressed the importance of, for example, silencing political and religious subjects in public spaces, such as the reunified Gymnasium. Moreover, they added that they would feel unsafe if they are 'at the other side' of the city, on the street or in a club, and somebody would shout their names (which are usually strongly associated with one ethnonational group or the other). Hiding their background, thus, is considered an important tactic to get by in their everyday life. One former teacher of Mostar Gymnasium explained how the division in schooling system also contributes to foster a sense of (exclusive) belonging and identification that might be used against people from the other school (and ethnonational background): 'You always have some street bullers, and they can always recognise you are from some school ... one student of mine from Gymnasium, who was completely lacking any division in his mind, went out in the Old City (predominantly Muslim side) for a drink, some people recognised he was from the Croatian side and he was attacked out of the blue'[8].

Therefore, we notice that different forms of silence are present in the everyday life of Mostar and they are closely related to practices of (in)security. Language, that supposedly enables dialogue and shared coexistence, is also used to justify a segregated scholar system, where 'sensitive' topics such as the historical events of the 1990s war have been silenced and designated to be discussed only in private spheres[9].

Vukovar: Silencing spaces of coexistance

Our analysis of the Vukovar case-study is based on the ethnographic research made between 2013 and 2016 with yearly visits to two other municipalities (Lipovljani and Šumeće) as well as to Vukovar through participant observations and semi-structured interviews. In total, one of the authors conducted nine interviews[10] and six observations[11] with the Ukranian community in Vukovar, to understand how a third ethnic community lives in the city and preserves its identity and culture. The educational system in Vukovar stood out as an important site to be studied, since it crystallises ethnonational distinctions.

Moreover, special strategies were created in order to resolve some of the issues regarding the unwillingness or discomfort of our participants. We conducted an extensive research of the official legislation regarding Education and Languages Status in Croatian, as well as academic and media texts, which would 'fill in' the silences that we perceived while doing the fieldwork. While conducting research, some interviewees mentioned the project of an intercultural school that was supposed to open in 2017, and which had received enough money to be built and operate in the city. This would become our case to study and present here as a example of the way silences and interdictions happen in Vukovar. Along with interviews and observations, we explore media articles that brought the intercultural school project into the public debate, creating a discourse quarrel by confronting different sides.

Before we go further in with our analysis we will comment briefly on the formal education in Vukovar and how language is a part of the division, based on the studies of Kasunić (2018), Čorkalo and Ajduković (2007; 2008; 2012), Milčić and Majsec (2010). The school system is divided as a direct result of the 1991–1995 war in Croatia and the Peaceful Reintegration, which ended in 1998, accompanied by a slow normalisation and integration of the East Sector in Croatian educational system with a lot of negotiations since the original 1995 Erdut Agreement. The right to minority education was later specified by the 2000 Act on Education of Minorities, acknowledging the right to have schooling in the native language and alphabet, establishing the 'A, B and C Model' as a part of The National Pedagogic Standard for Primary and Secondary Education[12].

The National Pedagogic Standard is a complex model, which brings three possibilities for the students and their parents, sometimes limiting the contact they have in everyday (school) life. The more present an ethnic minority is in the *županija*, *grad* and *općina* (county, city and municipality), the more options it has for education in its language. On the other hand, the more present it is, depending on the historical moment and context, the more the discourse of insecurity is evident, like in the case of the Serbian population in Vukovar. This is clear by the public discourses portraying the actions or the existence of an ethnonational group as a problem to Croatian national sovereignty.

As our ethnographic research showed, smaller groups such as the Ukranians, are, on one hand, really present as a group in everyday life (with presentations in events, publications and educational projects), but on the other hand, they are silent when they deem that interfering might cause them to be seen as a possible threat. Here we have to remember that they also use the Cyrillic alphabet and are mostly of Orthodox religion, just as the Serbians, which, as all interviewees highlighted, is a constant 'ethnic risk' of being compared and equalised to them.

An important discussion on language and security in the everydaylife of Vukovar relates precisely to the role of Serbian language and the Cyrillic scripts in the city. This is a right foreseen in the actual Croatian Constitution and the Law on Use of Languages and Scripts of National Minorities but questioned (violently) by part of Vukovar and Croatian political elites and population, even forcing the Croatian Supreme Court to give a ruling. From 2013 onwards, there is a growing reclaiming of giving the Serbian Cyrillic Alphabet a co-official status in the city. At the same time, other voices in the city question the 'peril' it brings, trying to silence communication through

Cyrillic scripts (using even physical violence, with several signs being destroyed covertly and overtly – many of them were filmed). As Kapović (2016, 2020) argues, for many in Vukovar the Cyrillic alphabet acts as a visual presence and is considered a threat, since it brings about the memory of the war suffering for the Croatian population[13].

Besides the Model and its three possibilities, there is space for new propositions, like the creation of an intercultural school in Vukovar. The school was supposed to have a different kind of curriculum that would combine alternative educational objectives and contents in order to provide a less segregated school environment. This would allow for desegregating the schooling model. The existence of the intercultural school would also prevent situations in which parents feel like they could be looked upon like traitors due to the school choice they made for their children (Kasunić, 2018).

So, we shall take as an example the intercultural school Dunav (Danube) which was brought to public debate even though, in our experience, was accompanied with silences. We believe it is a good example to analyse how language and education are intertwined within the ongoing (in)security practices of Vukovar everyday life. It was first revealed by the media at the end of 2016 when the decision to create the school was made by the local authorities. At the time, neither the ruling Croatian Democratic Union (HDZ) nor the five members of the Serbian minority were interested in the project. The project had already been discussed three years before by the social democrats from the Social Democratic Party of Croatia (SDP) on the local level, however, without the support of the central government. The project, then, was silenced, until it came up again through the pressure from the Ministries of Education and Regional Development, along with the Norwegians. They wanted to use a larger sum of European Union money, as the Norwegian government stated, according to Enis Zebić in his article 'Intercultural school in Vukovar: Croats unwillingly for and the Serbs against,' published on the website of Radio Slobodna Europa (Radio Free Europe).

Through Zebić's article (2016), it is clear that the two main parties – the ruling HDZ and oppositionist Independent Democratic Serb Party (SDSS) – were against the intercultural school. Other voices were heard, such as members of the SDP, which had a mixed Serbian and Croatian, and the liberal party Croatian People's Party (HNS). Both of them were in favour of the creation of the intercultural school, but received much less attention in the article and in that context more generally.

This debate reveals that those voices have been continuously silenced in the city, as their previous attempts to put forward an intercultural school. Two of our interlocutors stressed in 2016 that, in Vukovar, there is no space for a 'third voice,' i.e. a discourse in favour of connections in the city. So, the interdiction here is made by minimising the presence and importance of those 'third voices,' while not recognising them also as protagonists of the intercultural school project. Those who are in favour of stronger connections inside of the city are regarded as 'foreigners' by the two ruling parties as we will see below.

Silence as practices of (in)security 93

The following is indicative of the vocabulary used by the HDZ, when justifying why they were against the school project: 'the State ... should not bring foreign bodies in its legislative frame.' Similarly, SDSS was against the school project because it 'can jeopardise the existing educational programme.'

The metaphor of foreign bodies is representative of the non-Croatian, usually European, institutional pressures for changes and policy enactments, which can put at risk the commonly cited 'hardly conquered (Croatian) sovereignty and liberty.' So intercultural ideas are seen as pushed from 'outside' (even when they came from groups based in Vukovar) to threaten Croatian statehood and status quo. The 'threat' was explicitly cited in the second metaphor of jeopardy of the Educational system. Here the (seemingly) opposite sides (nationalist Croats and Serbs) come together to restrain the campaign in favour of the intercultural school, by arguing that the idea comes from the 'outside.'

Similar political moves were revealed to us in conversation with members of the Ukranian community in 2015 and 2016. As they argued, the two main local political parties would sometimes make silent agreements when they felt threatened by the central government and/or the European Union. In this sense, they presented themselves as local resistance to national or foreign propositions for the solution of ethnonational questions, 'preventing things to happen,' ignoring their requests or just interdicting a public debate about it.

Six months later, in 2017, the intercultural school situation reached a paradoxical state as Dragana Bošnjak writes in the article '*New school, old habits*' in the journal Novosti (News). The school building was built, while elected representatives of both Croats and Serbs were still reluctant. In this text we see that a common metonymy portrays the political representatives who were against the school as 'the community,' silencing all of those who were in favour of the project. For example when mayor Penava, introduced as 'City of Vukovar, the founder of the school,' said that: 'we are cautious because we are a very specific milleu'; his use of the pronoun 'we,' in our view, equalises the 'we – city' as 'we – people,' the official or political 'we' as the ethnic or all comprehensive 'we.' The only dissonant voice reported in this article is the local Hungarian minority, depicted through its president at the time as one of 23 minorities, which were supposed to attend the school. Most importantly, the Serbian minority is singled out in the text (here we have to take into account that the journal is financed by the Serbian People's Council) and pointed as a separate minority. The president of the Board of Education of Joint Serbian Municipalities even stated that the intercultural school represents a 'big trap for Serbs and a way to be assimilated.' Moreover, the mayor of Vukovar, member of the ruling party, declared scepticism towards the project because of the specific context in which the city is located, alluding to a particular tense and risky situation, where breaking the silences might trigger conflict and violence.

The last 'act' of this story was the cancellation of the project, in the end of 2018. At that point, the school buildings and installations were not yet completed and, more importantly, in the fall of that year there were no interested candidates. Drago Hedl sums it up well in the title '*What coexistence. The State, we found out, had to give back money for the failed project of the intercultural school*' in the journal Telegram. The term 'we found out' makes clear that those decisions were not transparent to the public. Several articles with similar content were published in 2018, trying to explain why the intercultural school did not succeed, which we can summarise through the idea of the 'intercultural school in Vukovar as a counter-state element,' as stated by Ivan Markešić in his column in Večernji list (Evening paper). The project that would allow for a shared educational system in a contested city, was considered a threat to the state-building and the current understanding of 'peace.'

In December of 2019 we contacted some of our interlocutors and two of them commented that the whole idea was again silenced. One of them argued that media articles on the case were not frequent, usually they related to some kind of official decision or individual journalistic research, and there was generally a lack of public debate about the future of language and education in the city. For all of them, remaining silent also represented a way of surviving in a tense environment, leaving room for other discussions that bring about less problematic topics; therefore, being inconsistent and not persistent on certain topics could also be understood a strategy to ensure the functioning of everyday interaction.

To conclude, there was an overt process of silencing the intercultural school project and interdicting the public debate by evoking, even indirectly, that it posed a threat to the painfully achieved status quo. A project like the intercultural school was transformed in public and media discourses into a 'foreign body,' embedded in 'foreign ideas,' unacceptable for the Serbian and Croatian political elites. In a sense, security concerns in everyday life in Vukovar created a situation where any proposition that did not corroborate to the status quo was dismissed as an external threat, while the local and national mistrust between the two dominant ethnonational groups was the fuel for perpetuating (in)security practices. The apparently two opposed groups in fact silenced other voices. The interdiction, in this case, concerns more alternative claims about a shared educational system and a less segregated everyday life.

Conclusion: *Silence and interdicts and the possibilities for post-conflict societies*

In this chapter, we have looked at struggles involving the educational system in two contested cities in the post-conflict, post-Yugoslav region – Mostar and Vukovar. We have exposed how, despite the absence of great linguistic differences that could make ethnonational distinctions strike out, language was still used to demarcate, identify, separate and segregate the educational system and other aspects of the everyday life in these two cities. We have also argued that silence – and silencing – is a prevalent feature of post-conflict societies. Instead of being only a sign of a lack of agency and absence of meaning, we have argued that silence can have different meanings and 'do' things, and it can even be an important aspect of 'everyday peace.'

The cases we have analysed show how silences fall often in a discomfort, if not fear, of speaking out about subjects deemed delicate in a post-conflict society. In this sense, silence might be understood as a possibility to co-exist without digging deeper in past events or a way to 'change the conversation,' by not engaging with some topics or by not abiding to specific (ethnonational) categories. More often, however, silence reveals the inability to promote a public debate about the recent past and the future of the nation. The political project in place in both Mostar and Vukovar produces lots of silences and, in some cases, interdicts the debate about the recent war and dissonant voices who promote agendas and initiatives that are not based on ethnonational lines.

Our research has suggested that silence can both enable and disable coexistence in these two cities. By avoiding 'sensitive' discussions and by keeping a certain degree of ambiguity, it is possible to create spaces where everyday interaction is made possible, as in the reunification of Mostar Gymnasium. On the other hand, attempts to silence proposals such as the intercultural school in Vukovar, which wanted to promote a shared space for all the communities in the city, corroborates to the feeling of insecurity and segregation, and to the political projects that thrive through segregation and fear.

Notes

1 According to the 1981 census, Serbo-Croat was the mother tongue of 73% of Yugoslavia population of 22.4 million (Bugarski, 2004).
2 Episode available at: https://www.youtube.com/watch?v=DztrX5dXmxU
3 For a linguistic-oriented analysis of the do Serbo-Croatian construction and dissolution, please refer to Bugarski, 2004.
4 So far, the "two schools under one roof" has been considered by both national and international courts as discriminating and violating human rights conventions ratified by BiH such as the Universal Declaration of Human Rights, the International Covenant on Economic, Social and Cultural Rights, the Convention on the Rights of the Child, the International Convention on the Elimination of All Forms of Racial Discrimination, the Convention against Discrimination in Education, the European Convention on Human Rights (OSCE, 2018).
5 A similar argument is advanced by Balkan Insight, in its article from 2017, "Pupils Challenge Ethnically-Divided Education in Bosnia". It describes the situation in one Bosnian town, Jajce, where local politicians were opening a new school specially conceived for Bosniak students - who used to attend the same, mixed school, until then. According to the article, many students were against segregation and were supported by "around 100 students of all ethnic backgrounds from across the country (and which) attended (a) conference in support of the students from Jajce". Again, students are portrayed as breaking the silence

around this question and working against attempts to interdict common education among different communities.
6 Interview with S. 7 May 2015.
7 "Students mingle – sort of – in post-war Bosnia's only integrated school"
8 Interview with V. 06.05. 2015, in the Gymnasium building.
9 In 2000, the Council of Europe issued a recommendation that Bosnian schools refrain from teaching about the Bosnian War "to enable historians from all communities [...] to develop a common approach." The topic has thus not been addressed in the schools of any of the cantons since 2000. In 2018, Canton Sarajevo has started teaching about the war, and other cantons followed suit. See: https://www.euroclio.eu/2019/08/19/dealing-with-the-past-challenges-as-sarajevo-tackles-the-bosnian-war-in-classrooms/
10 With three age groups: Between 20 and 35, 35 and 55, 55 and 75.
11 Two each year on different occasions: Festivals, schools events and folcloric rehearsals.
12 Basically the models establish the way the education has to be organised when it comes to minorities on Croatian territory, depending on the census which gives the percentages of specific ethnicities needed to confirm its existence, which in practical terms is always problematic. So the Model A permits that all of the schooling process is done in the minority language and script with no formal contact with the Croatian education, Model B is made within the Croatian schooling system with specific courses (History, Language, Geography, etc.) offered for minority students and Model C is entirely in the Croatian schooling system but with additional language and culture classes for the minority.
13 Recently, the Cyrillic question caused turmoil in the ruling HDZ party and they coalition partners, the SDSS (which represents the Serbs in Croatia), threatening the government to fall.

References

Ajdukovic, D., & Biruski, D. C. (2008). Caught between the ethnic sides: Children growing up in a divided post-war community. *International Journal of Behavioral Development*, *32*(4), 337–347.
Ajdukovic, D., & Biruski, D. C. (2007). Separate Schools – A Divided Community: The Role of the School in Post-War Social Reconstruction. *Review of Psychology*, *14*(2), 93–108.
Ajdukovic, D., & Biruski, D. C. (2012). Škola kao prostor socijalne integracije djece i mladih u Vukovaru', Zagreb.
Bollens, S. (2012). *City and soul in divided societies*. London: Routledge.
Bozic, Gordana (2006). Reeducating the Hearts of Bosnian Students: An Essay on Some Aspects of Education in Bosnia and Herzegovina. East European Politics and Societies: and Cultures, 20, 319–34210.1177/0888325404273502.
Bugarski, Ranko (2004). Language policies in the successor states of former Yugoslavia. Journal of Language and Politics, 3, 189–20710.1075/jlp.3.2.04bug.
Bush, Kenneth David, & Saltarelli, Diana (2000). The Two Faces of Education in Ethnic Conflict : Towards a Peacebuilding Education for Children. Research Report. Unicef Innocenti Research Centre.
Campbell, D. (1992). *Writing Security: United States Foreign Policy and the Politics of Identity*. Minneapolis: University of Minnesota Press.
Carabelli, G. (2018). *The divided city and the grassroots. The (un)making of ethnic divisions in Mostar*. London: Palgrave Macmillan.

Connerton, P. (2011). *The Spirit of mourning. History, memory and the body.* Cambridge: Cambridge University Press.
Čorkalo Biruški, D. Stavovi učenika, roditelja i nastavnika prema školovanju: što se promijenilo tijekom šest godina u Vukovaru?', *Migracijske i etničke teme 24*(3):189.
Charalambous, P., Charalambous, C. and Rampton, B. (2017). De-securitizing Turkish: Teaching the Language of a Former Enemy, and Intercultural Language Education, *Applied Linguistics, 38* (6):800–823.
Charalambous, C., Charalambous, P., Khan, K. & Rampton, B. (2018) 'Security and language policy'. In J. Tollefson & M. Pérez-Milans. *The Oxford Handbook of Language Policy and Planning* (pp. 633–653). Oxford: Oxford University Press.
Carabelli, G., Djurasovic, A. & Summa, R. (2019) Challenging the representation of ethnically divided cities: perspectives from Mostar. *Space and Polity, 23*(2): 116–124, DOI: 10.1080/13562576.2019.1634467.
Dingli, S. (2015). We need to talk about silence: Re-examining silence in International Relations theory. *European Journal of International Relations, 21*(4):721–742. doi: 10.1177/1354066114568033.
Djurasovic, A. (2016). *Ideology, political transitions and the city: The case of Mostar, Bosnia and Herzegovina.* London: Routledge.
Eastmond, M., & Mannergren Selimovic, J. (2012). Silence as possibility in post-war everyday life. *International Journal of Transitional Justice, 6*(3), 502–524.
Eastmond, M., & Mannergren Selimovic, J. (2020) Silence and Peacebuilding. In: O. Richmond, G. Visoka (eds.), *The Palgrave Encyclopedia of Peace and Conflict Studies.* Springer Nature.
Enloe, C, (1996). Margins, Silence and Bottom Rungs.
Forde, S. (2019). *Movement as conflict transformation. Rescripting Mostar, Bosnia-Herzegovina.* London: Palgrave Macmillan.
Guillaume X. (2018). How to do things with silence: Rethinking the centrality of speech to the securitization framework. *Security Dialogue, 49*(6):476–492. doi: 10.1177/0967010618789755
Gusic, Ivan (2020). Contesting Peace in the Postwar City. 10.1007/978-3-030-28091-8
Hromadžić, A. (2011). Bathroom mixing: Youth negotiate democratization in postconflict Bosnia and Herzegovina. *PoLAR, 34*(2), 268–289. doi: 10.1111/j.1555-2934.2011.01166.
Hobsbawm, E. (1996). Language, Culture and National Identity. *Social Research, Vol 63*(4).
Hromadžić, A. (2015a). *Citizens of an empty nation: Youth and state-making in postwar Bosnia and Herzegovina. The ethnography of political violence series.* Philadelphia: University of Pennsylvania Press.
Huysmans, J. (2014). *Security Unbound: Enacting Democratic Limits.* Abingdon, UK: Routledge.
Huysmans, J. (2006). *The Politics of Insecurity: Fear, Migration and Asylum in the EU.* New International Relations Series. London, UK: Routledge.
Jansen, S. *Yearnings in the Meantime. "Normal Lives" and the State in a Sarajevo Apartment Complex.* New York, Oxford: Berghahn Books, 2015.
Kent, L. (2016). Sounds of silence: Everyday strategies of social repair in Timor-Leste. *Australian Feminist Law Journal, 42*(1), 31–50.
Kreso, A. (2008). "The War And Post-War Impact On The Educational System Of Bosnia And Herzegovina," *International Review of Education, 54*(3).

Krishna, Sankaran (2001). Race, Amnesia, and the Education of International Relations. Alternatives: Global, Local, Political, 26, 401–42410.1177/030437540102600403.

Kamusella, T. *The Politics of Language and Nationalism in Modern Central Europe.* New York: Palgrave MacMillan, 2009.

Kapović, M. (2020). "Bosnian/Croatian/Montenegrin/Serbian: Notes on contact and conflict". European Pluricentric Languages in Contact and Conflict.

Kasunić, S. (2018). Pragmatic peace: the UNTAES peacekeeping mission as example for peaceful reintegration of occupied multiethnic territories.

Kolind, T. (2008). *Post-War Identification: Everyday Muslim Counterdiscourse in Bosnia Herzegovina.* Aarhus: Aarhus University Press.

Laketa, S. (2019) The politics of landscape as ways of life in the 'divided' city: reflections from Mostar, Bosnia–Herzegovina, *Space and Polity*, 23:2, 168–181, DOI: 10.1080/13562576.2019.1635444

Liddicoat, A. (2018). National security in language-in-education policy. *Un(intended) Language Planning in a Globalising World: Multiple Levels of Players at Work* (pp. 113–128).

May, Stephen (2016). Language, Imperialism, and the Modern Nation-State System, Oxford Handbooks Online10.1093/oxfordhb/9780190212896.013.12.

Mac Ginty. R. (2014). Everyday peace: Bottom-Up and local agency in conflict-affected societies. *Security Dialogue, Vol 45*(6) 548–564.

Maček, I. (2009) *Sarajevo Under Siege. Anthropology in Wartime.* Philadelphia: University of Pennsylvania Press.

Milčić, I. and Majsec, K. (2010). Reintegracija osnovnoga školstva u Vukovaru - u svijetlu nekih statističkih podataka. in Živić D and Cvikić S (eds), *Mirna reintegracija hrvatskoga Podunavlja: Znanstveni, empirijski i iskustveni uvidi* (Institut društvenih znanosti Ivo Pilar).

Milčić, I. and Majsec, K.. Language, Linguistics, Nationalism and Science. Etnološka tribina: Godišnjak Hrvatskog etnološkog društva 46/39, *25.30*.

Ochs, J. (2013). *Security and Suspicion. An Ethnography of Everyday Life in Israel.* University of Pennsylvania Press.

Orlandi, E. (2009). *Análise de Discurso: princípios & procedimentos.* 8. ed. Campinas: Pontes. 100p.

OSCE Mission to Bosnia Herzegovina (2018). "Two Schools Under One Roof" - The Most Visible Example of Discrimination in Education in Bosnia and Herzegovina. 3 December. https://www.osce.org/files/f/documents/3/8/404990.pdf

Palmberger, M. (2017) Nationalizing the streetscape: the case of street renaming in Mostar, Bosnia and Herzegovina. In *The Political Life of Urban Streetscapes Naming, Politics, and Place.* London: Palgrave.

Puh, M. Croats in Brazil as an Invisible Diaspora. *Journal of contemporary history*, v. *51*, p. 97–121, 2019.

Puh, M. (2017) Folklore as an educational activity in the constitution of language policies in and for rural communities of Ukrainian origin in Croatia and Brazil. 2017. 558p. Thesis (Doctorate). Faculty of Education, University of São Paulo, São Paulo,.

Pupavac, V. (2006). Discriminating language rights and politics in the post-Yugoslav states, Patterns of Prejudice, *40*:2, 112–128, DOI: 10.1080/00313220600634261

Rampton, B., & Charalambous, C. (2016). Breaking classroom silences: a view from linguistic ethnography. *Language and Intercultural Communication*, *16*(1), 4–21.

Sara Terry (2007). Students mingle – sort of – in postwar Bosnia's only integrated school. September 27. https://www.csmonitor.com/2007/0927/p20s01-wogn.html.
Shapiro, M. (1984). *Language and Politics*. New York University Press.
Stefansson, A. H. (2010). Coffee after cleansing? Coexistence, cooperation, and communication in post-conflict Bosnia and Herzegovina. *Focaal, 57*, 62–76.
Summa, R. (2021). *Everyday boundaries, borders and post conflict societies*. London: Palgrave McMillan.
Wollentz, Gustav, Barišić, Marko, & Sammar, Nourah (2019). Youth activism and dignity in post-war Mostar – envisioning a shared future through heritage. Space and Polity, 23, 197–21510.1080/13562576.2019.1635443.

5 Breaking taboos: The making of xenophobia as acceptable in Sweden

Emma Mc Cluskey

Introduction

This chapter draws on ethnographic research on refugee resettlement in Sweden to explore the increasing acceptability of xenophobic discourses and practices and the mainstreaming of so-called far-right parties throughout Europe. It adopts a transdisciplinary perspective, drawing on what has been labelled the 'PARIS' approach to thinking about questions of suspicion, exclusion and xenophobia, where PARIS is an acronym for Political Anthropological Research in International Sociology (Bigo & Mc Cluskey, 2018). As was discussed in chapter one, such an approach, on the interface of International Relations and Anthropology moves the discussion of capturing everyday practices of (in)security beyond a question of ethnography as method. Instead, it attempts to address what it means to foster an anthropological approach as a way of knowing about so-called international problems; looking in unexpected, quotidian spaces and seemingly 'insignificant' actors, attempting to engage with their everyday practices of (in)security before they reach the level of Discourse. In fostering this approach, it enables xenophobic or far-right political communities to be conceived of using a relational lens, forgoing the impetus to endow groups or individuals with pre-existing characteristics, or to impose on them prefabricated analytical grids. Instead, the chapter draws attention to the transformations and emergence of xenophobic discourse and practice within society, illuminating its entanglements with seemingly unrelated phenomena and sets of practices: hospitality, humanitarianism, and refugee 'solidarity.'

To achieve this, the chapter proceeds in the following ways. Firstly, it asks what it means to think transversally about 'the far right,' taking up Gusterson's (2017) call to pay ethnographic attention to communities attracted to far-right politics, a population usually ignored by anthropology. Moving onto the empirical case, the paper then proceeds to tell the story of Oreby, Sweden, a small village which housed a few dozen refugees from 2013 onwards. Using James C. Scott's (1990) conceptual tools of 'public' and 'hidden transcripts,' it traces the way taboos around speaking negatively about refugees and asylum policy were almost unnoticeably overturned,

DOI: 10.4324/9781003080909-5

rendering xenophobic and 'far right' discourses- sayable and actionable. Lastly, the chapter ponders what it means to 'scale up' from these local encounters in one village and speak to the broader politics of acceptability of far-right politics in contemporary times.

The emergence of political communities: Thinking transversally about 'the far right'

The refugee crisis of 2015 and 2016 in Europe called into question some of our modes of analysis and political assumptions. Even the relative 'openness' of Sweden and Germany turned rather quickly to resentment towards refugees with borders being closed to asylum seekers. Across Europe more broadly, far right parties made significant gains and political constellations shifted in quite unexpected ways. Xenophobic discourses, once confined to the fringes of society, became mainstream and considered as legitimate positions in day-to-day debate (see Antonsich, 2017 for an overview).

How can we think about the transformations of taboos and the politics of acceptability around being associated with 'the far right'? Conventional wisdom explains a lot of these changes as the effects of neo-liberal policies finally manifesting in an inevitable backlash; those who are left behind by globalisation expressing their unhappiness and anger with an uncertain world (Burns & Gimpel, 2000; Goodwin & Heath, 2016). Other studies however which investigate voters who identify themselves as 'far-right,' have found that the only thread which in fact unites these vastly different people throughout Europe is hostility to immigration, particularly regarding migrants from Muslim majority or Arab countries (Inglehart and Norris 2019). Though successful in illuminating and hierarchising the different factors which could determine voting for extreme right wing parties, analysis in this literature has tended to be quantitative, and based on survey data and opinion polls. Ethnographic perspectives on far-right voters and the life-worlds these voters inhabit- have been noticeably lacking.

In noticing this absence, Hugh Gusterson (2017) has called for anthropologists to devote research to groups of people attracted to the far-right, who he claims are populations usually widely ignored by anthropology. For Gusterson, these ethnographies would shed light on what makes the particular demographics of people likely to support Trump, Brexit, Le Pen etc. be attracted to what were once deemed quite extreme positions. Challenging anthropology to examine 'bad' civil society as intellectually within reach, especially in a time of Manichean interpretations of world politics, Gusterson argues, is extremely important. Holbraad (2017) pushes this research call even further, arguing that researchers should 'take seriously' stances we would otherwise think of as 'preposterous.'

My ethnographic research, which charted the disbanding of relations between villagers in Sweden and the refugees who were resettled there, and which forms the core of this chapter, demonstrates that any homogenising or essentialising narrative around 'populations' most likely to support far-right politics – be it social class, age, race, geographical location – is misplaced. What my research captured (quite inadvertently, as this was not the initial research question of the ethnography) was the much smaller shifts taking place, which normalised xenophobic and far-right politics more widely, attaching a *logic of suspicion and othering* to everyday practice around quite far removed and seemingly unrelated phenomena. Indeed, my interlocutors considered themselves as good and decent people, acting in solidarity with the refugees. From this perspective, it makes sense to think about 'good' and 'bad' civil society in relation and in terms of a transformation of the content of what is seen as 'acceptable,' sayable or sometimes even virtuous, as opposed to exceptional or extreme groups divided by ideology (De Orellana & Michelsen, 2019). Instead of focusing on 'far-right' or 'xenophobic' as an object of study or as already constituted agents, it thus became possible for me to focus on the practices and relations which produce these individuals as identifying themselves as such; how these became lived in categories and embodied subjectivities.

In this way, somebody identifying themselves with far-right movements may indeed be very ordinary and not see themselves as 'xenophobic.' They may not embody this political subjectivity whatsoever, and 'live in' the category of anti-migrant or right-wing subjectivity in interesting and unanticipated ways (cf. Hacking, 1986). Thinking in terms of the transformation from a pro-refugee dominant narrative to a xenophobic one for me involved studying actors traditionally conceived of as 'civil society' to see the way in which rationalisations of behaviour change over time. It is thus possible to move beyond dichotomies of xenophobia vs. openness, and an ideological or 'top-down' approach to xenophobia or securitarian politics to look at how actors who were open about voting for a far-right party (many of whom for the first time) justified their practices. The notion of political communities of 'far right' voters, therefore becomes emergent and contingent; a point I will return to in the conclusion. 'Capturing' this emergence and contingency and engaging with this empirically attempts to objectivise this normalisation of xenophobia as *it is happening* in everyday life.

This links to a core tenet of what Bigo and Mc Cluskey (2018) have relabelled as a 'PARIS' approach to studying processes and practices of (in)securitisation; placing ontological and epistemological primacy on the significance of lived experience of the 'subjects' of these security practices, be they 'direct or indirect victims, be they amateurs of security, or just indifferent to the debates but affected by them.'

This ethnographic perspective also enables the 'writing in' of the constantly shifting formations of these subjectivities as the ethnographic encounters unfold, engaging with the temporality of these subject formations as they transformed with the ever-changing relations that these individuals were embedded within. This story is always one informed by a practical reflexivity (Jeandesboz, 2018), built in to every step, paying heed to my situatedness in knowledge production particularly the activation of different relational positionalities which perhaps had not been anticipated (Blommaert, 2005).

Oreby, Skåne and transformations of Swedish 'solidarity'

Sweden is an interesting case; regarded as a 'humanitarian superpower' during Europe's so-called 'refugee crisis' for its relatively open policy and high standard of care provided to people arriving to claim asylum, the Swedish government subsequently adopted some of the strictest asylum policies at the midst of the 'crisis,' reintroducing border controls along the southern border with Denmark. With the failure of Europe to formulate any sort of coordinated response to the 'crisis,' these moves were articulated in terms of burden sharing and already having done one's fair share, but also in starker security terms, linked with anti-terrorist measures and public order. The anti-immigration *Sweden Democrats* party also made great gains during the same time period, increasing their proportion of votes from 13% in September 2014, to 19% in September 2018 making them the nation's third largest political party. It was just before what has been called the 'long summer of migration' in 2015, that I left Sweden, having spent around a year and a half conducting fieldwork for my PhD on the changing dynamics between refugees and villagers in a small enclave called Oreby (Mc Cluskey, 2019). During this time, I came to find myself forming relationships with volunteers and members of informal refugee solidarity groups, who became drawn to far-right politics for the first time.

I was based in Oreby, a picturesque little village in the county of Skåne, southern Sweden home to around 1600 inhabitants. A largely middle-class place, Oreby's main road was bordered on either side with large, detached well-groomed bungalows complete with generous front gardens housing all manner of children's play equipment. Though a rather tiny place, the village was well served with a good school, a library, a minimart and a pizzeria. On one February morning in 2013 however, Oreby's population increased by seventy when, without much notice, a few dozen Syrian refugee families were resettled by the Swedish Migration board in an apartment complex just off the main road. The proposed resettlement of Syrians in Oreby was initially met with some resistance by the villagers at a 'consultation' meeting organised in the school hall by the Migration Board. I was not present for this meeting but heard second-hand accounts of angry exchanges between locals and officials, along the lines of falling house price worries, fear of increase in petty crime and most strongly, sexual assaults. Despite this unease, a small volunteer group, the 'Friends of Syria,' mobilised quickly to provide the refugees with the material goods they needed for life in Sweden; bicycles, warm clothes and toys, as well as offering Swedish lessons to complement the official Swedish-for-immigrants (SFI) policy. My role, as both a researcher and volunteer, was that of translator between Arabic and Swedish, or Arabic and English, as all communication from government agencies was in Swedish, and the Migration Board declared themselves too overwhelmed to offer translation services.

The particular dynamics between the villagers and the refugees in Oreby were extremely illustrative of all the taboos, obligations and negotiations of norms in play amongst those who identified themselves as, 'good' and 'decent' citizens. The five women who made up the Friends of Syria were all local, middle class and in their forties or fifties. Thanks to the mobilisations and local advocacy of the group leader, Bodil, the NGO accumulated a huge amount of goods which she then took upon herself to distribute amongst the refugees. As a member of the village community, Bodil was not part of any wider humanitarian organisation and was loosely affiliated with the Swedish church. As opposed to the usual working practices of NGO workers, it was Friends of Syria who initiated contact with the Syrian refugees by knocking on each of their doors a few hours after the officials from *the Migration Board* had settled them into their new homes, introducing themselves as fellow villagers and neighbours and volunteering themselves as the first point of contact should the new arrivals be in need of any assistance. When the first Syrians in Oreby were joined by another dozen refugees from Eritrea, Uganda, Iran and Georgia, the Friends of Syria campaigned for a nearby house to be rented by *The Migration Board* to be used as an 'activity centre' for the resettled refugees. This became the scene of Swedish lessons, clothing donation and distribution, and general 'hanging out.'

With the realisation that the placement of the refugees in Oreby was something that they would be obliged to live with, rather than something that they were in discussions about, objections to the resettlement of the refugees were no longer voiced or articulated in formal settings, such as the various village events (which took place roughly once or twice a month), such as the Spring Festival or Children's Day. Instead, these fora became a terrain through which the villagers could perform the role of 'decency' to each other, demonstrating generosity and hospitality by regaling stories of how terrible the war in Syria is and advertising how much they had personally donated to the new arrivals. The meeting at the school was thus the only occasion of such vocal resistance to the housing of the refugees in Oreby. Indeed, many of those people present at the meeting later denied being present or raising any objections, dismissing the resistance to the resettlement of the refugees as demonstrations by 'ignorant people' or 'people who were simply a bit scared of the unknown.' With the inability to influence the Migration Board's decision to place refugees in Oreby, power relations reverted to maintaining a certain ideal of respectability, and all the taboos and obligations enabled by the national myth of 'humanitarian superpowerfulness' were brought back into play.

Grumbles or complaints I overheard about the perceived deficiencies and flaws of the new arrivals, however, took to the more informal, 'safer' settings of the school gates, the pizzeria and the slimming club. The Arab men were conceived of in familiar orientalized terms, as hypermasculinized, lecherous and deficient; as though it was only a matter of time before something terrible would happen in the village. Areas of the village in which the refugees congregated were deemed 'no go zones' of sorts, without ever needing to be openly articulated as such. For example Swedish children and refugee children were 'of course' permitted to play together according to many of the local parents, but this transpired to be only within the supervised settings of the school (during school time) or the football club every Saturday. During training, Syrian parents congregated along a far end of the football field and Swedish parents separately along the length of the pitch. After the game, most of the local parents left immediately and ensured that their children were quickly shepherded away into cars. A family living next to the area in which the refugees were housed even put their house on the market, claiming openly that they were moving to be nearer family in the city though Bodil admitted they were very uncomfortable about living so close to the refugees.

Such a tacit, unspoken understanding between the residents of Oreby as to where the line of 'solidarity' and 'hospitality' was to be drawn and where it was permitted to falter enabled any outward confrontation to be kept to a minimum, even completely avoided, and for everybody involved to maintain their 'good citizen' reputation. James C. Scott, though talking about domination, talks about this type of shared understanding between members of a group in terms of a 'hidden transcript' – a sort of collective resistance that maintains the illusion of a placid surface, whilst slyly making use of fleeting, seized opportunities that push the limits of what is permitted (Scott, 1990: 196). This hidden transcript co-exists with a 'public transcript'; which represents the maintenance work that is needed to uphold relations of domination through symbolic demonstrations and enactments of power (Scott, 1990:49). This 'public transcript' however has also been applied by Scott to less coercive relations of power; the choreography around 'good manners' and the avoidance of social taboos whilst in polite company. Venturing away from interpreting his framework in terms of a very narrow definition of domination, Scott (1990: 47) links his idea of a 'public transcript' with the concept of politeness and good taste. He asserts that 'some displays, some rituals ... are more elaborate and closely regulated than others' pointing out how events such as royal coronations are designed and choreographed with as little wiggle room as possible, connecting this to the way in which 'smaller daily ceremonies,' more day-to-day social intercourse, can also be spoken about with the same generalisation:

"Rules of etiquette represent, after all, a kind of grammar of social intercourse, imposed by the guardians of taste and decorum, which allows its users to safely navigate the sholas of strangers, especially powerful strangers" (Scott, 1990: 47). He goes on to add however, citing Pierre Bourdieu, that these 'performances' are too pervaded by power. 'The concession of politeness always contains political concessions ... the symbolic taxes due are from individuals' (Bourdieu cited in Scott, 1990: 48).

Though far from dominated, the taboos brought into being by obligations of 'decency' invoked by Sweden's humanitarian superpower narrative – meant that any resistance against the refugees was pushed into a more 'hidden' realm. Though able to be voiced behind closed doors amongst members of a trusted group; those who were certain to share these views, such sentiments were unable to be articulated in polite company if one were to uphold a certain image of oneself as a good person and good citizen.

The performance of the 'good citizen' was nonetheless permitted to lapse or alter somewhat around the notion of gender equality and the 'children's well-being.' Although the familiar orientalized conception of the Arab man as somewhat dangerous was an accepted truth in the village – unspoken in 'polite company' after the initial meeting, but coming to form a sort of common sense, nobody would now expressly label the men as threatening or undesirable. Instead, open discourse was along the lines of how terrible the suffering of the refugees must have been, how it must be so traumatic to be forced to adapt to such a new culture, and how much help and support they would need. In terms of gender and parenting, however, a great deal more room for manoeuvre was available to still behave decently; to divert slightly from never criticising the refugees whilst nonetheless still appearing very polite and welcoming from the acceptance of 'no-go' zones for the village children to the adoption of various 'female empowerment' strategies.

The demand for reciprocation: Appropriating solidarity as a free gift

As an intermediary between the village and the refugees, Bodil and the Friends of Syria were often the target of these grumbles and complaints and, thus, took on the role of helping the Syrians to 'integrate' and 'enter society.' Any attempt to directly force the Syrian men to 'mend their ways,' however, was deemed taboo. The Friends of Syria volunteers were aware that speaking about the Arab men as fanatical and potentially violent was in bad taste. Although acceptable to be articulated behind closed doors, to speak this way publicly would be seen as particularly unsavoury and something that was relegated in their imagination to the realm of the far right. Eva, for example, the volunteer in charge of running the weekly Swedish classes, would often roll off the platitude that 'sexism and racism are two sides of the same coin.' In this way the 'public transcript' of decency and generosity was able to be upheld. Nonetheless, the Friends of Syria, in accommodating the unease of the wider community, took it upon themselves to 'do something' to help the new arrivals adjust to Swedish life, particularly with regards to the notions of gender equality and the upbringing of children.

One way to avoid more open or direct criticism of the perceived patriarchy or sexism of the Syrian refugees, which would risk being viewed as breaking a taboo, was to articulate disapproval as though it was not completely serious – simply a 'joke' or light-hearted teasing that could be easily laughed off (for an exploration on the relationship between humour and prejudice, see Billig, 2001). This type of interaction was especially prominent between the volunteers in their dealings with the older Syrian men and fathers who had been settled in the village. To every new family who arrived, for example, Bodil would proclaim to the father that 'Sweden is the opposite of your culture; here, women are legally allowed to take four husbands but men are only allowed one wife,' before quickly adding that she was 'just joking.' This type of teasing took on the form of anything from trying to shock the Syrian men into dramatically altering their perceived norms of how they expected their wives to dress – 'Don't be surprised come summertime when your wife will be in a bikini! You're not in Aleppo now' – to gently mocking the men for what the volunteers perceived to be a lack of domestic skills – 'A Swedish woman would never let a man get away with that!' This type of advice, though with serious intent behind it, was always given playfully, and as such was easily disowned.

Within the same orientalist episteme, the Syrian women, viewed as more 'passive' and thus a somewhat easier target, were hence seen as a more receptive group at whom to direct advice. In addition to the Swedish lessons and general drop-in sessions held in the activity centre, the volunteers also devoted every Tuesday to holding cooking classes, whereby two or three of them would show the new arrivals how to make simple Swedish recipes like cinnamon buns and pancakes. The rationality of organising this event was precisely to attract the women, to facilitate an arena in which they could get to know the 'real' person in the absence of the perceived influence of the husband, and to create a separate form of 'female solidarity.'

The first few cooking lessons were deemed very successful, attended by around twenty or so women, both Syrian and non-Arab. The volunteers spoke to the women in English, but took care to teach them simple, Swedish words as they went along. 'They will never integrate or get a job if they can't even say basic sentences.' Bodil, the chief volunteer, encouraged the women to leave their children at home during these classes, citing the need for the women to have some well-deserved time to themselves, but also promoting the ideal of a more gender-equal style of parenting: 'Besides, now that you're living in Sweden, it's time that your husbands did some childcare for a change.'

After around five or six weeks, however, most of the Syrian women stopped attending the cooking classes, with only a family of two sisters and one of their husbands from Georgia, as well as three Ugandan women, making the weekly visit. This was a source of mild irritation to the Friends of Syria group who saw their time as wasted if the Syrian women would not even make the effort to get to know the Swedish culture and simply 'locked themselves away.' In the absence of any Syrians, conversations at Tuesday's cooking classes often centred on their perceived deficiencies; they were seen to be 'stuck in their ways' and weak-willed, unable to 'stand up to their husbands' about the changes needed to integrate in Sweden.

Engagement with the Syrian refugees, both male and female, therefore only took place in the more informal 'drop-in sessions' that the volunteers had arranged twice weekly, whereby the new arrivals could stop by to discuss any issues they were having with accommodation, to search through donations and take any clothes they needed, or to come with letters from The Migration Board or, the Employment Agency, to be translated into Arabic. The five volunteers thus utilised this opportunity to advise the women on what they should be doing to make 'entering society' easier, on subjects such as how to dress or how to control their children's behaviour. The perceived deficiencies of the Syrians' parenting was amplified during Ramadan when complaints about the refugee children being permitted to stay up late and 'run amok' came to a head, and the group received more and more complaints from fellow villagers.

The Swedish decision and the changing of the stakes

In October 2013, almost two years before Angela Merkel's *'Wir Schaffen das'* policy was implemented in Germany and the whole 'refugees welcome' movement, Sweden took the unilateral decision to grant every Syrian arriving at the border permanent residency. Up until that point, most of the Syrian refugees had been granted temporary five year residency permits, though many doubted that they would ever return.

I was working at the reception centre the morning after the announcement and sensed that this changed things somewhat for the volunteers. Susanne, one of the founders of the group, explained her reservations: "Sweden is such a good country, but sometimes I think we are being naïve, you know? What now if thousands arrive here? We can't manage on our own." Being from the UK, a de-facto 'xenophobic' country in the eyes of the volunteers, I was seen as a non-judgemental and a somewhat sympathetic set of ears. 'You lot over there must think we're all a soft touch.'

The move to grant permanent residency to the Syrians was defined by then minister for migration Tobias Billstrom as being one of rationalism and legal obligations. If other EU member states were not living up to their legal responsibilities, it was not up to Sweden to lower its standards or abandon its commitment to the right of asylum. Nonetheless, within Oreby, the volunteers interpreted this move (and the failure of other EU member states to live up to the standard) as one of generosity on the part of Sweden. 'Solidarity' was appropriated and transformed. To interpret notions of solidarity within the boundaries of generosity enabled a gift economy to be brought into play whereby any behaviour outside that of from the saviour vs saved paradigm was deemed problematic.

What was at play was a type of 'changing of the stakes' (Mauss, 2002). Perceptions that, with this decision taken by the Swedish government, something tangible had now changed. Though for many of the villagers, and indeed the volunteers, this move by the Swedish government was largely unrelated to the day-to-day goings on in Oreby (once the Syrians had been granted asylum, they were technically supposed to have been placed into alternative accommodation under the care of a separate government agency), this changing of the stakes permitted different demands to be placed on the refugees in terms of repaying the symbolic debt.

How did this move contribute towards the shifting of where the limits had been placed? The changing of the stakes made way for a small chink; a slight shifting in the norms of acceptable behaviour. The right to asylum was placed into a new relation and the move to grant permanent residency was instead seen as 'generous.' New demands could be legitimately placed on the refugees to adhere to a certain standard and the rules on what it was to be a worthy guest, more vigorously enforced. At play was a crystallisation; the volunteers, as well as others in the village, became more certain of the 'rightness' of the demands they placed on the refugees; the need to be stoic, the need to mend their ways and more forcefully integrate into the Swedish way of life, the need to demonstrate gratitude towards the 'host country.' A space for hierarchization of refugees was also created from the mobilisation of this gift economy; those who were deemed to adhere to this set of behaviours branded more worthy of the 'gift' of asylum than those who stepped outside.

Since the 'long summer of migration' and declaration of various 'crises,' a great deal of scholarship has been focused on the way in which volunteers, humanitarians and in some cases, even activists; falling broadly under the banner of 'civil society' reproduce the existing hierarchy of lives between the European citizen and the refugee 'benefactor' of care; between the saviour and the saved (see especially Fleischmann & Steinhilper, 2017; Vandevoordt & Verschraegen, 2019; Picozza, 2021). This scholarship has been most pronounced in relation to the German approach to the refugees, where Merkel's '*Wir Schaffen das*' policy saw the mobilisation of an unprecedented number of volunteers.

Some of these studies point to the way in which the depoliticisation of acts of refugee solidarity in this way took place *at the same time* as a series of legislative acts which rendered German asylum law the most restrictive it had ever been. The mobilisition of volunteers en masse was followed by border closures and a hardening of residency and family reunification policies. These studies are exceptional in illuminating the way in which 'civil society' can reproduce the European 'border regime' and exclusionary apparatus through practices which they deem apolitical – what Fleischmann and Steinhilper (2017) label the 'myth of apolitical volunteering.'

This has been read recently in post-colonial or racialized terms, in which the usually 'white' volunteers re-inscribe the non-white refugee as a permanently displaced 'other' (El-Tayeb, 2008). Most often however, it is read in broader biopolitical terms in which hierarchies of life are created between the carer and the cared for. However, these studies tend to consider these sets of humanitarian practices as separate to the rise of anti-migration sentiment, or 'bad' civil society actors. This reading re-transcribes the idea that 'good' and 'bad' civil society actors are separate categories of practice. That one cannot transform into the other. Perhaps this is more sociologically accurate in the German case, though more research is undoubtedly needed in this regard. However, in Sweden, where the majority of Sweden Democrats voters in the last election were in areas which house the majority of refugees and asylum seekers, the picture is more complex. Hence, a more dynamic reading- in which one can position the possibility of transformation from one type of political actor to another is important. Furthermore, it also becomes possible to position this transformation from 'good' to 'bad' civil society as a logical extension to the stratification of rights and mobilisation of gift economy brought into play by 'hosting' refugees.

Indignation and panic: The voicing of the hidden transcript

By never openly criticising or voicing objection to the resettlement of the refugees, the volunteers and residents of Oreby reinforced but also utilised the 'humanitarian superpower' myth to retain a sense of their own moral superiority. In this respect, a 'public transcript' was firmly in place, giving the appearance of a tranquil, placid surface in which everybody accepts the prevailing norms. Although there was a marked unease in the village over the resettlement of the refugees, any resistance to their resettlement, aside from the initial meeting, was forced into a more hidden realm in order to maintain a decent image. The only realm in which it became acceptable to let this public transcript 'lapse' somewhat was around concerns about the perceived gender inequality and parenting practices of the new arrivals, whereby the 'good citizen' image was still able to be maintained. Any allusion to the Arab men as violent or fanatical, though allowed to be voiced in the initial meeting, was no longer acceptable in public and would now immediately render the speaker a 'dreg'; a person of very low social standing (Gullestad, 2002), or at best, un-Swedish. As long as the refugees played by all the rules of being a 'worthy guest' (Rozakou, 2012), and accepted the advice of the volunteers on how to be more gender equal and on how to raise their children, then this 'public transcript' of complete acceptance was maintained, and talk of violent, suspicious men and passive, dominated women- was kept somewhat hidden. This delicate situation lasted for a good nine months before external events disturbed the balance.

As I was driving to Oreby on a dry, autumnal morning, I turned up the volume of the car radio to listen to the news of a Somali man who had been shot dead by the Swedish police in the north of the country, in a tiny village in the county of Jämtland. According to this report, the Somali man was an asylum seeker who had been drunk and brandishing a knife at police when he was killed.

When I reached the village, the atmosphere was extremely tense with a few dozen people gathered at the activity centre. Bodil was attempting to organise some sort of meeting and had asked as many of the Syrian refugees to attend as possible. It took a while to realise that the meeting Bodil had called was in relation to the incident in Jämtland, something I did not comprehend until she approached me quite aghast, asking if I had heard. She told me that her phone had not stopped ringing all morning with parents from the children's school reprimanding her for being so naïve and open to asylum seekers, when it was clear that they were traumatised and unstable people. "That little place in Jämtland is just like here, it's a place just like this". Although the Syrians had lived in Oreby for some eight months by then, with not so much as a bin bag being disposed of out of place, the incident in Jämtland had shifted the terrain of acceptable public discourse on what could be said about the migrants.

For the first time since their arrival, Bodil communicated this general anxiety of the villagers to the refugees themselves, dis-embedding herself from the position of intermediary between the villagers and the refugees and placing herself firmly as a spokesperson for the good people of Oreby: 'I just want to tell you men that you have to behave yourselves. This is what happens in Sweden if you don't behave yourself. It is a good country but if you come here, you have to respect our rules.' Bodil's speech to the thirty or so people who had gathered was short and to the point, directed at every Syrian man there.

The protests of an articulate, twenty-two-year-old male medical student from Aleppo that this man was 'Somali' and thus, in his reasoning, was completely uncivilised and backward, as opposed to Syrians who were cultured and peaceful people, was quickly dismissed by Bodil. True, he may be from another country, but he was also a 'guest' in Sweden, who the good people of Jämtland had been so kind as to protect.

This was the first time that there was a firmly demarcated line between the people of Oreby and the refugees. The incident legitimised, in the eyes of the Oreby dwellers, the move away from performances of hospitality and generosity– to an open articulation of an 'us and them.' Cohen (1980) famously articulates such an event as a 'moral panic,' recognising the way in which a person, or group of people, can emerge and come to be framed by the media as a threat to societal values and interests through exaggerated and somewhat distorted reporting. The resulting frenzy thus engenders a largely disproportionate response to the perceived 'deviancy.' Crucial to the success of a moral panic, however, is its capacity to tap into somewhat pre-existing societal orientations, perhaps not previously publicly voiced, but which become more crystallised and organised as the result of the panic, and hence more legitimate (Cohen, 1980: 47).

Indeed, this vignette of the police shooting and the subsequent reaction in Oreby is extremely telling. The Somali man in Jämtland had most spectacularly broken the rules of being a 'worthy guest' (Rozakou, 2012) by wielding a knife. The media articulation of the refugee as threatening and dangerous thus altered the power dynamics in Oreby and rendered sayable what had been taboo only a day previously. The repertoire of available actions for the 'decent' citizen became far more wide ranging. Although the episode did not take place in Oreby, or indeed anywhere near it, a subsequent moral panic ensued allowing Bodil to publicly voice what people had being saying more or less privately in phone calls and in conversations at the school gate.

Conclusion

This chapter has traced the almost imperceptible changes from a humanitarian approach to the resettlement of Syrian refugees in a Swedish village to the emergence of public xenophobic and exclusionary discourses and sentiments. These sentiments, deemed taboo only a year previously, became inhabited by the very people who had contributed towards rendering them taboo in the first place. In January 2016, activities at a national level mirrored what took place in Oreby, when the Swedish Prime Minister articulated refugees entering Sweden as a 'serious threat to public order and national security' (cited in Goodwin & Heath, 2016) and closed the southern border with Denmark to prevent any more refugees from entering. My final trip to Oreby was about a year before these changes to legislative policy took place, before the 'long summer of migration' and subsequent discourses of 'crisis' (Squire et al., 2021). Even so, during this trip, both Bodil and the other members of the 'Friends of Syria' had revealed to me that Oreby could no longer cope, that the far-right 'Sweden Democrat' party were the only party to speak on behalf of their struggles, and that blocking any more refugees from coming into Sweden would, paradoxically, help focus resources on the refugees who were already there, possibly even lowering the chance of vigilantes and hooligans threatening them or vandalising their dwellings.

A transdisciplinary approach grounded in ethnographic, situated analysis avoids 'ready-made' accounts of thinking about people or groups who align with far-right as already constituted agents, somehow predisposed to xenophobic tendencies through socioeconomic status or other reified identity markers. Instead, these transformations are seen to be emergent and becoming (Guillaume & Huysmans, 2019), tied to a host of other, seemingly unrelated and sometimes opposing sets of practices like hospitality, generosity, or even solidarity. It also avoids reading 'far right' in Manichean terms, which can serve to have a de-politicising effect, reproducing imaginaries of xenophobia as something 'over there,' an 'object' of study but not something that can come to penetrate imagined life-worlds of familiar middle-class ordinary people. By tracing the coexistence of xenophobia and solidarity, the boundaries between these two seemingly contradictory concepts are shown to be permeable and fluid at the level of everyday practice.

Instead of conceiving of far-right voters in Sweden as a single 'case study,' my encounters with the villagers and refugees in Oreby is better framed as a 'conjuncture of social relations'; a 'conjuncture of the national and the transnational' (De Genova, 2005: 7; Appadurai, 1996). In this way, going 'local' is never ignoring the international or national, but recognising that any form of national and international is simultaneously always a form of 'local.' In this sense, my ethnography is also multiscalar (Xiang, 2013; Williamson, 2015). Drawing on my encounters with Swedish villagers and the refugees resettled in this village, it becomes possible to 'scale up,' drawing connections with the wider transformations in political constellations through tracing these norms of sayability and breaking of taboos. Through being recognised as 'acceptable,' these previously taboo and hence marginal sentiments are able to circulate throughout different social universes. In the sphere of party politics, we see how the far-right Sweden Democrats party, once ostracised and excluded from any chance of participating in coalition government, has now become 'mainstream,' with more traditional centrist parties now declaring themselves ready to work with them in government (Helmerson, 2021). Through capturing these practices of (in)security in the quotidian realm before these sentiments reach the level of official political discourse, we are better able to explain the normalisation of xenophobic politics than through approaches which frame the issue of 'xenophobic' and 'far-right' political communities merely through the lens of ideology or through analyses which fashion these groups as somehow pre-existing.

This takes me to my final point, which was also discussed in the introduction of this book, and points back to some broader ramifications of working beyond bounded knowledge. In reflecting on this transdisciplinary endeavour and how this chapter can speak to the broader reflexive scholarly encounter, the normative assumptions, blind spots and sheer incommensurability of our disciplinary baggage become starkly illuminated. The stories that we choose to tell and how we frame our questions is a political act in itself; the everyday negotiations of taboos and norms of sayability described in this chapter for example are broadly similar across the four chapters that make up this section. The practices that chapter three views under the notion of 'everyday peace,' however, are labelled here as a 'public transcript of solidarity,' enacting violence in a more hidden realm. Only when placed alongside each other, and outside of disciplinary framings do the dissonances and tensions between how we frame questions, the stories we choose to tell and the labels we choose to give – become visible, enabling conversation and cross-fertilisation to take place across boundaries. Productivising this dissonance, as argued in chapter one, is as much part of reflexive scholarly practice as the 'fieldwork' itself.

References

Antonsich, M. (2017). The return of the nation: When neo-nationalism becomes mainstream. *Environment and Planning D: Society and Space* (Online blog) Available at https://www.societyandspace.org/articles/the-return-of-the-nation-when-neo-nationalism-becomes-mainstream (Accessed 19/03/2020).

Appadurai, A. (1996). *Modernity al large: cultural dimensions of globalization*, Minnesota: University of Minnesota Press.

Bigo, D. & Mc Cluskey, E. (2018). What Is a PARIS Approach to (In) securitization? Political Anthropological Research for International Sociology. In *The Oxford Handbook of International Security*. Oxford: Oxford University Press, 116–133.

Billig, M. (2001). Humour and hatred: The racist jokes of the Ku Klux Klan. *Discourse & Society*, *12*(3), 267–289.

Blommaert, J. (2005). Bourdieu the ethnographer: The ethnographic grounding of habitus and voice. *The Translator*, 11(2), 219–236.

Burns, P., & Gimpel, J. G. (2000). Economic insecurity, prejudicial stereotypes, and public opinion on immigration policy. *Political Science Quarterly 115*(2), 201–225.

Cohen, S. (1980). *Folk devils and moral panics: The creation of the mods and rockers*. Abingdon: Psychology Press.

De Genova, N. (2005). *Working the boundaries: Race, space, and "illegality" in Mexican Chicago*, Durham NC: Duke University Press.

De Orellana, P. & Michelsen, N. (2019). Reactionary Internationalism: the philosophy of the New Right. *Review of International Studies* 45 (5), 748–767.

El-Tayeb, F. (2008). 'The Birth of a European Public': Migration, postnationality, and race in the uniting of Europe. *American Quarterly 60* (3), 649–670.

Fleischmann, L. & Steinhilper, E. (2017). The myth of apolitical volunteering for refugees: German welcome culture and a new dispositif of helping. *Social Inclusion* 5 (3), 17–27.

Goodwin, M. J., & Heath, O. (2016). The 2016 referendum, Brexit and the left behind: An aggregate-level analysis of the result. *The Political Quarterly 87*(3), 323–332.

Guardian, The (2016). Sweden and Denmark crack down on refugees at borders.4th January. Available at http://www.theguardian.com/world/2016/jan/03/sweden-to-impose-id-checks-on-travellers-from-denmark. [Accessed 4/9/2020]

Gullestad, M. (2002). Invisible fences: Egalitarianism, nationalism and racism. *Journal of the Royal Anthropological Institute* 8(1), 45–63.

Gusterson, H. (2017). From Brexit to Trump: Anthropology and the rise of nationalist populism. *American Ethnologist 44*(2), 209–214.

Hacking, I. (1986). Making Up People. In Heller, Sosna, & Wellbery (eds.) *Reconstructing Individualism: Autonomy, Individuality, and the Self in Western Thought*. (pp. 222–236). Stanford: Stanford University Press.

Helmerson, E (2021). Liberalerna öppnar för Sveriges mest antiliberala parti [Liberals open to Sweden's most illiberal party] *Dagens Nyheter* 28th March. Available at https://www.dn.se/ledare/erik-helmerson-liberalerna-oppnar-for-sveriges-mest-antil-iberala-parti/ (Accessed on03/04/21)

Holbraad, M. (2017). *Critique, risqué: A comment on Didier Fassin. Anthropological Theory 17* (2), 274–278.

Guillaume, X., & Huysmans, J. (2019). The concept of 'the everyday': Ephemeral politics and the abundance of life. *Cooperation and Conflict 54*(2), 278–296.

Jeandesboz, J. (2018). Putting security in its place: EU security politics, the European neighbourhood policy and the case for practical reflexivity. *Journal of International Relations and Development 21* (1), 22–45.

Mauss, M. (2002). *The gift: The form and reason for exchange in archaic societies.* London: Routledge
Mc Cluskey, E. (2019). *From righteousness to far right: An anthropological rethinking of critical security studies (Vol. 2).* Kingston and Montreal: McGill-Queen's Press-MQUP.
Norris, P., & Inglehart, R. (2019). *Cultural backlash: Trump, Brexit, and authoritarian populism.* Cambridge University Press.
Picozza, F. (2021). *The Coloniality of Asylum: Mobility, Autonomy and Solidarity in the Wake of Europe's Refugee Crisis.* London: Rowman & Littlefield Publishers.
Rozakou, K. (2012). The biopolitics of hospitality in Greece: Humanitarianism and the management of refugees. *American ethnologist 39*(3): 562–577.
Scott, J. C. (1990). *Domination and the arts of resistance: Hidden transcripts*, New Haven: Yale Univ Press.
Squire, V., Perkowski, N., Stevens, D., & Vaughan-Williams, N. (2021). Narratives of 'crisis'. In *Reclaiming migration: Voices from Europe's 'Migrant Crisis'.* Manchester: Manchester University Press. (chapter 1).
Vandevoordt, R., & Verschraegen, G. (2019). Subversive humanitarianism and its challenges: Notes on the political ambiguities of civil refugee support. *In Refugee protection and civil society in Europe* (pp. 101–128). Palgrave Macmillan, Cham.
Williamson, R. (2015). Towards a multi-scalar methodology: The challenges of studying social transformation and international migration. In *Social transformation and migration* (pp. 17–32). London: Palgrave Macmillan.
Xiang, B. (2013). Multi-scalar ethnography: An approach for critical engagement with migration and social change. *Ethnography 14*(3), 282–299.

Part II
Managing suspicion and surveillance in everyday life

6 Embodying the US security state: Surveilling intimate spaces to counter violent extremism

Nicole Nguyen

Introduction

Given its concerns with the perceived rise of homegrown terrorism within its large Somali student body, Minneapolis Public Schools announced plans to 'hire and train experienced youth workers from the community to bridge the gap between youth and the school system.' More specifically, these youth workers would 'spend time in the lunchroom and non-classroom setting building relationships and trust' and 'spot identity issues and disaffection' believed to be the 'root causes of radicalization' among Somali students (Kiernat 2015). In Maryland, youth workers referred immigrant students experiencing 'acculturation related stress,' 'feelings of alienation,' and 'economic stressors' to intervention programs, on the premise that these experiences 'suggest they *may be* at risk of violent extremism' (World Organization for Resource Development and Education 2014:4 emphasis in original). Formalized under the Obama administration, these local initiatives have contributed to a broader Countering Violent Extremism (CVE) strategy in the United States, which has called on community leaders, social service providers, and families to prevent terrorist radicalization and recruitment. To do so, some CVE programs have encouraged social service providers like youth workers to identify, report, and work with individuals perceived to be vulnerable to or in the process of radicalization, often in collaboration with federal, state, and local law enforcement agencies. As one State Department official explained, 'having the government work closely with civil society' to 'create opportunities for dialogue,' 'address the root causes' of terrorist radicalization, and 'undo the terrible narrative of violent extremism' could stop 'disastrous terrorism in its track' (participant observation, August 2016). The CVE strategy therefore has sought to counter terrorist radicalization and recruitment through community-led programming.

Government officials and community leaders alike have promoted CVE as a progressive alternative to conventional counterterrorism methods like sting operations, preemptive prosecutions, and indefinite detention. Terrorism expert Daniel Glickman, for example, defined CVE as 'the solution to the problem of violent extremism that looks to non-kinetic and non-coercive

DOI: 10.4324/9781003080909-6

toolkits' because 'you can't kill or arrest every perceived threat' (participant observation, March 2017).[1] Recognizing the limits of coercive policing in the domestic war on terror, security professionals viewed CVE as a more sophisticated solution to the perceived problem of homegrown terrorism by mobilizing communities to intervene 'before the line of criminal activity is crossed' (Department of Homeland Security 2015:2).

Local practitioners also described the CVE strategy as a way to increase community control over the domestic war on terror, amplify Muslim American voices in the political process, and improve community-police relations, especially after decades of deceptive and deleterious surveillance programs that secretly infiltrated community spaces like mosques, without community input or oversight. Somali practitioner Abdi Mahdi endorsed CVE as a 'mom and pop' solution to the problem of homegrown terrorism by facilitating collaborations between communities and law enforcement to achieve 'zero terrorism' (interview, April 2017). Wanting to protect children from arrest and from the lure of terrorist recruiters, practitioner Aeden Warabe facilitated Somali youth's access to an athletics center, where staff could support and monitor their character development. Warabe argued that providing these resources effectively responded to 'the reality that…there are some kids who are radicalized, and they are radicalizing fast, efficiently, using social media.' By frequenting the athletics center, young people 'bring their friends. They say, 'check out my muscles.' They're not paying attention to social media when they're here. They're playing soccer and getting strong' (informal conversation, April 2017). For Warabe, investing in community resources like sports leagues offered a powerful antidote to terrorist radicalization.

Despite these appraisals, academic scholars and community organizers have challenged the United States' CVE strategy (Anon 2017; Kumar 2012; Kundnani 2014; LoCicero & Boyd 2016; Patel 2011; Patel & Koushik 2017; Price 2015; Shafi & Qureshi 2020). These contestations have disproven the radicalization research organizing CVE programs, refuted the premise that Muslim children merited access to services like soccer leagues as 'ticking timebombs' rather than as deserving members of society, disputed the strategic narrative that CVE offered an alternative to police-led antiterrorism initiatives, and called attention to how this framework disproportionately has cast suspicion on Muslim communities (participant observation, April 2017). For example, one youth organizer criticized a Somali elder who 'pushed this notion that hoards and swarms of [Somali youth] are becoming radicalized and if you don't send them on camping trips, they're going to radicalize.' This narrative then justified the introduction of CVE 'into schools and libraries' to 'deradicalize boys aged 8-16 years old and deradicalize them before they become radical.' Given these experiences, this youth organizer concluded that CVE is 'an Islamophobic and anti-Black push that helps make political careers and nonprofits' (participant observation, April 2017). Across the United States, communities have argued that CVE is an anti-Muslim program that has extended the reach of the security state into libraries, schools, athletics centers, therapists' offices, and other intimate spaces of everyday life.

As community organizers have challenged CVE through direct actions, political education forums, and public statements, practitioners have constantly managed public objections to their work. For example, one practitioner explained in a CVE workshop, 'This work is always fraught with pushback. We've had some significant pushback from some entities. We've had some of our events disrupted and so on. But aside from a few of those...we've been able to actually win over a number of community organizations and faith-based organizations to help work with us' (participant observation, June 2018). Given this pushback, this practitioner implored me to talk with 'regular people who are trying to speak in a fair and balanced way,' rather than 'high-level' national security operatives who advanced simplified yet 'politically charged' narratives that flattened the everyday realities of CVE programs (informal conversation, March 2017). Talking to 'regular people' could provide insight into how CVE programs were lived and made in situ, rather than discussed in federal offices disconnected from local communities. Such conversations also could offer a window into how practitioners managed arguably 'incorrect information' and 'superficial critiques' that challenged their daily work (interview, January 2017), revealing how 'the policies of the state are enacted amid tension and difference,' even as 'higher-level bureaucrats and communications employees construct[ed] coherent narratives for the public' (Mountz 2010:58).

Given this contested context, I conducted a two-year interpretive qualitative research study to better understand the practices and perspectives of 'regular' CVE actors as they confronted claims that their daily work intensified the racialized policing of Muslim communities, relied on disproven theories of radicalization, and transformed trusted adults into informants. Through interviews, participant observation, and document analysis, I came to learn how practitioners defended their work by defining CVE as a national security approach that effectively balanced 'liberties and securities' by mobilizing 'civil society and private actors' to 'steer people away from a trajectory that leads them to violence' (interview, January 2017). Practitioners, however, varied in their understandings of their work, their responses to community resistance, and their relationships with their constituents. Governing social, geopolitical, and economic conditions, in addition to their own personal and professional experiences, shaped how CVE practitioners and policymakers thought about national security threats and effective antiterrorism strategies.

My fieldwork challenged the myth of the monolithic and disembodied security state by revealing how CVE practitioners exercised discretion in designing and implementing local national security programs initiated by federal agencies like the Department of Homeland Security. As feminist geographer Alison Mountz (2004) explains, 'embodying the state by studying the day-to-day locations and challenges of bureaucrats shows a far more diverse, diffuse, and conflicted state' (340). A deeper ethnographic analysis of security state practices 'complicates the monolithic characterization of 'the state' and proves its institutional networks to be socially embedded' (Mountz 2010:57). For example, one researcher reminded me that tracking new national security developments was especially difficult because:

> It depends on who you talk to. And, not surprisingly, DHS and FBI are huge bureaucracies and the people who work in them don't see things all the same way. So depending on who you talk to, you get very different outlooks and perspectives on how much we should be emphasizing things like intervention versus just being law enforcement only. (interview, February 2017)

In fact, this researcher warned that 'even the same person isn't necessarily consistent with what they're saying,' making the CVE policy environment 'very difficult' to navigate. One FBI agent even reported that he would refuse to facilitate deradicalization interventions because 'our job is to arrest people,' while also saying, 'we can't arrest our way out' of the problem of homegrown terrorism (interview, February 2017). By examining the daily work of CVE practitioners, this analysis challenges dominant representations of the state as a coherent body politic disembedded from governing social contexts and disconnected from the agency of its actors. Focusing on the contradictory and contentious work of CVE actors illustrates how 'the practices and sites of governance have also become ever more dispersed, diversified, and fraught with internal inconsistencies and contradictions' (Hansen & Stepputat 2001:16). Significantly, an embodied analysis of the security state has supported youth-led community resistance contesting the implementation of CVE programs as organizers could challenge specific practitioners, some of whom eventually resigned, returned federal funding, withdrew support for CVE, or ended local initiatives (Bharath 2018; Ruppenthal 2017; Zerkel 2019).

Drawing from my analysis of these contestations, I argue that the case of CVE contributes to studies that demystify the myth of the monolithic state by illustrating how security regimes are unevenly enacted and implemented as practitioners differently interpret the role, utility, and risks of emerging antiterrorism initiatives and the social contexts in which they are embedded. Although high-level officials advanced a unified message about the purposes and effects of CVE programming, practitioners regularly managed public objections to their work, often laboring amid controversy and contestation. Practitioners refused to adopt the blunt scripts offered by federal policymakers, instead initiating narratives and programs that reflected their own understandings of their community's most pressing problems and effective solutions to such problems.

An analysis of the daily work of CVE practitioners reveals a more contentious set of policies and practices seeking to increase access to the intimate spaces of everyday life while appearing to rein in governmental overreach, racial profiling, and constant surveillance. As the federal government outlined a national framework for countering violent extremism, it also deferred on-the-ground programming and accountability to local practitioners left to defend and reform a flawed antiterrorism initiative unevenly developed and implemented across the country. By examining the perspectives and practices of CVE actors, this analysis explores how the US security state has gained access to intimate spaces otherwise unavailable to it by cultivating community relationships and mobilizing social service providers, processes fraught with conflict, contradiction, and complexity.

Studying up to map the geographies of the embodied security state

In her institutional ethnography of immigration bureaucrats, Mountz (2004) reminds us that 'rather than a coherent, hidden strategy awaiting discovery, states are comprised of persons with distinct objectives and perspectives, often struggling amongst themselves over state projects' (328). Taking a cue from feminist geographers like Mountz (2004), I conducted a research study that sought to 'center people within conceptual understandings of the [security] state' and 'locate[power relations and contextualize[decision-making within workplace settings and life histories' by examining the practices and perspectives of those most involved in CVE work: researchers, practitioners, political leaders, policymakers, and community members (328). To do so, a research assistant and I conducted a two-year interpretive qualitative research study attentive to the uneven and chaotic implementation of this national security strategy. As a highly mobile and fast-moving initiative, CVE required flexible fieldwork that began with collecting, coding, and analyzing hundreds of relevant documents such as national security policies, white papers, and research briefs that provided insight into the emergence of CVE programs in the United States. We also filed dozens of Freedom of Information Act (FOIA) requests, which gave us access to hundreds of public records such as CVE training guides, grant applications, e-mail exchanges, and working budgets. We analyzed these documents using qualitative analysis software (Dedoose), developing and then refining codes as patterns of themes, words, and phrases emerged. These documents importantly illustrated how practitioners and policymakers publicly and privately discussed the domestic war on terror, homegrown terrorism, and national security initiatives. We continued to collect, code, and analyze relevant documents throughout the course of this research study.

Using these documents to guide local fieldwork, we then traveled across the United States to key CVE hotspots where we initially observed more than forty events, such as industry conferences and professional workshops, some of which convened over a few days. Through our participation in these events, we came to informally talk with dozens of practitioners, policymakers, and researchers involved in CVE policy making and taking. Sometimes chance meetings in hotel lobbies or between conference sessions led to hour-long breakfasts or walks that allowed me to learn more about the work of CVE actors outside of the formal interview setting. Oftentimes if I sat at a table with other participants during a training or conference session, they provided me with running commentary about the presentation or offered a historical overview that located the talk in the shifting politics of the local community. Finding people to chat with me was never an issue; CVE was so controversial at the time that everyone had something to say about it.

Through this social network, we formally interviewed sixteen CVE actors from a range of different backgrounds, from powerful state employees to local community practitioners. In these interviews, CVE actors discussed their strategies, struggles, and successes in designing and implementing national security policies and programs. Six other CVE practitioners wanted to contribute to this study, but without formally enrolling as participants; these extended informal conversations offered background knowledge on local CVE programs and their articulation with the needs of their communities. During this time, my research assistant and I continued to attend additional CVE events, primarily hosted by community organizations seeking to end the criminalization of Muslim communities. Four years later, I continue to track CVE developments, collaborate with community organizations, and observe public events.

Taken together, this fieldwork provided insight into how CVE programs affected local communities and how practitioners sought to legitimize and execute this antiterrorism approach. As I traveled the country, I came to understand that CVE was a controversial federal initiative that local practitioners unevenly implemented depending on their own interpretations of the national security threat, their understandings of community concerns, their access to resources, and their community relationships. Left to improvise alone, CVE practitioners struggled to gain community support, respond to public objections to their work, and reform already-existing programs in the face of mounting resistance. Although some relished the opportunity to 'win over' critics, my broader fieldwork demonstrated how the security state is 'multiple, conflicted, and in perpetual negotiation' as street-level bureaucrats and state-sponsored practitioners labored amid controversy and discord, especially as federal officials often discussed CVE in ways that intensified local resistance (Mountz 2004:339).

Rethinking research reciprocity when studying up

By investigating powerful institutions and their workers to better understand pressing social problems (Nader 1972), I came to understand how research participants enjoyed varying degrees of power and privilege in their workplaces as they differentially reported to supervisors, funders, and communities. In addition, some CVE actors were Muslim, meaning they negotiated anti-Muslim racism in the CVE policy world as well as in their daily lives, even if they held powerful positions in elite institutions. Throughout this research study, I needed to account for how participants' social locations shaped their work and their understandings of their work.

As a qualitative researcher and non-Muslim woman of color, I also needed to be reflexive about how my relational positionality with participants organized the research encounter. Some Muslim participants, for example, preemptively contextualized their responses to my questions on the assumption that I was unfamiliar with the everyday experiences of Muslims in the United States. One participant described the visceral anti-Muslim racism he experienced growing up in the United States and how this drove his desire to reform domestic antiterrorism practices to be more inclusive of and less harmful toward Muslim communities. Such interactions forced me to more generously engage the perspectives and practices of these participants as these racialized experiences invariably shaped their understandings of countering violent extremism initiatives.

Other participants approached me with suspicion by responding to my interview questions in guarded ways, by treating me as unknowledgeable of national security policies, or even by interrupting me to joke with colleagues or answer phone calls. When I asked a former law enforcement agent to help me understand these responses, he explained that 'law enforcement don't respect the perspectives of anyone who hasn't walked in their shoes,' which meant I sometimes struggled to build rapport and develop trust in interviews with law enforcement officials. Like all researchers, my place in the world shaped how I interacted with and interpreted the experiences of CVE actors.

To account for my positionality, I engaged in reflexive practices such as member checking and memoing through which I interrogated my own assumptions, intellectual politics and positionality and their impact on my fieldwork. In some instances, I shared my research findings with participants so they could confirm or correct my interpretations. In fact, in one case, a research participant called me to clarify his position after a local newspaper ran a story where I discussed how CVE programs often targeted Muslim communities. Although participants could challenge or reject my ideas, I maintain the power to represent their work in my writing (for more on reflexivity, please refer to Nguyen 2019).

As a part of these ethical considerations, I carefully weighed the feminist practice of reciprocity through which scholars 'return the research' by 'empowering the informant and [their] community' in exchange for their participation (Blee 1993:605). For example, I was sympathetic to how local community leaders like Warabe struggled to secure funding, connect with more powerful national security experts, and gain community support, even if I disagreed with their work. In fact, Warabe agreed to talk to me because he thought his participation in the study could help him develop relationships with more prominent practitioners. Recognizing Warabe's precarious position as an underfunded community leader seeking to 'prevent kids from doing bad things,' I introduced him to a state-level practitioner and prominent CVE researcher, both of whom could increase his profile, credibility, and access to resources. Because Warabe was a Somali elder working in a disinvested community, I felt some ethical responsibility to 'return the research' as a condition of talking with him about his work while also worrying that doing so could enhance programs that treat Muslim youth as incipient terrorists.

Although I willingly connected Warabe with other CVE practitioners, I also resisted other requests by more powerful and prominent state and federal actors. For example, state law enforcement agent Tanvir Rahman admitted in a follow-up conversation that he participated in a formal interview with my research assistant because he thought I could give him access to local schools. Given my fears that the introduction of CVE into this school district would harm Muslim, Black, and immigrant children, I made no attempts to 'return the research.' In this case, I determined that it was unethical to agree to such an exchange and at no time during our conversation did I indicate a willingness to take such action. As these examples illustrate, conducting research with participants working in fields 'regarded with suspicion or antipathy' raises unique ethical questions related to the feminist practice of reciprocity such that determining when and how to return the research is a fraught and tense process (Thiem and Robertson, 2010: 5).

Throughout my fieldwork, I struggled to make these ethical decisions, especially as I developed collegial relationships with CVE practitioners. Like other researchers engaged in oppositional research, I often found myself reflecting on my own conflicted interpretations of CVE practitioners, at once understanding their desire to 'do the right thing' and disagreeing with what 'doing the right thing' looked like (informal conversation, November 2016). I empathized with the pain and fear Mahdi felt when he received 'face-to-face death threats' from 'anti-people CVE' who said, 'You're calling us terrorists. You have no soul. You're selling out your community' (interview, April 2017). Other practitioners mourned the loss of young people who traveled to Syria to fight President Bashar al-Assad's brutal regime, losses that drove their desire to contribute to local CVE programming (interview, March 2017). My fieldwork therefore forced me to consider the complex personhoods of practitioners who were irreducible to their roles as national security workers (Gordon 1997). In doing so, my fieldwork captured how state security regimes often are enacted amid tension and conflict as practitioners' own life histories, workplaces, and community contexts shaped the uneven implementation of CVE programs.

Taxonomizing terrorists: Radicalization research and the co-production of national security

At a peacebuilding conference, a former FBI senior advisor argued that the United States focused its police-led antiterrorism efforts on 'handcuffs, body bags, and closed case files' that sometimes missed 'real' threats, such as Omar Mateen. Since security professionals could not 'kill or arrest' every perceived threat or accurately conduct thousands of threat assessments, the United States needed to develop a meaningful alternative that mobilized adult mentors, like wrestling coaches, to protect children from the lure of terrorist recruiters and disrupt the regenerating capacity of insurgent networks (participant observation, October 2016). Another security professional similarly explained that there were three main police-led solutions to the problem of homegrown terrorism, particularly given the 'pre-criminal dilemma' where an individual may express radical views but has not yet committed a crime: sting operations, labor-intensive surveillance, and doing nothing. In this context, CVE served as 'the fourth way,' an additional approach that could prevent terrorist violence by mobilizing communities to intervene in the 'pre-criminal stage' (participant observation, March 2017). Echoing these understandings of CVE as the 'fourth way,' a senior officer at the National Counterterrorism Center called for a 'professionalized mental health approach' that could deter young people from terrorist violence (participant observation, October 2016). In this view, the 'diffuse, complex, and multi-tiered' nature of the global war on terror necessitates that everyday members of society 'remain vigilant, alert, and aware' (Andrejevic 2006:441). Effective CVE programs therefore task community members and social service providers with identifying, reporting, and working with individuals vulnerable to terrorist violence by monitoring their workplaces and surveilling their communities for the signs of terrorist radicalization.

Domestic war on terror initiatives increasingly ask ordinary members of society to identify and report suspicious activities on behalf of the security state. In a post-9/11 context in the United States, the 'threat of a pervasive and indiscriminate risk underwrites the invitation to participate in the policing function by providing a capillary extension of surveillance into households and surrounding neighborhoods' (Andrejevic 2005:486). The 'ostensibly democratic character of such participation' implies that this 'monitoring process is no longer solely the province of professionals, but can be shared with those normally excluded from the command centers of the intelligence industry' (Andrejevic 2006:450–51). Participatory surveillance regimes transform everyday citizens into proxy national security agents, ultimately extending the reach of law enforcement into intimate spaces of everyday life. For example, one CVE practitioner explained that she anchored her own program in a 'collective impact approach' dedicated to 'increasing the citizen's role in public safety [by] intervening in the lives of vulnerable individuals before they choose a path of violence' (participant observation, August 2016). CVE further institutionalizes such participatory surveillance by providing federal funding, community trainings, and academic research that support the daily monitoring of neighbors, clients, and students in the name of national security.

In the United States, contemporary surveillance regimes reconfigure earlier slave patrols, which imbued already-existing groups of armed white men with the power to police and punish enslaved people, capture escapees, and suppress insurrection. CVE programs, for example, mobilize community members and social services providers as terrorist watchdogs, both reporting potential threats and intervening in the lives of vulnerable individuals, especially when working with 'faith communities, Black Lives Matter, diverse communities, refugee communities, and LGBTQ communities, among others, facing disenfranchisement by society' (Denver Police Department 2016:3). Targeting disenfranchised communities, these surveillance regimes further infiltrate the intimate spaces of everyday life, including the body's interior and exterior surfaces that can be read for signs future dangerousness and modulated to thwart such threats.

Today, public institutions like police departments increasingly use this type of 'community-based surveillance' to 'extend their own capacity for surveillance, as is illustrated by the spread of public vigilance campaigns against terrorism' (Purenne & Palierse 2016:79). Participatory surveillance therefore enhances and expands police powers, while appearing to empower communities, increase access to social services, and limit the role of law enforcement. Political officials and community leaders have celebrated these collaborations as an effective mechanism to facilitate community control over domestic war on terror initiatives and increase the political participation of Muslim Americans, while restraining coercive policing practices. Yet, as we will see, the case of CVE demonstrates how such liberal reforms to security regimes strengthen the criminalizing functions of state institutions like schools and mental health departments and expand the reach of law enforcement agencies.

To support these community policing efforts, academic scholars and law enforcement agencies have produced reports that map the radicalization process by detailing how an ordinary person arguably transforms into an ideologically inspired violent actor. These reports also outline the early warning signs police officers can use to identify individuals vulnerable to or in the process of terrorism racialization. For example, the New York City Police Department (NYPD) published the influential report, *Radicalization in the West: The Homegrown Threat,* which outlined a four-stage radicalization process defined by a changing relationship to Salafi Islam. The NYPD concluded that each stage of this process comes with its own 'distinct set of indicators and signatures,' such as 'wearing traditional Islamic clothing,' 'growing a beard,' 'becoming involved in social activism and community issues,' 'giving up cigarettes,' and participating in activities like 'camping, white-water rafting, paintball games, target shooting, and even outdoor simulations of military-like maneuvers' (Silber & Bhatt 2007:7, 31, 44). Police officers and community members could look for these warning signs to identify individuals in the process of terrorist radicalization. By abstracting political violence from its formative conditions, the NYPD report and other studies root the radicalization process in the cultural, psychological, and/or theological pathologies of individual actors.

As these radicalization theories matured, terrorism scholars responded to the growing empirical research disproving and discrediting the premise that 'there is a predictable path toward terrorism' and the idea that 'potential terrorists have identifiable markers' (Patel & Koushik 2017:2). John Horgan (2008), for example, encouraged his colleagues to pivot away from developing terrorist profiles and documenting the root causes of extremist violence, especially since 'no terrorist profile has yet been found' (p. 83). Instead, terrorism scholars refocused their efforts on identifying 'predisposing risk factors for involvement in terrorism as a prelude to some form of risk assessment for prediction of involvement' (Horgan 2008:84). Rather than predict future terrorists, these studies outlined the risk factors that could detect individuals vulnerable to terrorist radicalization, such as 'the presence of some emotional vulnerability' among 'some alienated young British Muslims' who look for 'guidance and leadership' outside of the mosque because their leaders are perceived to be 'too old, too conservative, and out of touch with their world' (Horgan 2008:84–85).

Terrorism scholars conceded they had not yet developed an accurate terrorist profile while insisting that certain risk factors could be useful in identifying individuals vulnerable to or in the process of terrorist radicalization. Across interviews, observations, and documents, CVE practitioners recognized the scientific limitations of radicalization research while using these same studies to inform their work. The World Organization for Resource Development and Education (WORDE) (2016), for example, acknowledged that 'there are no studies to date that have demonstrated a causal link between any one risk factor, or combination of factors, and an individual becoming a terrorist' (p. 44). Yet, WORDE (2016: 44) also argued that these risk factors could serve as a 'structured guide to explore the variables that have the *potential* to contribute to one's radicalization' (emphasis in original). A CVE researcher similarly explained, 'We can say that there's certain factors that are *associated with*…entry into nonstate ideologically motivated violence,' without making any of 'those kinds of strong causal claims' (interview, January 2017, emphasis in original). CVE practitioners both affirmed the scientific limitations of radicalization research and insisted that this research still provided reliable tools to identify individuals vulnerable to terrorist violence.

Rather than focus on 'crude religious markers,' more recent radicalization research has included 'more coded references to ideological viewpoints, such as concerns about US foreign policy or the belief that [the] West is at war with Islam' (Patel & Koushik 2017:14). For example, the Los Angeles Police Department (2012) listed 'being passionate about Somalia,' 'having absolute trust in the mosque,' 'feeling fear and mistrust,' 'having a large community with powerful mosques,' and 'not talking about the war' as 'possible risks for terrorist recruitment'. In Massachusetts, the United States Attorney's

Office for the District of Massachusetts (2015: 3-4) argued that isolation, alienation, and frustration with 'US policy and events around the globe' make some young people 'more vulnerable to recruitment by violent extremists' (p. 3-4). To interrupt the radicalization process, communities could 'utilize schools, community and faith-based programs, and private providers' to assist young people with 'fostering effective interpersonal and self-advocacy skills,' 'developing critical thinking and conflict resolution skills,' and 'constructively work[ing] on public issues that matter to them, thus helping them gain skills, motivation, democratic values, and a sense of belonging' (United States Attorney's Office for the District of Massachusetts 2015: 4). Informed by newer radicalization theories, local CVE programs increasingly call on community members and social service providers to identify individuals vulnerable to terrorist radicalization and then provide tailored interventions that address the underlying psychological, cultural, and/or theological dispositions perceived to drive the turn to violence.

Following other jurisdictions that have turned to CVE to fight homegrown terrorism, the Cook County Department of Homeland Security and Emergency Management (Illinois) developed *Countering Targeted Violence Against Our Communities* (CTVAC) trainings for law enforcement agents, law enforcement executives, and community leaders. The community leader training teaches communities how to 'recognize potential indicators of radicalization to violence and activity related to targeted violence' and 'identify the process of radicalization to violence' (Cook County Department of Homeland Security and Emergency Management, and Cardinal Point Strategies, 2015:13). In this model, 'family and friends' play an important role in identifying individuals vulnerable to terrorist radicalization, providing 'counter-narratives' that challenge and delegitimize 'violent narratives,' and cultivating 'safe spaces' where individuals feel 'they have freedom to discuss their ideas without fear of repercussion' (p. 58). These 'inhibitors' can prevent, slow, or stop the radicalization process. The training module concludes that 'the vulnerability to acts of targeted violence can only be reduced by each person understanding radicalization to violence and recognizing the indicators of people that are on this path' (p. 58). Informed by radicalization research, the Cook County training directs practitioners to monitor community spaces like classrooms and counseling centers and to target the minds, bodies, and psyches of Muslim youth.

The creep of security regimes into intimate and interior spaces

Given the demand for a 'professionalized mental health approach' to countering violent extremism and the continued prominence of radicalization research in the national security arena, the Los Angeles Police Department (LAPD) began adapting its Crisis Response Support Section to address the perceived threat of homegrown terrorism. To do so, the LAPD collaborated with the LA County Department of Mental Health (DMH) to develop its Providing Alternatives to Hinder Extremism (PATHE) program.[2] To institutionalize this antiterrorism program, the LAPD situated PATHE within in its already-existing Mental Health Unit, a 'co-housed' division where 'approximately 110 sworn detectives and officers and about 55 clinicians from the Los Angeles County Department of Mental Health' share the same office (participant observation, February 2019). As a 'risk assessment strategy,' the PATHE program first identifies individuals 'suffering from a mental illness or mental health crisis' and exhibiting behaviors 'which are indicative of being on a pathway to future act(s) of targeted mass violence' (Los Angeles Police Department n.d.:1).

Explicitly targeting individuals with psychiatric disabilities, the PATHE program identifies, reports, and works with individuals perceived to be vulnerable to terrorist radicalization.

The PATHE process begins when the LAPD receives a referral from behavioral health professionals, community members, and federal, state, and local law enforcement agents. For example, 'psychiatric emergency department doctors' would call the LAPD 'in regards to individuals who have access to weapons because they're concerned' (participant observation, February 2019). To facilitate these referrals, PATHE personnel established 'quarterly stakeholder meetings' to increase community willingness to report vulnerable individuals. As one LAPD detective explained, 'one of the most important things is developing a relationship with the community, ensuring that the community engagement is strong, and that we're very open in why we're doing what we're doing,' such that community members are 'willing to engage us and help us in identifying people of concern who may be demonstrating behaviors which obviously causes them concern' (participant observation, February 2019). After 'identifying a person of concern,' a PATHE questionnaire directs stakeholders to evaluate 'statements and behaviors that would lead [them] to believe that the individual [they] contacted is at risk of being on a pathway to commit a future act of targeted mass violence' (Los Angeles Police Department n.d.:1). The questionnaire asks questions such as: 'Do you have a religious community affiliation?'; 'Do you have a political or other community affiliation?'; 'Do you have animosity towards any religious, community, or political group?'; and 'Have you sought others who share similar animosities, views, or grievances?' (Los Angeles Police Department n.d.:3). These questions explicitly direct stakeholders to consider religion and political orientation in the threat assessment process, engaging speculative techniques in an effort to preemptively prevent future threats, such that each subject's interiority provides clues about their future dangerousness.

After this initial evaluation, the PATHE coordinator then contacts the Joint Regional Intelligence Center, which conducts a 'full workup' on the individual using 'comprehensive information about the individual, including social media analysis, criminal records, probation and warrants, weapons, travel details, financial records, and any other information deemed to be relevant.' Using this workup as a guide, the PATHE coordinator then directs the referred individual to one of two joint LAPD-Department of Mental Health programs: 1) the Case Assessment Management Program (CAMP) which 'tracks incidents created by individuals who may be suffering from mental illness' or 2) the System-Wide Mental Assessment Response Team (SMART) which 'responds to situations and provides crisis intervention.' After the CAMP or SMART team evaluates the individual, it suggests one of three options: an involuntary 72-hour psychiatric hospitalization, outpatient therapy, or social services such as mentorship or cross-cultural programs (National Academies of Sciences Engineering and Medicine 2017: 40). Finally, the PATHE coordinator submits an updated report to the Joint Terrorism Taskforce.

The PATHE program ultimately relies on law enforcement to coordinate the provision of mental health treatment and other social services, on the presumption that integrating mental health into domestic antiterrorism initiatives and intervening in the interior spaces of individual subjects can cultivate a 'culture of first preventers rather than first responders to counterterrorism' (National Academies of Sciences Engineering and Medicine 2017:40). In this view, offering 'therapeutic, non-punitive measures to ameliorate or eliminate those problems early on' could effectively deter a person perceived to be 'in the process of mobilizing to commit violence' (participant observation, November 2016). Such participatory surveillance reaches not only into 'households and surrounding neighborhoods,' but also into the offices of therapists, social workers, and guidance counselors to monitor and (re)modulate the interiority of potential threats. Such surveillant activities have intensified, even as researchers have recognized that 'there is no indication that violent extremists act out of mental illness' (Weine et al. 2015:1) and that individuals with psychiatric disability labels are ten times more likely to be victims of violence than the general public and less likely to be perpetrators of it (Desmarais et al. 2014).

Although public institutions like schools and their inhabitants engage in social control as a part of their daily work, CVE and similar national security regimes facilitate new kinds of policing, surveillance, and criminalization that further creep into the spaces of everyday life and jeopardize children's relationship with adults whose work depends on trust, privacy, and confidentiality. These practices constitute what I refer to as *carceral care work*: care work that intensifies policing, while appearing to rein in the criminalization of communities of color and enhance the provision of social services. The carceral care work CVE facilitates harms Muslim youth, particularly by turning 'safe spaces' into sites of suspicion, transforming trusted adults into the 'eyes and ears' on the frontlines of the domestic war on terror, and treating common experiences such as outrage over US foreign policy or feelings of hopelessness as early warning signs of terrorist radicalization, especially when exhibited by Muslim youth. Carceral care work both legitimizes national security regimes as progressive alternatives to coercive policing and increases law enforcement's access to community spaces, such as therapists' offices, school cafeterias, and youth centers.

Unfortunately, antiterrorism programs that facilitate participatory surveillance risk increasing school and health disparities as Muslim children and their families fear seeking services that could lead to their criminalization, arrest, and incarceration (Morgan 2018). For example, in a Minneapolis forum led by youth organizers, one Somali student criticized the school district's hiring of youth intervention workers to counter violent extremism, reporting, 'We already face disparities being in school' and CVE merely 'adds to the barriers we're already facing' (participant observation, April 2017). Another Somali student reported that CVE practitioners 'try to come after our safe spaces we've created for ourselves' and 'come to our school and tell us how to walk and talk and what to do [as] America wants you to act a certain way and if you don't, they're not having it.' In fact, the youth organizers lamented that some of their peers withdrew from their mosques in fear of increased surveillance. Even though many in Minneapolis 'say the mosque is bad,' youth argued that it was where they learned to be a good person, learned a third language, and learned to be charitable. Somali youth experienced community sites like the mosque as important 'safe spaces' that contributed to their coming of age and provided critical services that supported their development. Youth reported that CVE programs eroded these safe spaces by casting suspicion on their everyday activities and by circulating damaging narratives predicated on the assumption that 'their humanity is subpar' (participant observation, April 2017). Prominent Muslim leaders affirmed young people's position, concluding,' 'We cannot support CVE. We don't support it. We're against it. And we believe there's problems with it, and nothing of benefit will come out of it' (interview, April 2017). Although some viewed CVE as an effective antiterrorism initiative through the provision of 'therapeutic, non-punitive measures,' others considered it to be yet another program that criminalized, demonized, and harmed Muslim communities.

Conscripting community leaders and social service providers into the domestic war on terror

Given the persistent resistance to local CVE programs, many practitioners used their interviews with me or their public presentations to forcefully explain why they participated in this national security strategy. Tanvir Rahman, for example, insisted that he wanted to 'do the right thing' through his CVE work, reporting that his own childhood experiences with anti-Muslim racism shaped his engagement with antiterrorism initiatives. Rahman explained that, as a 'practicing Muslim and immigrant,' he understood how some CVE programs could 'stigmatize' Muslim children, while arguing that 'the flip side…is that it's not just sexual predators out there that are trying to recruit vulnerable kids, but there's other bad actors that are trying to take advantage of vulnerable people' (interview, November 2016). In this view, CVE programs 'implemented incorrectly' risked stigmatizing Muslim children, a problem that should not deter communities from participating as terrorist recruiters still posed a serious threat. Like Rahman, Mahdi criticized community leaders who viewed CVE as a surveillance program, referring to these critics as 'ostriches' because 'they plant their heads deep in the ground' and ignore the 'reality' that young people were radicalizing.

In interviews, Muslim leaders reported that a wave of terrorism-related arrests encouraged them to bring CVE programming to their own communities. Masoud Kaleel, for example, explained that, in his community, 'ten young Muslims were arrested over the past two years' for terrorism-related crimes, which 'devastated' their families. In response, local Muslim organizations began 'developing programs to build resilience' to terrorist radicalization, despite concerns that an 'overreaction' to homegrown terrorism could lead to the criminalization of entire communities (participant observation, November 2016). Religious leader Bassem Ali also detailed his entry into CVE work by describing how the radicalization of his former student and his eventual death while fighting on behalf of al-Qaeda on the Arabian Peninsula (AQAP) made CVE 'very close' to his heart. Although Ali willingly spoke at quarterly roundtables organized by the Department of Homeland Security, he told federal agents that 'their reputation in the Muslim community is that they are just trying to entrap people' and that he 'thinks that the problem of Muslim radicalization is very severely overplayed compared to something like white supremacy.' Ali therefore focused his efforts on 'giving people an approach to Islam, an approach to life that will be of use to them beyond just memorizing a bunch of names and things like that.' Although CVE proponents argued that such religious training could militate against radicalization, Ali viewed his teachings as 'guiding people on how to think [about] and practice Islam in our contemporary context' (interview, March 2017). I observed several community leaders express similar conflicted views, where they both contributed to and criticized local CVE programs.

In helping me make sense of these contradictions, Muslim activist Yusuf Elmi explained that many community leaders believed that 'there's a table created and if we're not at the table, somebody else will be there'; even if 'they don't like the table, they still have to be there.' Although Elmi argued that 'this is a table we don't want to be at,' other community leaders understood 'the value of the power they may gain by aligning themselves with law enforcement and government affairs' (interview, April 2017). Throughout my fieldwork, I heard several community leaders describe their desire to 'have a seat at the table,' even if that meant advancing a national security strategy that conflicted with their own principles. Other community organizers like Bashir Cilmi rejected this logic, stating that 'having any people yield to dictatorship practice and implement programs that single out the Somali community – to have people who look like you tell you it's better to be at the table, if you're not at the table you're on the menu, but who is at the table? The people at the table are people who honestly want opportunities and people there out of fear.' In Cilmi's experience, community leaders participated in CVE programming because 'they're there for the job' while others were 'raised in a dictatorship' and therefore 'give over to what they're told to do,' even if it meant implementing a 'counterterrorism effort to infiltrate the community.' Community organizers concluded that local practitioners contributed to harmful CVE programs because 'the incentive is money, political power' (participant observation, April 2017).

Practitioners also argued that CVE programs could provide federal funding otherwise unavailable to their communities. For example, Mahdi reported that federal CVE funds 'paid for afterschool programs, paid for coaches, paid for job training, paid for parents being aware of their kids in school, and paid for a lot of good things within my community.' Although some critics told Mahdi that 'money for afterschool programs is surveillance,' Mahdi insisted that this was 'bullshit. And the parents are struggling with their kids' education because they're not educated, you know? And the kids need tutoring. If someone else is willing to pay for it, let's go for the money' (interview, April 2017). Some parents therefore viewed federal CVE funds as an antidote to the chronic disinvestment in their communities by providing resources that could help their children to flourish. For Mahdi, CVE offered a community-driven alternative that prevented terrorist radicalization by intervening in the lives of young people through community-police relationships and through the provision of vital resources.

Other CVE practitioners, however, objected to the use of these resources to enact a national security program and gain community support. Practitioner Aysha Khoury, for example, argued that 'providing resources to underserved communities that should have been filled' constituted 'good governance,' not CVE. For Khoury, all communities deserved access to these resources, independent of broader national security objectives. In fact, Khoury troubled the working assumption that 'if you give poor people money, then they will stop becoming terrorists,' as this approach ignored how violent actors often are 'deeply engaged and politically active' (interview, January 2017). Although the federal CVE strategy exploited the state's continued disinvestment in immigrant communities to enlist local practitioners like Mahdi, others, like Khoury, challenged the assumption that Muslim communities only deserved access to these resources to fight terrorism.

Like Ali, Khoury questioned the racial impetus driving the federal CVE framework. Rather than abandon this national security approach, Khoury diligently worked to eschew the problems of racial profiling by developing CVE programs 'for everyone.' For example, Khoury refused to teach internet security only to Muslims vulnerable to predatory terrorist recruiters, instead focusing on the 'whole spectrum' of online threats to 'protect[them from pornography, pedophiles, and cyberbullying,' such that 'people who might be trying to recruit young people online' was 'just a piece of' that larger training. While some community leaders refused to participate in CVE given its explicit targeting of Muslim communities, some practitioners sought to reform their programs to engage a wider audience and address a broader range of security issues.

Unlike Khoury, some CVE actors refused to take community concerns seriously. For example, one CVE researcher reported that 'although there are some very, very genuine concerns people have about their liberties, about their privacy, about their civil rights,' the 'narratives and descriptions of what people, especially CVE critics, have described CVE as…are tantamount to alternative facts' (interview, January 2017). Across interviews and observations, other practitioners dismissed community concerns as 'conspiracy theories' and 'unintelligent analyses' undeserving of their attention. These practitioners rebuffed these criticisms, declining the opportunity to alter their programs, arguing that collaborating with the government to identify vulnerable individuals could effectively result in 'zero terrorism' (interview, April 2017).

Even as some practitioners refused to respond to community concerns, higher-level officials admitted in public presentations that 'mistakes were made during the launch of CVE' and that they had 'learned from those mistakes' (participant observation, October 2016). One National Counterterrorism Center staffer, for example, explained that 'CVE people had learned from earlier mistakes,' a sentiment reiterated throughout my fieldwork (participant observation, October 2016). In this view, 'second generation' CVE programs abandoned past practices of 'focus[ing] exclusively on the Muslim and Arab communities' and 'securitizing relationships between law enforcement and these minority communities' (interview, November 2016). In a CVE training for mental health professionals, DHS representative Nabil Soliman similarly described himself as a 'former civil rights attorney who prosecuted crime [committed] by DHS.' Soliman reported that DHS was now a 'different agency' dedicated to 'advancing civil rights and civil liberties,' which would 'help us reach our goal of securing our communities and campuses' (participant observation, October 2017). These higher-level officials circulated a common narrative that framed CVE as a product of hard lessons learned, especially given the Department of Homeland Security's new commitment to Muslim civil rights and civil liberties.

In addition to these CVE actors, I also encountered social service providers like librarians who had been conscripted into CVE work through strategic narratives that portrayed this national security approach as a way to increase access to services, reduce hate crimes, and even protect children from coercive policing. For example, one librarian reported that she viewed a local CVE practitioner as a 'good egg' and 'good resource' who could further develop the library's work on 'building programs to empower people to be at the aid of others.' She was interested in the practitioner's 'upstander/bystander training' used to identify individuals vulnerable to or in the process of terrorist radicalization, which she (mis)understood to be a 'training about being attacked' and how to respond. Wanting to prevent hate crimes in her city, this librarian agreed to participate in this CVE program, without necessarily realizing that this national security strategy focused specifically on terrorist violence (informal conversation, December 2018).[3] A religious leader similarly reported that he expressed initial interest in applying for a federal CVE grant to fund community outreach efforts or aid refugees who attended his mosque. After learning the fuller details of the grant, he withdrew support for the application (Ruppenthal & Mustafa 2020).

As these examples illustrate, CVE actors with varying degrees of power and privilege differentially understood and enacted this national security strategy depending on their own personal and professional experiences. Rahman's childhood experiences with anti-Muslim racism informed his desire to increase community participation in antiterrorism initiatives while Ali's observation of anti-Muslim policing made him suspicious of law enforcement initiatives. Mahdi understood that his community lacked resources and viewed the CVE strategy as a way to secure federal funding and protect children from the lure of terrorist recruiters. Khoury intentionally sought to modify her CVE program to reduce the racial profiling of Muslim communities and to militate against other threats, such as cyberbullies. Higher level officials discussed CVE with a less impassioned tone, describing more technical aspects of this national security strategy, such as describing the differences between 'lone actors' and 'lone wolves' (participant observation, March 2017). In fact, when DHS senior policy advisor Jaylani Darden described 'increased religiosity' as a sign of terrorist radicalization, National Counterterrorism Center officer Emily Evans interrupted him to remind conference participants that such increased religiosity represented a 'change in behavior,' making it a valuable risk factor to identify vulnerable individuals (participant observation, October 2016). In doing so, Darden and Evans worked together to reassert the dominant narrative that CVE targeted behaviors, rather than engaged in racial profiling, while local practitioners sought to address the anti-Muslim impetus underwriting CVE programs.

My conversations with CVE practitioners and observations of CVE events revealed how individuals within the US security state unevenly made sense of terrorism and their role in preventing it. High-level officials issued strategic narratives about their countering violent extremism strategy. Local practitioners, however, developed more nuanced accounts that responded to community concerns, such as emphasizing how CVE programs served 'everyone,' offered 'therapeutic, non-punitive' services to deter individuals from terrorist violence, and sought to achieve the shared goal of 'zero terrorism.' Drawing from their own experiences with racism and responding to community pushback, local CVE practitioners often expressed conflicting and contradictory understandings of their work, reflective of how state security regimes often are enacted amid controversy and chaos.

Conclusion: Embodying the security state

Articulating with feminist theorizations of the embodied state, community organizers regularly mapped the individuals responsible for their criminalization, recognizing how dominant narratives and federal frameworks could not provide insight into the intimate yet fraught ways state actors policed their minds, bodies, and psyches. Community organizers deeply understood how 'policy on paper ... narrates only a partial story, the idealized ways in which events should take place, rather than the ways things actually happen on the ground,' as they worked to uncover and then challenge local CVE programs (Mountz 2004:329). Community contestations therefore assigned responsibility to individual actors who unevenly implemented CVE programs and encountered various barriers to success, even as high-level officials offered coherent narratives of a unified and uniform national security strategy. In doing so, community organizers exploited the unease some practitioners expressed about CVE programs, such as their 'laser beam' focus on ISIS (interview, February 2017), their role in 'securitizing relationships between law enforcement and these minority communities' (interview, November 2016), and their status as fomenters of suspicion feeding the 'internal destruction' of Muslim communities (interview, April 2017).

Through this embodied analysis of state security regimes, community organizers identified how the integration of Muslim communities and social service providers into the domestic war on terror has transformed Muslim youth's 'safe spaces' into sites of surveillance and increased the reach of the security state into their most intimate spaces. Youth organizer Assad argued that CVE practitioners 'want us to leave the places we've created for ourselves and then they pick us off one by one on the street—for thought crimes, for gangbanging' (participant observation, April 2017). Another community organizer described CVE as 'the criminalization of services,' explicitly exploiting how 'our community is extremely underserved regarding our mental health issues and underserved regarding our social services.' In this person's experience, security professionals 'come into our community and say, 'Well, if you want money for mental health services that you desperately need, well, you're going to have to come under the government guise of CVE. You'll first have to admit that there's some kind of radical extremist problem in the community, and if you do that, well, then you'll get money for your services" (participant observation, June 2016). Through these government-funded CVE programs, mental health professionals would be expected to 'report people who might have some social problem, might have some difficulty making friends, or some difficulty in school or the community' and then subject them to 'counseling and reeducation' (participant observation, June 2016). The federal government has used its disinvestment in immigrant communities to entice Muslim leaders to apply for CVE grants and implement local programs that mobilize social service providers as terrorist watchdogs.

This broader analysis indicts CVE programs for targeting Muslim minds, bodies, and psyches; subjecting them to 'tailored interventions' to remodulate their behaviors and beings; and surveilling their political ideologies, emotional states, and social networks to detect the early warning signs of terrorist radicalization. Such surveillant activities 'attempt to capture the hitherto 'unmarked' or 'un-inscribed' aspects of the subject—either their psychoanalytic state, bodily content, or intimate behavior, as it surfaces and becomes enacted at the body boundary' (Ball 2009:643). Transforming spaces of everyday life into sites of surveillance and turning social service providers into proxy national security agents imbued with police powers has extended the reach of the security state into our most intimate spaces, such as therapists' offices, school lunchrooms, and soccer fields.

By surveilling the interiority of Muslim youth and their 'safe spaces,' CVE programs have intensified, not mitigated, the targeted criminalization of Muslim communities and strengthened the school-to-prison and clinic-to-prison pipelines. In this way, 'the racialization of state surveillance regimes [are] underpinned by the entanglement between notions of Islam and terrorism' that treat Muslims as a suspect community (Sharma & Nijjar 2018:73). Although Haggerty and Ericson (2000) suggest that such all-pervasive surveillant assemblages participate in the 'democratic leveling of the hierarchy of surveillance' such that 'no major population groups stand irrefutably above or outside of the surveillant assemblage,' the case of CVE demonstrates the racial charge of such rhizomatic surveillance (618). As some practitioners defended their work as an 'ideologically ecumenical approach' to 'deal with' individuals 'associated with al-Qaeda and ISIS' as well as 'violent far-right and even violent far-left actors' (interview, January 2017), social scientists and community organizers have identified how radicalization research and corresponding CVE programs explicitly have identified Muslims as uniquely susceptible to terrorist radicalization and recruitment (Kundnani 2014; Patel & Koushik 2017). Even as practitioners like Khoury have modified their programs to reduce the role of racial profiling, CVE still largely targets Muslim communities, evident in funded grant applications, program descriptions, and young people's lived experiences.

Understanding how contemporary national security regimes rely on the active participation of social service providers like mental health professionals offers a political opening to contest these practices. Because such surveillance regimes depend on community participation, organizers have mobilized political education campaigns that reveal CVE's harms and that call on social service providers to refuse contributing to local programs. Psychologist Alice LoCicero (2018), for example, encourages 'very nice and caring professionals' to refuse to participate in CVE programs, warning that 'the actual partnering between paid law enforcement and various paid service providers runs the risk of failing, and even harming, unpaid members of the partner community.' Furthermore, organizers have challenged individual CVE practitioners by exploiting their own uncertainties with and critiques of CVE. Ethnographies of the security state can support these organizing efforts by mapping local practitioners, dispelling the myths used to justify emerging surveillance regimes, and identifying pressure points ripe with political possibility, such as practitioners' desires for career advancement, concerns with racial profiling, or personal experiences with government surveillance.

Notes

1 I have given all research participants and public presenters pseudonyms. I also have changed other identifying information, such as the workplaces or titles of participants.
2 PATHE originally launched under the name Recognizing Extremist Network Early Warnings (RENEW).
3 This conversation was initiated by the Freedom of Information Act (FOIA) officer, who arranged a meeting with this librarian as a part of fulfilling my public records request.

Bibliography

Andrejevic, Mark. 2005. The Work of Watching One Another: Lateral Surveillance, Risk, and Governance. *Surveillance & Society* 2(4):479–497.

Andrejevic, Mark. 2006. INTERACTIVE (IN)SECURITY: The Participatory Promise of Ready.Gov. *Cultural Studies* 20(4–5):441–458.

2017 Anon. 2017. *Statement: AMEMSA Groups Oppose Expansion of the Countering Violent Extremism Program.*

Ball, Kirstie. 2009. EXPOSURE: Exploring the Subject of Surveillance. *Information, Communication & Society* 12(5):639–657.

Bharath, Deepa. 2018. LA Mayor Turns down $425K in Federal Funding to Counter Violent Extremism after Opposition from Civil Rights Groups Stalls Process. *Daily News*, August 16.

Blee, Kathleen M. 1993. Evidence, Empathy, and Ethics: Lessons from Oral Histories of the Klan. *The Journal of American History* 80(2):596–606.

Cook County Department of Homeland Security and Emergency Management, and Cardinal Point Strategies. 2015. *Facilitator Guide: Community Leaders' Course: Countering Targeted Violence against Our Communities.* Chicago, IL: Cook County Department of Homeland Security and Emergency Management.

Denver Police Department. 2016. *Countering Violent Extremism Collaborative Grant Program Grant Proposal.* Denver, CO: Denver Police Department.

Department of Homeland Security. 2015. *Factsheet: A Comprehensive US Government Approach to Countering Violent Extremism.* Washington, DC: Department of Homeland Security.

Desmarais, Sarah L., Van Dorn, Richard A., Johnson, Kiersten L., Grimm, Kevin J., Douglas, Kevin S., & Swartz, Marvin S. (2014). Community Violence Perpetration and Victimization Among Adults With Mental Illnesses. *American Journal of Public Health*, 104, 2342–234910.2105/ajph.2013.301680.

Gordon, Avery. 1997. *Ghostly Matters: Haunting and the Sociological Imagination.* Minneapolis: University of Minnesota Press.

Haggerty, Kevin D. & Ericson Richard V. 2000. The Surveillance Assemblage. *British Journal of Sociology* 51(4):605–622.

Hansen, Thomas Blom & Finn Stepputat. 2001. Introduction: States of Imagination. In T. B. Hansen and F. Stepputat edited by *States of imagination: Ethnographic explorations of the postcolonial state* (pp. 1–38),. Durham, NC: Duke University Press.

Horgan, John. 2008. From Profiles to Pathways and Roots to Routes: Perspectives from Psychology on Radicalization into Terrorism. *The Annals of the American Academy of Political and Social Science* 618(1):80–94.

Kiernat, Kourtney. 2015. *Minneapolis Public Schools CVE Program*.White House Summit on Countering Violent Extremism, C-Span (Feb. 18, 2015), https://www.c-span.org/video/?324398-102/white-house-summit-countering-violent-extremism. (quoting Courtney Kiernat, former Executive Director, External Partnerships for Minneapolis Public Schools).

Kumar, Deepa. 2012. *Islamophobia and the Politics of Empire*. Chicago, IL: Haymarket Books.

Kundnani, Arun. 2014. *The Muslims Are Coming! Islamophobia, Extremism, and the Domestic War on Terror*. London: Verso Press.

LoCicero, Alice. 2018. #StopCVE: Well-Meaning Psychologists May Find Themselves Doing Harm. *Psychology Today*, March.https://www.psychologytoday.com/us/blog/paradigm-shift/201803/stopcve.

LoCicero, Alice, and J. Wesley Boyd. 2016. The Dangers of Countering Violent Extremism (CVE) Programs. *Psychology Today*, July 19. https://www.psychologytoday.com/blog/almost-addicted/201607/the-dangers-countering-violent-extremism-cve--programs.

Los Angeles Police Department. 2012. *Countering Violent Extremism Outreach Activities for State, Local, and Tribal Law Enforcement*. Los Angeles, CA: Los Angeles Police Department.

Los Angeles Police Department. n.d. *PATHE (Providing Alternatives to Hinder Extremism) Questionnaire*. Los Angeles, CA: Los Angeles Police Department.

Los Angeles Police Department. n.d. *PATHE Procedural Guide*. Los Angeles, CA: Los Angeles Police Department.

Morgan, Kelly. 2018. Pathologizing 'radicalization' and the Erosion of Patient Privacy Rights. *Boston College Law Review* 59(2):791–820.

Mountz, Alison. 2004. Embodying the Nation-State: Canada's Response to Human Smuggling. *Political Geography* 23(3):323–345.

Mountz, Alison. 2010. *Seeking Asylum: Human Smuggling and Bureaucracy at the Border*. Minneapolis, MN: University of Minnesota Press.

Nader, Laura. 1972. Up the Anthropologist: Perspectives Gained from Studying Up. In D. H. Hymes edited by *Reinventing anthropology* (pp. 284–311). New York: Random House.

National Academies of Sciences Engineering and Medicine. 2017. *Countering Violent Extremism through Public Health Practice: Proceedings of a Workshop*. Washington, DC: The National Academies Press.

Nguyen, Nicole. 2019. *Suspect Communities: Anti-Muslim Racism and the Domestic War on Terror*. Minneapolis, MN: University of Minnesota Press.

Patel, Faiza. 2011. *Rethinking Radicalization*. New York, NY: Brennan Center for Justice at New York University School of Law.

Patel, Faiza, and Meghan Koushik. 2017. *Countering Violent Extremism*. New York, NY: Brennan Center for Justice at New York University School of Law.

Price, Michael. 2015. *Community Outreach or Intelligence Gathering? A Closer Look at "Countering Violent Extremism" Programs*. New York, NY: Brennan Center for Justice at New York University School of Law.

Purenne, Anaïk, and Grégoire Palierse. 2016. Towards Cities of Informers? Community-Based Surveillance in France and Canada. *Surveillance & Society* 15(1):79–93.

Ruppenthal, Alex. 2017. Agency Awarded $200K Grant without Approval from 'partner' Organizations. Chicago, IL: *WTTW*, May 23. https://news.wttw.com/2017/05/23/agency-awarded-200k-grant-without-approval-partner-organizations.

Ruppenthal, Alex, and Asraa Mustafa. 2020. As Trump Relaunches Countering Violent Extremism, Records on Past Illinois Program Reveal Links to FBI, Law Enforcement. Chicago, IL: *Chicago Reporter*, August 14.

Shafi, Azfar, and Asim Qureshi. 2020. *Stranger than Fiction: How "pre-Crime" Approaches to "Countering Violent Extremism" Institutionalize Islamophobia*. Amsterdam: Transnational Institute

Sharma, Sanjay, and Jasbinder Nijjar. 2018. The Racialized Surveillant Assemblage: Islam and the Fear of Terrorism. *Popular Communication* 16(1):72–85.

Silber, Mitchell D., and Arvin Bhatt. 2007. *Radicalization in the West: The Homegrown Threat*. New York, NY: New York City Police Department.

Thiem, Claudia Hanson, & Robertson, Morgan (2010). Behind enemy lines: Reflections on the practice and production of oppositional research. Geoforum, 41, 5–610.1016/j.geoforum.2009.11.001.

United States Attorney's Office for the District of Massachusetts. 2015. *A Framework for Prevention and Intervention Strategies: Incorporating Violent Extremism into Violence Prevention Efforts*. Boston, MA: United States Attorney's Office District of Massachusetts.

Weine, Stevan, Ellis, Heidi, Haddad, Ronald, Miller, Alisa, Lowenhaupt, Rebecca, & Polutnik, Chloe. 2015. *Supporting A Multidisciplinary Approach to Violent Extremism: The Integration of Mental Health in Countering Violent Extremism (CVE) and What Law Enforcement Needs to Know*. College Park, MD: The National Consortium for the Study of Terrorism and Responses to Terrorism at the University of Maryland.

World Organization for Resource Development and Education. 2014. *COPS Application*. Montgomery Village, MD: World Organization for Resource Development and Education.

World Organization for Resource Development and Education. 2016. *Developing a Community-Led Approach to Countering Violent Extremism (CVE): An Instructor's Manual*. Montgomery Village, MD: World Organization for Resource Development and Education.

Zerkel, Mary. 2019. *Head of Controversial Illinois Program Resigns*. Chicago, IL: American Friends Service Committee.

7 Goffman and the everyday experience of surveillance[1]

Ben Rampton and Louise Eley

According to the first page of the *Routledge Handbook of Surveillance Studies*, contemporary developments in surveillance have produced 'social changes in the dynamics of power, identity, institutional practice and interpersonal relations on a scale comparable to the changes brought by industrialization, globalization or the historical rise of urbanization' (Lyon et al., 2012, p. 1). And yet there are empirical uncertainties: '[the] effects [of surveillance] are difficult to isolate and observe, as they are embedded within many normal aspects of daily life' (p. 1; also p. 9). Comparably, Green and Zurawski (2015) argue from an anthropological perspective that Surveillance Studies tends to operate with an '*a priori* categorization of what constitutes surveillance,' treating 'surveillance as so large, and such a complex set of processes, that it can best be researched and understood through its systems and structures, at the expense of attention to embeddedness in everyday life' (p. 31; see also Ball, 2002, 2005, 2009; Ball & Wilson, 2000; Ball et al., 2015).

In sociolinguistics, our own sub-discipline, there is a long tradition of ethnographic work that examines power, ideology and social change in everyday communicative practice. This covers class, ethnicity, sexuality, gender, generation, etc. across a host of sites (including homes, communities, schools, workplaces, clinics, mass & new media). So, in principle, sociolinguistics ought to be able to contribute to the studies of everyday surveillance relations advocated by Lyon et al. (2012) and Green and Zurawski (2015), particularly if surveillance is an interactional relationship between watcher and watched, as many suggest. But somewhat remarkably, there is very little sociolinguistic research on surveillance (see however Jones, 2015, 2017; Rampton, 2016, 2017, pp. 11–12; Lyon et al., 2012, p. 6).

To understand everyday experiences of being surveilled, the ambient monitoring that everyone engages in as a routine matter-of-course provides one obvious starting point. This is the kind of 'side-of-the-eye,' 'half-an-ear' awareness of other people, objects and events that we rely on wherever we go, and there is a detailed account of how it operates in social situations in Erving Goffman's work on 'unfocused interaction' – the interaction that occurs between people who are physically co-present but engaged in separate activities, focusing on different things. In studies of surveillance,

DOI: 10.4324/9781003080909-7

Goffman is sometimes brought into descriptions of the surreptitious practices with which people in subordinate positions transgress, resist or otherwise adjust to rules and regimes that they are unable or unwilling to follow to the letter (e.g. Jacobs & Miller, 1998; Collinson, 1999; Helten & Fischer, 2004, p. 343; Ball, 2005, pp. 96, 102; Simon, 2005, pp. 6–8; Cherbonneau & Copes, 2006; Lyon, 2007, pp. 82, 166–167; Smith, 2007, pp. 290, 302, 308; Gilliom & Monahan, 2012, p. 409; Marx, 2009, p. 299). But notions like 'by-standing' and 'civil inattention' – key elements in unfocused interaction – hardly feature. In sociolinguistics, Goffman has had a huge influence, providing concepts that are now accepted as basic to the description of communicative interaction, and he is also a foundational influence in interactional sociolinguistics (Schiffrin, 1994, p. 102ff; Jones, 2016, p. 37). But both here and in adjacent fields of communication research, the overwhelming emphasis has been on what Goffman calls '*focused* interaction,' in which people do things together, rather than on people carrying out independent activities in each other's presence.[2]

So in what follows, we first outline Goffman's conception of the 'interaction order' (Section 1), and then within that, 'unfocused interaction,' a notion that treats surveillance-like activity as inextricably bound into everyday social life everywhere, regardless of the institutional domain (Jones, 2017, p. 170) (Section 2). In the three sections after that, we focus on scenes from everyday life in Germany in order to bring out the links between unfocused interaction and surveillance commonly understood as 'the focused, systematic and routine attention to personal details for purposes of influence, management, protection or direction' (Lyon, 2007, p. 14). Section 3 examines a video recording of a woman's brief walk down the street from one shop to another, and it shows how ambient monitoring, a relatively relaxed demeanour and institutional surveillance are closely interwoven, contributing to the normalisation of surveillance. Section 4 shifts to two men who engage in the (mildly) illegal practice of posting up stickers, and uses data from participant observation and interviews to bring out differences in their sense of the risks from surveillance, drawing on Goffman to attempt a more systematic account of thought and action at the point of committing an offence under surveillance. This is followed by a brief discussion of the interactions with surveillance technology described in Ole Pütz's (2012) study of airport scanning (Section 5). These three empirical analyses are then drawn together in a rudimentary model (Section 6), before the final section places our account within broader discussions of the changing forms of contemporary surveillance. (For an extension of this perspective beyond the surveilled to the agents of surveillance, see Rampton & Eley, 2018, Appendix; Heath et al., 2002; Luff et al., 2008; Smith, 2007.)

Methodologically, our discussion is offered as an interdisciplinary contribution to opening up the everyday interactional experience of being surveilled (Ball, 2009, p. 640). In the cumulative process of comparative analysis that informs our (modest) theory-building, we draw on different types of data (audio-video recordings, participant observation, interviews) as well as different studies, not just our own. The only technical vocabulary we use is Goffman's (bolding the first use of terms which are especially significant in our analyses), and for the most part, this is treated ethnographically as a framework of 'sensitising constructs,' which 'suggest directions along which to look' rather than 'definitive' concepts which 'provide prescriptions of what to see' (Blumer, 1969, p. 148). In this way, we seek to contribute to ethnographic 'research on the constitution of surveillance relations and processes in everyday life' (Green & Zurawski, 2015, p. 38).[3]

With this view of the paper's scope and limitations in place, we should now turn to a sketch of the interaction order, within that concentrating on unfocused interaction.

Goffman and the interaction order

Goffman's *oeuvre* roams rather eclectically across a plurality of empirical and documentary sources in the pursuit of a rather coherent, cumulative career-long project of analytic distillation, focusing on what he came to call the '**interaction order**' (1983).[4] This involves the very basic structural arrangements, forms of attention and ritual sensitivities that arise whenever individuals are physically co-present, and his argument is that this underpins social activity everywhere. The interaction order is certainly always clothed in the kinds of cultural and institutional particularity that ethnographies describe, and these particularities have to be addressed in any empirical analysis of the interaction order. But Goffman insisted that the interaction order is only 'loosely coupled' with institutional systems, roles and relationships, social statuses (age-grade, gender, class, etc.), cultural styles and so forth (what he called 'social structure' (1983, p. 2)),[5] and as a result, the framework of concepts he developed is unaffected by 'standard [sociological] contrast[s] between village life and city life, between domestic settings and public ones, between intimate, long-standing relations and fleeting impersonal ones' (1983, p. 2).

So what exactly does the interaction order consist of? The interaction order has a 'body to body starting point,' and it comes into operation in 'environments in which two or more individuals are physically in one another's… presence,' whether they are on their own ('**singles**') or in company (in '**withs**') (1983, p. 2). This 'co-presence renders persons uniquely accessible, available and subject to one another' (1963, p. 22), and much of this happens in **focused interaction**. Prototypically as in e.g. a conversation, focused interaction covers 'arrangements in which persons come together into a small physical circle as ratified participants in a consciously shared, clearly interdependent undertaking, the period of participation itself bracketed with rituals of some kind' (1981, p. 7), but it also extends to activities in which talk plays a secondary role like 'card games, service transactions, bouts of love making, and commensalism'; activities involving an audience and platform format (plays, movies, formal meetings, etc.); quite large-

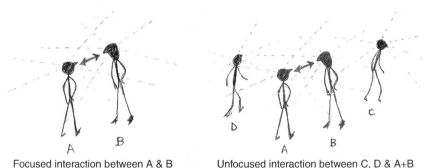

Focused interaction between A & B   Unfocused interaction between C, D & A+B
Key: ↔: mutually ratified & reciprocated attention
- - - - : ambient awareness

Figure 7.1 Focused and unfocused interaction.

scale celebratory occasions; and to mediated communication such as 'telephonic connection and letter exchange' (1983, pp. 6–7).[6] In all these settings, participants 'share a joint focus of attention, perceive that they do so, and perceive this perceiving' (1983, p. 3). But as well as encompassing focused interaction, the interaction order also involves the presence of people (either as singles or withs) who are engaged in adjacent activity within visual range but *beyond* the circle in which one is principally occupied, and in the **unfocused interaction** that takes place in a larger gathering of this kind, people glean information from (and about) one another in glancing or in passing (1963, pp. 24, 18; see Figure 7.1). In fact, people are continuously giving off signs of their intentions: 'It is not only that our appearance and manner provide evidence of our statuses and relationships. It is also that the line of our visual regard, the intensity of our involvement, and the shape of our initial actions, allow others to glean our immediate intent and purpose, and all this whether or not we are engaged in talk with them at the time' (1983, p. 3). Participants' patterns of attention, 'engrossment and involvement' play a constitutive part in the interaction order, and 'emotion, mood, cognition, bodily orientation, and muscular effort are intrinsically involved' (1983, p. 3). 'Ease and uneasiness, unselfconsciousness and wariness are [also] central' (1983, p. 3), because '[w]hen individuals come into one another's immediate presence, **territories of the self** bring to the scene a vast filigree of wires which individuals are uniquely equipped to trip over' (1971, pp. 135–136). These territories cover a variety of preserves – our bodies, our personal space, our possessions, our reputations, the information about us (1971, Chapter 2) – and in one another's presence, we 'become vulnerable [not only] to physical assault, sexual molestation, kidnapping, robbery and obstruction of movement,' but also 'through their words and gesticulation to the penetration of our psychic preserves, and to the breaching of the expressive order we expect will be maintained in our presence' (1983, p. 4). But these preserves aren't just the focus of constraint, prohibition and threat – when we invite or allow others into them, they are also vital resources for courtesy, affection and intimacy (1983, p. 4).

To reiterate: focused and unfocused interaction always takes place in settings that are culturally and historically specific.[7] Both individualising and/or collective classification frameworks feature in our identification of others (Goffman, 1983, p. 3), and the semiotic signs, expectations and material circumstances informing our interaction will vary from location to location. Nevertheless, within all the social and cultural variability, Goffman sees this embodied orientation to the co-presence of others as universal, maybe with roots in animal behaviour (1983, pp. 3, 10), and this gives his work a significance that reaches well beyond the classification of tactics in the under-life of institutions, valuable though this can certainly be.

Unfocused interaction

Within the framework that Goffman develops, *unfocused* interaction is the most obvious place to start considering surveillance relations. In unfocused interaction in multi-party gatherings, people are conscious of co-present others with whom they are not themselves directly engaged, and whether these others are singles or withs, they themselves will also be monitoring their surroundings in some way or other, since in Goffman's account, every social situation involves '**mutual monitoring possibilities**' (1964/1972, p. 63). In fact, to map these social relations, operating either outside or at the margins of face-to-face encounters, Goffman develops quite an elaborate account of how people distribute their attention, organise their bodies, and display ritual respect for one another.

When individuals participate in focused and unfocused interaction simultaneously, orienting both to 'ratified participants' inside particular conversational enclosures and 'bystanders' within range (who may simply overhear parts of the talk or actively listen in as eavesdroppers (1981, p. 131ff)), their attention is necessarily divided. As well as being involved in the talk or task that is the main focus for ratified participants, they remain alert to the wider field of 'communication in the round' and particularly in gatherings and public places, they may scan the surroundings out of the corner of their eye, checking that there is nothing nearby to alarm them (1971, Chapter 1). Both within and beyond the project or encounter in which they are principally engaged, people notice but actively **disattend** objects and activities that can be safely ignored (1974, Chapter 7; 1981, p. 132), although this distribution of involvement can shift, either gradually or suddenly, so that a person changes from 'placidly attending to easily managed matters at hand' to being 'fully mobilised, alarmed, ready to attack ... or flee' (1971, p. 282; 1981, pp. 101–104).

Within these mutual monitoring environments, people also usually design their own behaviour and appearance in ways that display to others that they're not a threat themselves. As well as being able to 'transmit' linguistic signs in talk, people 'exude' information through their **body idiom**, which is open to interpretation by anyone within perceptual range (1970, pp. 5–11; 1963, pp. 33–35).[8] In addition, 'this kind of controlled alertness to the situation will [often] mean suppressing or concealing many of the capacities and roles the individual might be expected to play in other settings' (1963, pp. 24–25), and there are a host of 'involvement shields' 'behind which individuals can safely do the kinds of things that ordinarily result in negative sanctions' – pieces of furniture, objects, items of clothing, etc. (1963, p. 39ff; 1971, pp. 344–345).

In fact, in situations of co-presence, there is 'strict normative regulation, giving rise to a kind of communication traffic order,' and this is different from 'the moral rules regulating other aspects of life... (codes of law, regulating economic and political matters; codes of ethics, regulating professional life)' (1963, p. 24). As well as observing these **situational proprieties** in their own body idiom, participants usually collaborate in the maintenance of this normative order, and much of the time they do so through **civil inattention**. In civil inattention,

> 'one gives to another enough visual notice to demonstrate that one appreciates that the other is present..., while at the next moment withdrawing one's attention from [him/her] so as to express that [s/he] does not constitute a target of special curiosity or design... By according civil inattention, the individual implies that [s/he] has no reason to suspect the intentions of others present and no reason to fear the others, be hostile to them, or wish to avoid them' (1963, p. 84).

Occasions do arise when civil inattention is abandoned. For a variety of reasons (acquaintanceship, business, etc.), someone may seek to transition from unfocused interaction to a face-to-face encounter, displaying to the person they're approaching that they're no threat with an **access ritual** like a greeting. Alternatively, some violation of situational propriety may (be thought to) occur – someone steps on a toe, talks too loudly or drops something – and this can instigate either a **remedial ritual**, which involves a variable sequence of interactive moves like 'primes' ('oi!'), explanations, apologies, remedies, appreciations ('thanks') and minimisations ('no problem'), or alternatively, a 'run-in' if for example the alleged source of the infraction pointedly refuses to provide a remedy (1971, Chapter 4; 1967; see also Pütz, 2018). There are also 'non-persons' – for example, children, servants and animals – who don't (or aren't expected to) observe situational proprieties and aren't accorded civil inattention (1963, p. 40, Chapter 5), while there are others in **opening positions**, like police officers, who have 'a built-in license to accost others' (1963, p. 129; see Jones, this volume).

In summary, unfocused interaction involves:

a   perceiving other people's activity from the outside, without being a ratified co-participant in the talk or task they are engaged in, and assuming that they are also aware of you;
b   styling your appearance and bodily conduct in non-threatening ways, broadly in accordance with the proprieties of the situation;
c   actively displaying civil inattention and a respect for the boundaries around the joint activity of 'withs' and the territories of the selves of 'singles';
d   only shifting into a focused encounter with an access ritual that provides reassurance that the approach is non-threatening, or if some un-ignorable infraction is jeopardising situational proprieties.

There are a lot more subtleties in Goffman's work, but this initial sketch should be sufficient to show that he sees unfocused interaction and the ambient monitoring it entails as an ineradicable aspect of our behaviour in social situations. But how is ambient monitoring in unfocused interaction linked with experiences of surveillance, defined as 'the focused, systematic and routine attention to personal details for purposes of influence, management, protection or direction' (Lyon, 2007, p. 14)? We will explore this in the rest of the chapter, and use the resources that Goffman provides to address their connection in everyday experience, beginning with data from Eley's fieldwork in the streets of Frankfurt.

Walking in a street and the normalisation of surveillance

Eley's doctoral ethnography developed an interactional perspective on the regulation, perception and emplacement of signage in a large public thoroughfare in Frankfurt,[9] and the analysis here focuses on a 3 minute 52 second audio-video recording of a woman leaving one shop, going out into the street in search of another, seeing it and then crossing the road to go into it – all in all, a process that would be hard to beat in terms of day-to-day mundanity (Green & Zurawski, 2015, p. 40). As such, it is a good test of our ability to document some lived experience of unfocused interaction with Goffman as a guide, and in what follows, we will consider the woman's humming and general demeanour, different types of ambient attention, and fleeting experience of the city traffic police, which we recorded with a tiny audio-visual device built into the spectacles that the woman was wearing. Here is a sketch of the background and the main actions recorded on the video.

Background: It's around three p.m. on Friday in mid-March. The walker (henceforth 'Inge') is a middle-aged white German woman, who lived for several years in Turkey and speaks Turkish. She lives outside the neighbourhood, but likes to visit it from time to time, when 'I'll run a few errands. I'll go to Her Şey [a kiosk (not its real name)], chat with [the owner]. Buy fruit. The usual. Drink tea' (taken from Eley's conversation with Inge about her plans before she set off wearing the video glasses). But Inge hasn't been in the neighbourhood for a while, and is looking for Her Şey because 'every time I look for Her Şey, I [can] never find it.' She starts wearing the video glasses at around three p.m. and stops at around four p.m. A video-replay discussion takes place immediately afterwards.[10]

Broad outline of actions:

27.42: Inge starts to leave the Turkish bookshop with her purchase and begins humming softly as she moves to the door. (Inge hummed when walking on other occasions during Eley's fieldwork, including when walking with Eley without the video-glasses);
27.46: turns left onto the pavement and walks along it, humming;
28.28: crosses a side road (without stopping humming);
28.46: briefly interrupts humming to comment on an Indian bakery with papered up windows: 'Oh it's closed or something. Gosh!' Then resumes;
29.12: moves closer to the left to the shop window and slows down for four seconds in front of a display of Turkish books and CDs;
29.26 and 29.37: Inge has been looking across to the opposite side of the main road from time to time (28.52–29.02) and continues to do so later (29.58–30.00; 30.10–30.14), but now she stops and looks across the road for five seconds and then again for eight seconds at a small shop missing a shop front sign displaying its name, with four men standing outside (still humming) (Inge during replay: 'there I'm looking for Her Şey'). Then carries on walking (and humming);
30.03: comments looking up at a shop: 'This is new here. Okay?' Resumes humming;
30.23: approaches a second side road, glances left twice at a small cluster of men (two in city traffic police uniforms), momentarily stopping the humming during the first glance (see below). Crosses the side road (humming again);
30.40: moves to the right of the pavement, and while looking up and down the main road, says: '(*unclear word*) there seen it';
30.43: crosses the main road (humming until she reaches approximately half-way, resuming when she reaches the pavement);
31.05: slows down as she approaches Her Şey's shop front, which is covered with stickers and posters, and stops humming;
31.09: stops walking for nearly 20 seconds to read a poster stuck to the wall outside, going close up to one (no humming);
31.28: moves along towards the shop door (resuming humming);
31.30: turns right through the door, sees the shop-owner close at hand, and slips straight from humming to a greeting.

There are important clues to Inge's shifts of attention and experience of the surroundings in the humming that she keeps up for most of the walk, stopping at particular moments, and Goffman facilitates three observations.

First, Goffman sees humming as a 'side involvement,' one among a number of activities that 'an individual can carry on in an abstracted fashion without threatening or confusing simultaneous maintenance of a main involvement,' such as '[h]umming while working and knitting while listening' (Goffman, 1963, pp. 43, 70; Rampton, 2006, Chapter 3). This fits the video: Inge's main involvement is finding Her Şey, but she drops her humming when she refers out loud to changes that she notices (the shops that have closed and opened since her last visit [28.46, 30.03]), as well as when she stops outside Her Şey to look at a poster (31.09) – in other words, she stops humming when particular things catch or require her closer attention. Second, whereas full-voiced singing would draw attention, the softness of her humming is consistent with situational propriety and the display of civil inattention. This kind of private orientation to music (and other auditory artefacts) involves an 'inward migration from the gathering': '[w]hile outwardly participating in an activity within a social situation, an individual can allow [their] attention to turn from what [they] and everyone else consider the real or serious world, and give [them]self up for a time to a playlike world in which [they] alone participate' (1963, p. 69). Third, Inge's humming suggests that she feels relatively safe in the street, presupposing an environment that doesn't demand full alertness, where she can 'placidly attend to easily managed matters at hand' (1971, p. 282). There is, though, one episode relevant to *institutional surveillance* when this situation seems marginally less stable.

As Inge approaches the second side road, a man, who has just crossed it and is walking towards her, briefly turns his head right to look down the side road (30.18, see Figure 7.2), looks ahead again, and then glances back once more (30.19). He passes Inge on the inside of the pavement, and then as she moves closer to the corner with a view down the side road, she also turns her head to look down the side road. A group of three men standing and talking come into view, one of them behind a pedestrian barrier (30.22, see Figure 7.3). Two are in city traffic police uniforms, one with arms folded (behind the barrier), the other with hands held behind his back, while the un-uniformed man has his hands in his pockets. Another pedestrian, who had been walking ahead of Inge and has turned down the side street, can be seen glancing back in the direction of the group. As the threesome comes into view, Inge stops humming for about two seconds (30.22–24). She then resumes the tune, turns her head back to the direction she's going (to avoid the bollard ahead 30.26), but then looks back down the side-street once more for a couple of seconds, with the group of three to the left of her vision. After that, she turns her head back in the direction she's going, humming and walking forward across the side road.

152 *Ben Rampton and Louise Eley*

Figure 7.2 Oncoming pedestrian turning head right to look down side road (circled). (A slightly clearer colour image can be found online open-access in Eley & Rampton, 2020.)

Figure 7.3 The scene recorded by the video-glasses at the moment when Inge is turning her head down the side-street and stops humming. Note: The two uniformed men are marked out with the darker oval ring furthest left, the un-uniformed man with his hands in his pockets is marked with the lighter oval ring second from the left, and the pedestrian glancing back is marked with the circle. (A slightly clearer colour image can be found online open-access in Eley & Rampton, 2020.)

So what can we learn from all this about ambient monitoring and experiences of surveillance in unfocused interaction? To answer, we can first focus on the walker, turning to studies of surveillance afterwards.

The video we've described lasts less than four minutes, but it provides quite a rich socio-cognitive view of Inge's fluctuating and multi-track attention to the circumstances around her (cf Goffman, 1974, Chapter 7). Her overall *intention* is to locate and reach Her Şey, and the video captures her actively looking, walking forwards and from time to time *scanning* the opposite side of the road, at one point stopping for over ten seconds to look more closely (29.26 and 29.37). There are also moments of *noticing* when she slows down (29.12; 31.05), stops (31.09) or comments (28.46; 30.03; 30.40) near things that catch her attention and speak to her cultural interests (in Turkish culture, in the poster at the kiosk which she thought was advertising a reading/exhibition, in the changing neighbourhood). For much of the time, she is '*away*' in the tune that she is humming, although she does this in a way that displays respect for the situation (1974, p. 345). In fact, she passes more than 20 pedestrians coming towards her on the pavement without any problem, and in doing so, she employs a '*dissociated vigilance*' that 'provide [s] a running reading of the situation, a constant monitoring of what surrounds... out of the further corner [of the] eye, leaving the individual [her] self free to focus [her] main attention on the non-emergencies around [her]' (1971, p. 282). Of course the passers-by also contribute to avoiding collision, mutually monitoring and adjusting their own paths as well (Goffman, 1971, p. 28; Ryave & Schenkein, 1974; Haddington et al., 2012, para. 40–42, 47).

But beyond the different kinds of (often simultaneous) awareness displayed in Inge's practices, what about her experience of organised institutional surveillance? There is a non-smoking sign on the door of the bookshop that she leaves, and as Jones (2017) notes, this implies that 'someone... is watching... to make sure that [customers] do not engage in these prohibited activities' (p. 154). But in the recording, it appears only very briefly at the edge of the screen – Inge doesn't appear to pay any attention to this on the video (and doesn't light up when she gets outside). Nor does she look up at any of the Closed-Circuit Television (CCTV) cameras that she passes.[11] It is most likely that both types of surveillance are just taken-for-granted, but this is *not quite* the case with the two uniformed employees of the city traffic police she passes, even though their 'opening position' means that they might also be taken for granted. Here it looks as though she is alerted to something non-normal by the two rightward glances of the pedestrian coming towards her, and she appears to pay greater attention to the scene with the traffic police when she glances towards the group for four seconds (30.22–30.26), momentarily stops humming (30.22–30.24), and then looks back for two seconds as she moves past (30.26–30.29). But that's it. The body idiom of the three men suggests nothing untoward (arms folded, hands clasped behind back, hands in pockets); 'as the individual moves, some potential signs for alarm move out of effective range (as their sources move out of relevance)' (Goffman, 1971,

p. 301); and 'the actions of passers-by form a chain of embodied events that signal and help maintain normalcy' (Haddington et al., 2012, para. 35) – the oncoming pedestrian whose sideways glancing Inge copied didn't look unduly concerned, and nor does anyone else. All in all, the official surveillance supported by organisations here seems to be inextricably interwoven with the routine practices of unfocused interaction that everyone performs in Inge's vicinity.

If we turn to the literature in surveillance studies, this account of the subjective experience of surveillance is very broadly compatible with the phenomenological approach suggested by Friesen et al. (2009) and Ball (2005, pp. 96–8, following Crossley, 1995, 2001), addressing 'lived space, lived time, lived body, lived human relations' and 'a-thematic consciousness' ('awareness that is not intellectual, interpretive or deciphering') (Friesen et al., 2009, pp. 85, 88). But as an empirical method, the introspectively generated narratives that Friesen et al. recommend are unlikely to be able to capture the synchronised interplay of physical movement, built environment, body idiom, gaze and vocalisation recorded in the ten seconds of video in which Inge oriented to (non-) events with traffic police down the side-street. Indeed, more generally, the narratives produced in interviews are likely to have quite serious limitations as sources of insight into the lived experience of surveillance. This is because narratives tend to dwell on what's tellable (and often a little bit more dramatic), thereby missing the mundane unremarkable-ness of surveillance in a scene like the one that Inge experienced during her walk (cf Green & Zurawski, 2015, pp. 28, 31). And yet it is essential to address this humdrum ordinariness if we are interested in the *normalisation* of surveillance (Lyon et al., 2012, p. 1). In fact, the combination of Goffman and an audio-video recording like this allows us to spotlight the very practices with which the normality of surveillance is produced and maintained – mid-afternoon on a Friday for Inge.

But, of course, our account has been closely tuned to the experience of one particular person, a respectable middle-aged white woman. The links we've made to Goffman show that this case isn't utterly idiosyncratic, but even so, experiences of surveillance differ considerably, and it is worth now turning to a case study of two people with everyday interests that bring them closer to the borders of legality. In the process, we will develop another angle on how surveillance is experienced, and start to build a model to represent this.

Posting up stickers and the experience of feeling surveilled

It is a civil offence in Frankfurt to post up stickers (small pieces of adhesive material carrying text and/or images) in the street, and the local authorities and public transport operators employ cleaners to take them down. Eley's PhD fieldwork included a number of individuals and groups who regularly put up stickers in the neighbourhood she was researching (which also had more CCTV cameras than any other part of the city). While some engaged in stickering for fun, because they liked particular stickers and enjoyed seeing interesting or amusing ones around, others used them in social, political and commercial projects that they were committed to, and their stickers carried messages about welcoming migrants, new musical outlets and so forth (cf Eley, 2019). In both categories, people said that they liked to have some stickers ready in their pockets whenever they went into the streets. We didn't video anyone placing stickers, but we asked about and/or observed the process, and it is worth comparing what two of them told us.

'Adnan' was in his late twenties, was born in Turkey, came to Germany as a child, now ran a small business, and put up stickers if he liked the political message or found them entertaining. Talking about putting up stickers on trains, he said:

> 'Yeah because vandalism is anti-social (*laughs*). It's vandalism vis-à-vis the City... There are cameras everywhere... Yeah or ticket inspectors are there' (translated from German).

And he explained how he actually posted them up (see also the illustration in Figure 7.4):

> 'Just like that, put it in your hand... Sticker is here, you hold it so like (*bends fingers inwards to cup hand, traces with other hand the rectangle shape of the sticker*) you take the backing away and (*stretches arm out as*

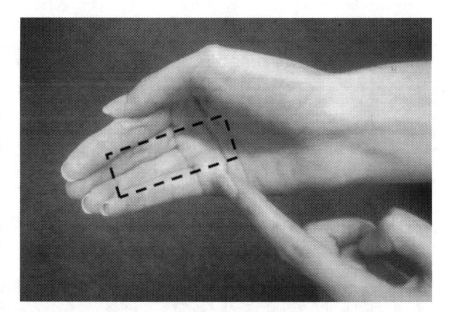

Figure 7.4 Preparing to place a sticker covertly (not demonstrated by Adnan).

if leaning with hand against surface)… Looks as though it was already there' (translated from German).

In Goffman's terms, Adnan was using his hand as an 'involvement shield,' concealing the sticker and disguising his action as a mundane stretch or lean.

'James,' also in his twenties, was born in the UK but spent a lot of time growing up abroad. During a stay in Frankfurt he became increasingly involved in a third sector organisation and remained in the city, supporting himself by working as a waiter. His stickers promoted the work, projects and politics of the organisation, and when we asked him about stickering, he said:

> '[N]o, I don't care about cameras. A lot of people care about cameras, I don't… like I don't think anybody is gonna look at a camera twenty-four hours. and even if they see somebody sticker something they're like okay. like if you go graffiti something maybe be a bit more wary. But a sticker like yeah it's not much.'

And here is Eley's field diary about walking with him from one of his organisation's events to the nearest tram stop:

> 'James left a trail of stickers along the route that we walked. While he walked, he took the backing from the back of the stickers and placed them on objects along our path, including two bollards, and he left one unstuck on a car. He appeared calm and unconcerned with who may be watching him, not looking around or over his shoulder at all, for example to see if CCTV cameras or any individuals were watching him. He took care and time to place the stickers straight, by holding them at the corners, and then wiped his hand over the top to stick them securely.'

There are obvious differences in James and Adnan's approaches to being surveilled, and Goffman's account of the remedial interchanges that sometimes turn unfocused into focused interaction helps to systematise them. In remedial interchanges, says Goffman, it is important to distinguish between (a) an act and (b) its categorisation or not as an offence, and (c) the interaction following the act in which the moral status of the act and its perpetrator is negotiated (1971, pp. 99, 102, 106). So when, for example, a person does something which appears to breach situational propriety ('the deed'), people in the vicinity are likely to display some concern, and it is how the actor then responds to their display – whether or not s/he appears repentant, convincingly disowns it, etc. – which determines whether the deed is deemed 'inoffensive' and normal order is restored, or whether further sanctions need to be pursued. Both Adnan and James are committed to the act of stickering, but in Adnan's account, bystanders and CCTV watchers would object to the act and initiate an interaction that could lead to sanctions. Adnan's concealment strategy was not only designed to hide the act but to provide

Goffman and everyday experience 157

Table 7.1 Comparison of how Adnan and James anticipate the act of stickering leading to remedial interchanges

a. *who could observe the act and/or its outcomes, when?*:
Adnan: CCTV cameras and ticket inspectors – now, during the emplacing
James: nobody will be looking at the CCTV; later on, local business and car owners, cleaners

b. *what would they think of it?*:
Adnan: CCTV operators and ticket inspectors – vandalism
James: CCTV operators – too minor to pursue; local car and business owners – a nuisance, requiring time-consuming removal; cleaners – a work task

c. *what actions would they be likely to pursue if they spotted the act?*
Adnan: CCTV operators and ticket inspectors – they'd pick you out and intervene, now or later
James: CCTV operators – nothing; locals – scrape off the stickers, and think badly of the project being publicised; cleaners – scrape them off

d. *what are the implications of all this for the here-and-now performance of the act?*
Adnan: conceal the act of stickering, and be ready with a disclaimer
James: ignore the CCTV and carry on stickering as normal; don't post stickers up on local businesses, or use adhesive on local cars; put them on surfaces that cleaners seldom work on

---

him with a ready denial if held to account ('the sticker was already there'). In contrast, James didn't think that anything could happen (no one would be watching CCTV and stickering wasn't serious enough to pursue). But he did imagine other people reacting to his stickers, and this influenced where he placed them: he didn't put them up on surfaces belonging to local and migrant-run businesses as 'they're… in the same bracket as us who are working class. They're the people we wanna get on our side.' So overall, James worried less about being spotted doing something illegal than about creating a bad impression on people that he didn't want to alienate. Comparing the two, Adnan's concerns were much more immediate – being seen committing the act and being accused of an offence – and their differences are laid out in Table 7.1.

It is likely that this difference reflects, at least in part, differences in their experiences of racialised insecuritisation. On other occasions, Adnan referred to racial profiling in his encounters with security personnel and police stop-and-searches, and we discuss the wider implications of this in the final section. But staying with the close-up exploration of experiences of surveillance while stickering for the time being, we can bring in Goffman's notion of the *Umwelt* to differentiate Adnan's perspective from James'. The *Umwelt* refers to 'the sphere around the individual within which… potential sources of alarm are found' (1971, p. 297), and when stickering, Adnan's sense of *Umwelt* threats was quite pressing. We can't say for sure whether James' *Umwelt* orientation was closer to Inge's than Adnan's when he was posting up stickers, but if we bring Inge back into the account, we can differentiate experiences of surveillance more clearly.

As Inge walked down the street, there was a ten second period when the gaze direction of another pedestrian and the sight of a scene in which there were uniformed men drew her attention, but there was no inkling of any untoward event, transgressive act or perpetrator. More generally, other than the cars, oncoming pedestrians and street furnishings that her dissociated vigilance helped her to avoid, there was little sense that Inge was watching out for particular threats or types of people who were likely to draw her into remedial interchanges. This was ambient monitoring in unfocused interaction, running along with a respectfully conducted side-involvement (humming), interspersed with noticings and scannings in search of her destination.

There was much more than dissociated vigilance or being 'away' in the stickering conduct that Adnan described. Rather than operating like Inge with a generalised awareness of whoever happened to be in the vicinity, Adnan was alert to the threat from very particular social types when he posted a sticker up – officials nearby or behind the CCTV – and he engaged in fabrication: 'an intentional effort... to manage activity so that... others will be induced to have a false belief about what it is that is going on' (1974, p. 83). His actions appeared to take a determinate shape that he was able to reflect and report on, and if we combine this with concepts offered by Goffman, we can suggest a general structure for the experience of surveillance that Adnan described:

i. the experience starts when an individual considers carrying out an act that they know is sometimes regarded as an offence;
ii. s/he reckons with the *Umwelt,* and imagines co-present observers who are likely to see her/his act as an offence, to view him/her as a suspect, and to initiate particular kinds of remedial sequence (see Table 7.1);
iii. s/he decides whether to abandon the act or go ahead with it, concentrating on body idiom to conceal it if they opt for the latter;
iv. the experience ends either when s/he moves out of range of the observers and relaxes, or when the surveillers declare themselves, maybe in uniform or through a public address system, at which point some kind of synchronous focused interaction takes over (an arrest, a remedial interchange etc.) (Jones, this volume).[12]

As a short-hand for this kind of experience of surveillance, with its heightened but disguised concern with surveilling bystanders, we can refer to Adnan's only-apparently unfocused conduct as 'crypto-focused' interaction under surveillance, distinguishing this from the fluid and multi-track ambient monitoring in unfocused interaction that we saw with Inge on the one hand, and on the other, the kind of focused encounter with officials that his targeted concealment seeks to evade.

Adnan's conduct broadly matches the accounts of deception that feature most commonly when Goffman is cited in surveillance studies, but we have elaborated it here within a fuller account of unfocused interaction. Indeed, Goffman's framework can also be extended to at least some of the everyday practices that arise when human bodies intersect with surveillant technologies, at 'the surfaces of contact or interfaces between… life-forms and webs of information,… between organs/body parts and entry/projection systems' (Bogard, 1996, p. 33, cited in Ball, 2005, p. 94; also Simon, 2005, p. 17; Ball, 2005, 2009; Ball & Wilson, 2000; Lyon, 2007, p. 164). This is demonstrated in Ole Pütz's ethnographic study of scanning at an airport security check point, which is briefly discussed in the next section.

Close-up interaction with surveillance technology

Pütz (2012) focuses on the brief but highly standardised process of preparing for an airport security check, stepping through a metal detector scanner, and being patted down by security staff if the scanner raises the alarm (p. 164). This is a situation in which it is hard for travellers to ignore the fact that they are being actively surveilled as a potential security threat, but Pütz details the ways in which everyone intensifies the effort to act as if nothing untoward is happening. He notes that the closer passengers come to the checkpoint itself, the quieter they become, dropping conversation and turning off their cell phones (p. 172). Individuals enter the walk-through metal detector one at a time and 'if the scanner detects metallic objects, screeners must identify who raised the alarm and pat this traveller down to locate the source of the alarm on [their] body' (p. 168). At this point, Pütz brings Goffman into the analysis, and proposes that this patting-down potentially violates the travellers' personal space (cf 'territories of the self' in Section 1). But the screeners and travellers conduct this 'breach of personal space in a way that reduces the social implications of bodily proximity' (p. 173). The screeners use a hand-metal detector, 'a lifeless technical object'; they wear gloves so there is no skin to skin contact; and they avoid 'private parts and do… not linger long on any part of the body' (p. 173). The travellers who are stopped and patted down 'avert their eyes while being patted down and focus visually on a point in the middle distance. They thus minimise the appearance of [focused] interaction, because eye contact is a clear indicator of [this]… [But they] do not fully avert the eye or stare dreamily into space; they are able to observe the situation out of the corner of the eye and stay cooperative' (p. 173).

In Goffman's terms, this seems to be one of those "blind' transactions, in which persons come together to accomplish a joint activity but do not bracket this spate of mutual coordination ritually, that is, do not sustain a social encounter,' which would involve 'an exchange of words or other recognition rituals and the ratification of mutual participation in an open state of talk' (1971, p. 97; also 1963, p. 88ff). Pütz uses the notion of civil inattention (cf Section 2) to explain the participants' conduct at the scanner, and in fact remedial interchanges are also potentially relevant, since at this particular point of the security process, the unstated question motivating the scanning of bodies (and personal possessions) is: 'Do you carry weapons or contraband which is a source of risk?' (2012, p. 169). This question is in principle potentially offensive to travellers, casting doubt on their character, and this may also contribute to the de-personalising avoidance strategies that Pütz outlines (2012, p. 175).[13]

This airport scene obviously differs in a number of ways from our characterisation of stickering. The surveillance technologies work differently: CCTV scans the street and picks out individuals, often differentiating them by age, ethnicity, gender as well as activity and appearance, whereas the step-through substance detector at the airport is used on all the passengers, regardless of social and personal identity. Stickerers vary in their interpretations of potential reactions to their acts of sticker emplacement, whereas in the airport scanner, a standardised interpretation of *Umwelt* risks takes over and governs everyone's behaviour. And their orientations to remedial interchanges are different: The stickerers wanted to avoid them, whereas airport passengers were already drawn into a remedial sequence, positioned as suspects and probed with technologies which investigated whether they were carrying material they shouldn't. Even so, it looks as though Goffman's account of unfocused interaction, remedial interchanges and the *Umwelt* are relevant to both.

Surveilled experiences: A rudimentary model

Our discussion of scenes from everyday life has tried to show that Goffman's work provides a multitude of empirical 'entry points' into the (inter-) subjectively lived experience of surveillance, in all its 'ubiquity and relative normalization' (Lyon et al., 2012, p. 9). Pütz (2012) characterises the airport scanning process as a 'non-event' because it does not acknowledge the passenger as an individual (p. 158), and if we accept this, we can use Goffman to develop the following schematisation of the experiences of surveillance that we have considered. So to begin with, we have

- focused interaction, which we can see, for example, whenever security staff abandon their surveillant position as overhearers/eavesdroppers and engage the (erstwhile) surveilled in a mutually acknowledged encounter such as a remedial interchange (as in stop-&-search). Alternatively, the (formerly) surveilled act up to the cameras (Smith, 2007).

Then we have:

- *un-focused* interaction, exemplified by Inge's ambient awareness, her ease in an *Umwelt* characterised by normal appearances, doing nothing likely to provoke a remedial sequence, displaying only a very fleeting

interest in uniformed personnel, taking surveillance for granted for the rest of the time;
- *crypto-focused* interaction under surveillance, involving the appearance of unfocused interaction even though the actor's attention and actions are directed towards co-present observers. This was Adnan, concealing his activity from the CCTV and uniformed personnel that he was now more acutely aware of, and was keen to avoid any remedial engagement with;

and lastly with Pütz:

- *non-focused* interaction under surveillance, involving surveillers and surveilled in a collaborative refusal to initiate a ritually ratified engagement, already finding themselves in a highly standardised remedial interchange, with the surveilled seeking to relinquish the status of suspect as soon as possible.

The lines between these four types of interaction are obviously porous – un-, crypto- and non-focused interaction can swiftly become focused, crypto- can slip back to unfocused, and so forth. And this list certainly isn't offered as a comprehensive typology. But it does show that Goffman's framework allows rather a differentiated account of the experience of surveillance, and with recognition of this in place, a number of more general points are in order.

Broader implications

Looking beyond the experience of being surveilled that we have taken as our central concern, our account of Goffman speaks to at least four issues in the wider discussion of surveillance.

First, it reaches beyond Lyon's (2007) widely cited definition of surveillance as 'the focused, systematic and routine attention to personal details for purposes of influence, management, protection or direction' (p. 14), and connects instead with Green and Zurawski's (2015) interest in surveillance 'as one form or mode of the social, becoming apparent in other activities and practices, something that is created, performed and perceived as such (in all its technical, discursive and interactional modes) – or not' (p. 29).

Lyon's canonical definition addresses modes of attention, the objects attended to and the purposes guiding this attention, but it skirts over the two-way dynamics of interaction and the relationship between watcher and watched. In contrast, to get closer to the experience of being surveilled, we have brought interactional relations into the account, concentrating on 'unfocused interaction' in Goffman's specialised sense. Unfocused interaction involves: being alert to others beyond the task or encounter that you're focused on, and knowing you're also visible to them; styling your conduct and outward appearance to conform to the proprieties of the situation, restricting intrusive gazes either way with civil inattention; and shifting to direct engagement only if you can display benign intent or there's some unignorable infraction. Most if not all these forms of awareness, practices and concerns seem fundamental to sociality, and in the three case studies that we have cited, we have seen how different ways of enacting unfocused interaction contribute to the normalisation of institutional surveillance, as well as to the ways in which sharper experiences of being surveilled are differently configured. In Green and Zurawski's (2015) discussion of the ethnography of surveillance, one of the central questions is: can surveillance be approached as a basic 'mode of the social' that is elaborated in different ways in different environments (pp. 29, 35; Simon, 2005)? Our answer is an unequivocal 'yes.'

Whereas institutionalisation and power stand out in Lyon's definition ('systematic,' 'purposes of management, protection or direction') (cf Marwick, 2012), a Goffmanian approach to surveillance foregrounds the relations between people and the activities that connect them. In doing so, it provides more scope to investigate the *emergence* of surveillance in a range of different settings.[14] Obviously, in settings like the airport security check point, the surveillance is very well-established and the roles are relatively fixed. But in principle, an approach centred on interactional relations can also cover much less systematic cases which participants might or might not call 'surveillance' (Green & Zurawski, 2015, pp. 28–29, 34–35), where there is less sophistication in the targets, in the technological supports, in the ideas of who could observe and what is looked for, and in the reporting requirements – for example, children or next-door neighbours; net curtains; late arrivals home; reprimands or gossip. With Goffman, we can address the question of what 'counts' as or what constitutes surveillance in the context of people's actual experiences, attending to classifications of surveillance that are 'created and produced within social interactions in everyday life' (Green & Zurawski, 2015, p. 29). As we have documented, Goffman's work on unfocused interaction provides a foundational framework for grasping the vital details of the particular ways in which people enact vigilance to outsiders, to the surroundings, to situational propriety and body idiom in particular environments. And whether or not the people involved in any particular relationship between watcher and watched experience it as oppressive, intrusive, necessary, acceptable, normal or nothing of note is subject to the kinds of variation we have described.

Second, building on Adnan's account of racial profiling, Goffman provides a path into everyday experiences of what Bigo (2008) calls the 'banopticon,' the politically cultivated suspicion and surveillance of migrants and minorities that has intensified since 9/11 in many parts of the West (and elsewhere). The experiences and enactments of surveillance that we have considered are themselves influenced and informed by prior knowledge, experience and discourses in society, and in Mangual Figueroa's (2020) formulation, regardless of their actions, certain types of people physically '*embody* the breach' that surveillance watches for (see also Nguyen, this volume). As a result, 'what for some people are practices relatively free of precarity, such as walking down the street, are, for others, sites of constant uncertainty in which at any moment they might be detained, accosted, searched, or even shot by the very agents of state security that promise to keep them safe' (Jones, 2020, pp. 94–95). It is not difficult to bring these broader characterisations back to the kinds of interactive experience we have described. Goffman recognised that 'whether we interact with strangers or intimates, we will find that the fingertips of society have reached bluntly into the contact, even here putting us in our place' (1963a, p. 70). In interactional sociolinguistics and linguistic anthropology, there are well developed accounts of how circumambient ideologies infuse activity in the here-and-now, explaining how a person's prior knowledge and experience of (in)securitised environments could inform their situated interpretation of the *Umwelt* on hand. As we have argued, differences in Adnan and James' experiences of racialised insecuritisation are likely to account (at least in part) for the differences in their perceptions and experiences of surveillance while stickering, as well as in their fleeting in-the-moment anticipations of remedial interchanges.

Following on from this, third, Goffman's recognition that mutual monitoring is a fundamental part of human sociality is also relevant to recent reappraisals of Foucault's (1977) claims about the mono-directionality and non-mutuality of surveillance (p. 200), as well as to growing interest in the role of agentive practice in surveillant relationships. So for example, contemporary technologies like digital phone cameras enable '*sous*veillance,' in which subordinates 'watch back' at the surveillers who hold institutional power over them, recording and publicising their conduct (Jones, 2020, this volume), and in on-line 'social surveillance' by friends and family on social media, 'each participant is both broadcasting information that is looked at by others and looking at information broadcast by others' (Marwick, 2012, p. 379). Goffman certainly wrote a great deal about people being the 'object [s] of information,' as in Foucault's (1977, p. 200) conception, but his starting assumption was that monitoring is *mutual* even though people's agendas, resources and constraints might be very different. Without this starting assumption, it would be easy to miss, for example, the mutual monitoring practices that contributed to the normalisation of institutional surveillance during Inge's walk in a street, as well as the ways that security personnel and travellers collaborate in the production of unfocused interaction at the airport scanner. Turning to questions of agency, Haggerty (2006) argues that studies of surveillance need to attend more to the activity of the governed: 'while governance inevitably involves efforts to persuade, entice, coerce or cajole subjects to modify their behaviour in particular directions, the targets of governance are understood to be a locus of freedom... subjects as active agents' (p. 40). As Haggerty suggests, some of this agency may be expressed in 'resistance, avoidance or subversion' (p. 40), but these terms themselves cover a host of intricate practices, and they overlook a multiplicity of other possibilities, including those we could loosely gloss as 'acceptance,' 'cooperation' and 'normalisation.' The subtlety of practices like these does not mean that they are rare – on the contrary, they are very ordinary and all the more consequential because of it.

Finally, remaining with the subtlety of such practices, we can use Goffman's framework to interrogate large-scale generalisations about surveillance, such as the claim that 'technological innovations fundamentally alter the organisation, practice and effects of surveillance relationships' (Simon, 2005, p. 1), changing 'the dynamics of power, identity, institutional practice and interpersonal relations on a scale comparable to... industrialization, globalization or the... rise of urbanization' (Lyon et al., 2012, p. 1). If some of the practices and relations that Goffman described in embodied, off-line interaction can be found in technologically mediated surveillance, then surveillance before and after technological change can be compared, examining the alteration more closely. All the cases we have discussed involved at least partly embodied interaction, but the concepts we have used are also relevant to surveillance in the environment of entirely web-based communication (Jenkins, 2010), such as between peers on social media.[15] Off- and on-line communication are obviously different, but with Goffman, we can investigate the differences with more specific questions, such as: what semiotic strategies and resources take the place of body idiom in displays of situational propriety in online gatherings? How far and in what ways does digital platform architecture provide new or different resources for concealing negatively sanctionable acts ('involvement shields') and so forth (cf Westlake, 2008)?

In sum, especially if it is supported by a methodological framework like linguistic ethnography, Goffman's *oeuvre* provides a foundational vocabulary for understanding the dynamic interactional enactment of surveillance and for grasping – empirically – its hugely varying significance in everyday life.

Notes

1 We are indebted to discussions with Emma Mc Cluskey and Constadina Charalambous.
2 In ethnomethodological and conversation analytic micro-sociology, there is a growing body of work that uses video-recordings to look at how people interact on the move in public places (visiting museums, walking, driving, cycling), but intentional communication remains the central concern, whether this is person-to-person or mediated by material texts or objects (Kendon, 1990; Mondada, 2009, 2016, p. 347ff; McIlvenny, Broth & Haddington, 2014; Haddington & Rauniomaa, 2014; but see Ryave & Schenkein, 1974; Hindmarsh et al., 2001, pp. 18-19; vom Lehn, Heath & Hindmarsh, 2001, pp. 203-207; Haddington et al., 2012; Liberman, 2013). In sociolinguistics, there is also a body of research that examines public signage in 'Linguistic Landscapes,' and this now extends beyond the analysis of verbal and visual text to a view of how people interact around

signs, moving through space (Scollon & Scollon, 2003). This is certainly one significant source of nascent sociolinguistic interest in surveillance (Eley, 2019; Jones, 2017; Kitis & Milani, 2015; Stroud & Jegels, 2014), but even so, the potential significance of Goffman's account of *un*focused interaction for understanding surveillance remains largely unexplored.

3 We recognise that surveillance takes many forms (Green & Zurawski, 2015, p. 29; Walby, 2005, p. 158; Haggerty, 2006) and at least two dimensions of surveillance that fall outside our concerns here: 'dataveillance' and the administrative design and management of information about individuals (Simon, 2005, p. 4; van Dijck, 2013; Lyon, 2007, p. 23), and the surveillance that is pervasive in focused interactional encounters with bureaucracy (cf Ball et al., 2015). The institutional dynamics of surveillance are considered in more detail by Nguyen (this volume), and some observations about these can be found in Rampton and Eley (2018, notes 28 & 31).

4 In earlier work, this is referred to as the 'situational' rather than merely 'situated' (e.g. 1963, pp. 22–23).

5 It may help to clarify Goffman's account of the interaction order as a partly autonomous dynamic within social process if we compare it with the way that linguists think of phonology, grammar and lexis as separate levels of language. It takes different analytical vocabularies to account for the forms and rules structuring each of these linguistic levels, and there are, for example, variations in phonological structure which have no consequences for the patterning of grammar. Goffman extends the analogy: the "workings of the interaction order can easily be viewed as the consequences of systems of enabling conventions, in the sense of the ground rules for a game, the provisions of a traffic code or the rules of syntax of a language" (1983, p. 5).

6 This surely also extends to something like solitary book reading, a literacy event in which for example, there are clearly recognisable opening and closing sequences (picking it up, opening the covers, resuming at particular points etc.) and the reader takes up a ratified recipient role intended by the text's author.

7 "Each participant enters a social situation carrying an already established biography of prior dealings with the other participants – or at least with participants of their kind; and enters also with a vast array of cultural assumptions presumed to be shared" (Goffman, 1983, p. 4).

8 "In American society," says Goffman, "it appears that the individual is expected to exert a kind of discipline and tension in regard to his [*sic*] body, showing that he has his faculties in readiness for any face-to-face interaction that might come his way in the situation.... In short, a kind of 'interaction tonus' must be maintained" (1963, pp. 24–25; 1971, pp. 326–327).

9 Eley, 2019; see also Scollon & Scollon, 2003; Blommaert, 2013; Jones, 2017; Stroud & Jegels, 2014.

10 Eley wasn't in audio contact with Inge during the walk, and did not follow her.

11 Judging from Eley's photographs of the street, there are at least three CCTV cameras that she walks past.

12 There is another possibility: the surveilled address the surveillers, turning them into an audience – see Smith (2007, pp. 293–294, 299).

13 Rampton and Eley (2018, Section 5) elaborate the possibilities in more detail.

14 Opening up possibilities for investigating the emergence of surveillance in a host of settings could also be considered ever more necessary in light of the extension of security strategies into intimate and everyday spaces (see Nguyen, this volume).

15 For example, in their investigations of US teenagers' concerns about social surveillance, Marwick and boyd argue that social media present people with entirely new experiences of exposure because of on-line 'context collapse.' *Off-*

line, they suggest, "different social contexts are typically socially or temporally bounded, making the expected social role quite obvious" (Marwick, 2012, p. 386), but "social media technologies collapse multiple audiences into single contexts" (Marwick & boyd, 2010, p. 114; boyd & Marwick, 2011). There is, though, a challenge to this notion of context collapse in Goffman's civil inattention, deriving as it does from our ability to divide attention and handle the co-presence of a lot of different people as a matter of routine, managing a main involvement with ratified participants at the same time as disattending – but remaining alert to – others in the vicinity, known and unknown.

References

Ball, K. (2002). Elements of surveillance: A new framework and future directions. *Information, Communication & Society 5*(4), 573–590.
Ball, K. (2005). Organisation, surveillance and the body: Towards a politics of resistance. *Organization 12*(1), 89–108.
Ball, K. (2009). Exposure: Exploring the subject of surveillance. *Information, Communication & Society 12*(5), 639–657.
Ball, K., Canhoto, A., Daniel, E., Dibb, S., Meadows, M., & Spiller, K. (2015). *The Private Security State? Surveillance, Consumer Data and the War on Terror*. Frederiksberg: CBS Press.
Ball, K., Haggerty, K., & Lyon, D. (Eds.). (2012). *Routledge Handbook of Surveillance Studies*. London: Routledge.
Ball, K., & Wilson, D. (2000). Power, control and computer-based performance monitoring: Repertoires, resistance and subjectivities. *Organization Studies 21*(3), 539–565.
Bigo, D. (2008). Globalized (in)security: The field and the ban-opticon. In D. Bigo & A. Tsoukala (Eds.), *Terror, insecurity and liberty: Illiberal practices of liberal regimes after 9/11* (pp. 10–48). London: Routledge.
Blommaert, J. (2013). *Ethnography, Superdiversity and Linguistic Landscapes: Chronicles of Complexity*. Bristol: Multilingual Matters.
Blumer, H. (1969). *Symbolic Interactionism: Perspective and Method*. Berkeley: University of California Press.
Bogard, W. (1996). *The Simulation of Surveillance: Hypercontrol in Telematic Societies*. Cambridge: Cambridge University Press.
boyd, d., & Marwick, A. (2011). Social privacy in networked publics: Teens' attitudes, practices, and strategies. Retrieved from https://www.danah.org/papers/2011/SocialPrivacyPLSC-Draft.pdf
Cherbonneau, M., & Copes, H. (2006). 'Drive it like you stole it': Auto theft and the illusion of normalcy. *The British Journal of Criminology 46*(2), 193–211.
Collinson, D. (1999). 'Surviving the rigs': Safety and surveillance on North Sea oil installations. *Organization Studies 20*(4), 579–600.
Crossley, N. (1995). Body techniques, agency and intercorporeality: On Goffman's *Relations in Public*. *Sociology 29*(1), 133–149.
Crossley, N. (2001). Merleau-Ponty, the elusive body and carnal sociology. *Body & Society 1*(1), 43–63.
Eley, L. (2019). *Linguistic Landscape: An Interactional Perspective* [Unpublished doctoral dissertation]. King's College London.

Eley, L., & Rampton, B. (2020). Everyday Surveillance, Goffman, and Unfocused Interaction. *Surveillance & Society 18*(2), 199–215.
Foucault, M. (1977). *Discipline and Punish: The birth of the prison* (A. Sheridan, trans.). Harmondsworth: Penguin.
Friesen, N., Feenberg, A., & Smith, G. (2009). Phenomenology and surveillance studies: Returning to the things themselves. *The Information Society 25*(2), 84–90.
Gilliom, J., & Monahan, T. (2012). Everyday resistance. In K. Ball, K. Haggerty & D. Lyon (Eds.), *Routledge Handbook of Surveillance Studies* (pp. 405–411). London: Routledge.
Goffman, E. (1963). *Behavior in Public Places: Notes on the Social Organization of Gatherings*. New York: Free Press.
Goffman, E. (1963a). *Stigma: Notes on the Management of Spoiled Identity*. Harmondsworth: Penguin.
Goffman, E. (1967). *Interaction Ritual: Essays on face-to-face behavior*. Harmondsworth: Penguin.
Goffman, E. (1970). *Strategic Interaction*. Oxford: Blackwell.
Goffman, E. (1971). *Relations in Public: Microstudies of the Public Order*. London: Allen Lane.
Goffman, E. (1972). The neglected situation. In P.P. Giglioli (Ed.), *Language and social context: Selected readings* (pp. 61–66). Harmondsworth: Penguin. Reprinted from *American Anthropologist* 66(6), 133–136 (1964).
Goffman, E. (1974). *Frame Analysis: An Essay on the Organization of Experience*. Boston: Northeastern University Press.
Goffman, E. (1981). *Forms of Talk*. Philadelphia: University of Pennsylvania Press.
Goffman, E. (1983). The interaction order. *American Sociological Review 48*(1), 1–17.
Green, N., & Zurawski, N. (2015). Surveillance and ethnography: Researching surveillance as everyday life. *Surveillance & Society 13*(1), 27–43.
Haddington, P., Frogell, S., Grubert, A., Huhta, H., Jussila, P., Kinnunen, J., Korpela, A.,… Vesisenaho, L. (2012). Civil inattention in public places: Normalising unusual events through mobile and embodied practices. *Forum: Qualitative Social Research 13*(3), Article 7.
Haddington, P., & Rauniomaa, M. (2014). Interaction between road users: Offering space in traffic. *Space and Culture 17*(2), 176–190.
Haggerty, K. (2006). Tear down the walls: On demolishing the panopticon. In D. Lyon (Ed.), *Theorizing Surveillance: The Panopticon and Beyond* (pp. 23–45). Cullompton: Willan Publishing.
Heath, C., Luff, P., & Sanchez Svensson, M. (2002). Overseeing organizations: Configuring action and its environment. *The British Journal of Sociology 53*(2), 181–201.
Helten, F., & Fischer, B. (2004). Reactive Attention: Video Surveillance in Berlin Shopping Malls. *Surveillance & Society 2*(2/3), 323–345.
Hindmarsh, J., Heath, C., vom Lehn, D., Ciolfi, L., Hall, T., Bannon, L., Best, K., & Hall, J. (2001). *Interaction as a public phenomenon*. Stockholm: CID, Centre for User Oriented IT Design.
Jacobs, B.A., & Miller, J. (1998). Crack Dealing, Gender, and Arrest Avoidance. *Social Problems 45*(4), 550–569.
Jenkins, R. (2010). The 21st-century interaction order. In M. Jacobsen (Ed.), *The Contemporary Goffman* (pp. 257–274). New York: Routledge.

Jones, R. (2015). Surveillance. In A. Georgakopoulou & T. Spilioti (Eds.), *The Routledge Handbook of Language and Digital Communication* (pp. 408–411). London: Routledge.
Jones, R. (2016). *Spoken Discourse.* London: Bloomsbury.
Jones, R. (2017). Surveillant landscapes. *Linguistic Landscape 3*(2), 149–186.
Jones, R. (2020). Accounting for surveillance. *Journal of Sociolinguistics 24*(1), 89–95.
Kendon, A. (1990). *Conducting Interaction: Patterns of Behavior in Focused Encounters.* Cambridge: Cambridge University Press.
Kitis, D., & Milani, T. (2015). The performativity of the body: Turbulent spaces in Greece. *Linguistic Landscape 1*(3), 268–290.
Liberman, K. (2013). *More Studies in Ethnomethodology.* Albany: SUNY Press.
Luff, P., Heath, C., & Sanchez Svensson, M. (2008). Discriminating Conduct: Deploying Systems to Support Awareness in Organizations. *International Journal of Human-Computer Interaction 24*(4), 410–436.
Lyon, D. (2007). *Surveillance Studies: An Overview.* Cambridge: Polity Press.
Lyon, D., Haggerty, K., & Ball, K. (2012). Introducing surveillance studies. In Ball, K., Haggerty, K., & Lyon, D. (Eds.), *Routledge Handbook of Surveillance Studies* (pp. 1–11). London: Routledge.
Mangual Figueroa, A. (2020). Embodying the breach: (In)securitization and ethnographic engagement in the US. *Journal of Sociolinguistics 24*(1), 96–102.
Marwick, A. (2012). The public domain: Social surveillance in everyday life. *Surveillance & Society, 9*(4), 378–393.
Marwick, A., & boyd, d. (2010). I tweet honestly, I tweet passionately: Twitter users, context collapse, and the imagined audience. *New Media & Society 13*(1), 114–133.
Marx, G. (2009). A tack in the shoe and taking off the shoe: Neutralization and counter-neutralization dynamics. *Surveillance & Society 6*(3), 294–306.
McIlvenny, P., Broth, M., & Haddington, P. (2014). Moving together: Mobile formations in interaction. *Space and Culture 17*(2), 104–106.
Mondada, L. (2009). Emergent focused interactions in public places: A systematic analysis of the multimodal achievement of a common interactional space. *Journal of Pragmatics 41*(10), 1977–1997.
Mondada, L. (2016). Challenges of multimodality: Language and the body in social interaction. *Journal of Sociolinguistics 20*(3), 336–366.
Pütz, O. (2012). From non-places to non-events: The airport security checkpoint. *Journal of Contemporary Ethnography 41*(2), 154–188.
Pütz, O. (2018). How strangers initiate conversations: Interactions on public trains in Germany. *Journal of Contemporary Ethnography 47*(4), 426–453.
Rampton, B. (2006). *Language in Late Modernity: Interaction in an Urban School.* Cambridge: Cambridge University Press.
Rampton, B. (2016). Foucault, Gumperz and governmentality: Interaction, power and subjectivity in the twenty-first century. In N. Coupland (Ed.), *Sociolinguistics: Theoretical Debates* (pp. 303–330). Cambridge: Cambridge University Press.
Rampton, B. (2017). Interactional sociolinguistics. *Working Papers in Urban Language & Literacies* #205.
Rampton, B., & Eley, L. (2018). Goffman and the everyday interactional grounding of surveillance. *Working Papers in Urban Language & Literacies* #246.
Ryave, A.L. & Schenkein, J. (1974). Notes on the art of walking. In R. Turner (Ed.) *Ethnomethodology: Selected Readings* (pp. 265–274). Harmondsworth: Penguin.

Schiffrin, D. (1994) *Approaches to Discourse.* Oxford: Blackwell.
Scollon, R., & Scollon, S. (2003). *Discourses in Place: Language in the Material World.* London: Routledge.
Simon, B. (2005). The return of panopticism: Supervision, subjection and the new surveillance. *Surveillance & Society* 3(1), 1–20.
Smith, G. (2007). Exploring relations between watchers and watched in control(led) systems: Strategies and tactics. *Surveillance & Society* 4(4), 280–313.
Stroud, C., & Jegels, D. (2014) Semiotic landscapes and mobile narrations of place: performing the local. *International Journal of the Sociology of Language 2014*(228), 179–199.
van Dijck, J. (2013). *The Culture of Connectivity: A Critical History of Social Media.* Oxford: Oxford University Press.
vom Lehn, D., Heath, C. & Hindmarsh, J. (2001). Exhibiting interaction: Conduct and collaboration in museums and galleries. *Symbolic Interaction* 24(2), 189–216.
Walby, K. (2005). Institutional ethnography and surveillance studies: An outline for inquiry. *Surveillance & Society* 3(2/3), 158–172.
Westlake, E. (2008). Friend me if you Facebook: Generation Y and performative surveillance. *The Drama Review* 52(4), 21–40.

8 Auditor design and accountability in encounters between citizens and the police

Rodney H. Jones

Introduction

On the 25th of May, 2020, Minneapolis police officer Derek Chauvin killed George Floyd, a 46- year-old African American man, by kneeling with his knee on the man's neck for nine minutes and twenty-nine seconds while multiple witnesses, including some who were videoing the incident with their cell phones, begged the officer to stop. The videos of the incident that circulated on social media sparked widespread protests and renewed calls for racial justice, not just in the US but worldwide. The first video of Floyd's death to go public was shot by a high school student named Darnella Frazier. It shows Chauvin looking down at Floyd for most of the incident as the black man pleads for his life, saying 'I can't breathe' and 'Don't kill me' until he becomes unconscious and the pleading stops. There are a few moments in the video, however, where Chauvin looks up and gazes directly at Fraizer's camera with an almost nonchalant expression on his face. 'You're enjoying it,' one witness can be heard saying. 'Look at you. Your body language explains it.' There were other videos taken on that day from other angles by other witnesses, by the surveillance camera mounted outside a nearby Chinese restaurant, and by officer's body cams, but Fraizer's video remained the most widely circulated public document of the killing, and the moment in the video that became the still photograph that appeared in newspapers around the world was of Chauvin gazing up at his audience while his victim died.

The proliferation of video cameras in the hands of private citizens has altered the relationship between police officers and the public, making incidents of police abuse like the one described above more visible and easier to document (Sandhu & Haggerty, 2017). Along with this 'new visibility' (Goldsmith, 2010; Thompson, 2005) has come the hope that the presence of cameras would make police more accountable for their actions after years of allegations of police misconduct being dismissed for lack of corroborating evidence (Meyer, 2015), and that this increased accountability would result in a reorganisation of the power dynamics between police and the community.

DOI: 10.4324/9781003080909-8

Much of discussion around this new regime of visibility has focused on the power of the technology itself—the portable video camera embedded into nearly every cell phone sold today—to 'reverse the gaze' (Sandhu & Haggerty, 2017: 80), creating what Manuel Castells (2007: 238) refers to as 'counter-power' (see also Monahan, 2006). Engineer and inventor Steve Mann (Mann et al., 2002; Mann & Ferenbok, 2013) has famously used the term *sousveillance* to describe the reversal of the gaze made possible by portable technologies such as cell phones and wearable cameras. *Sur*veillance, or 'veillance' from above, Mann argues, depends for its power upon being unobserved; sousveillance counters this power by making surveillance and those who practice it visible, and, crucially, by making them aware that they are visible. For Mann, this is a key difference between surveillance and sousveillance—while those involved in surveillance often seek to remain unobtrusive, those engaged in sousveillance derive much of their power from making their presence known with the aim not just of documenting abuses by authority figures, but of *preventing* them, based on the notion that the awareness of being visible inevitably alters people's behaviour (Brighenti, 2007; Foucault 1975; Thompson, 2005). The degree to which making police officers aware of their visibility actually makes them more accountable, however, is far from clear, as is dramatically illustrated by Officer Derek Chauvin's apparent impunity before the witnesses gathered to watch his murder of George Floyd, including the electronic witness of Darnella Frazier's cell phone camera.

One reason for this uncertainty is that technologies of visibility are, as surveillance scholar David Lyon's (2001) puts it, 'Janus faced,' able to be used for a range of different purposes with a range of different effects. How these technologies are used depends on the interactional contexts into which they are deployed and the ways their deployment alters those interactional contexts. In other words, the camera itself does not confer power on the witness using it; rather it constitutes just one of a range of different tools with which people can negotiate power in interactions with police. As Bock (2016: 15) argues, 'most scholarship [on citizens' use of cameras], so far, has focused on the technology and texts rather than grounded practices,' resulting in an 'impoverished' analysis (see also Allan, 2013). In contrast, Bock urges us to focus on these technologically mediated interactions between citizens and police as *embodied* practices which unfold over time, an approach in line with Brighenti's (2007: 323) call for increased attention to 'the relational, strategic and processual aspects of visibility.'

From this perspective, technologies are seen not as causing accountability, but as part and parcel of the 'material orderings in which the production and consumption of accounts is instantiated' (Neyland & Coopmans, 2014: 4), and accountability itself is seen not an inevitable by-product of visibility, but as a dynamic and contingent interactional accomplishment, something that needs to be continually negotiated over the course of citizens' encounters with police. It might be better to think of these negotiations in terms of what

Ericson (1995) calls 'account-ability': the capacity of different parties to create credible accounts of their activities (and elicit accounts from others) using whatever means are available to them (including what Garfinkel [1967: 1] calls 'situated practices of looking and telling').

Account-ability, says Ericson, always involves strategies of disclosure and concealment, selection and distortion, a point Goffman (1959) makes more generally about public performances of the self. More importantly, account-ability is always a matter of negotiating and organising the roles and responsibilities associated with looking and telling afforded to the different parties in the interaction, including interlocutors, involved third parties, uninvolved witnesses, and other present and non-present audiences, roles and responsibilities which Neyland & Coopmans (2014: 2) refer to as 'accountability relations.' Finally, such negotiations rest on a foundation of normativity: The relationship between visibility and accountability is always, as Goldsmith (2010) points out, predicated on participants' ability to maintain 'normal appearances' (Goffman, 1971) and 'proper performances' (Goffman 1959). This, of course, brings to the fore questions about what counts as 'normal' and 'proper' for particular kinds of people in particular situations, and how people act on their assumptions about normativity. To some degree, the very act of citizens videoing police officers already constitutes a *disruption* of normative relations of power and accountability. At the same time, it is clear that different police officers in different circumstances manage such disruptions differently, sometimes even exploiting them for their own advantages, and different citizens in different circumstances are viewed as (potentially) more disruptive than others.

In this more dynamic interactional approach to the role of video cameras in encounters between citizens and police, the important question, then, is not whether or not cameras make police more accountable, but how police and citizens *use* cameras (along with other mediational means such as speech, gesture, and aspects of the built environment) to identify 'relevant audiences for the discharge of accountability' (Neyland & Coopmans, 2014: 4; see also Neyland & Woolgar, 2002) and to *manage* visibility and its impact on the distribution of power and the possibility for action (Fyfe & Law, 1988).

Empirical studies of the ways police respond to citizens videoing them reveal a range of different strategies for managing visibility. Sometimes officers attempt to get people to stop recording them, often appealing to some nebulous law or regulation that prohibits it (see Example 1 below), and even going so far as forcing them to delete footage or confiscating their cell phones (Potere, 2012; Wilkinson & Glazer, 2016). When police do allow themselves to be recorded, many report that they alter their behaviour based on how they think they might appear to those viewing the video footage later on, and they sometimes express frustration with the degree to which the presence of cameras changes the interpersonal dynamics between them and citizens and more generally 'alter[s] the interactional context of policing' (Sandhu & Haggerty, 2017: 83; see also Brown, 2016; Kapok, 2014).

Sometimes, however, officers see the presence of cameras as potentially beneficial and engage in strategies such as pointing cameras out to interlocutors as a way to try to control their behaviour (Goold, 2003; Sandhu & Haggerty, 2017) or producing utterances designed to shape how audiences might interpret the footage. Haggerty and Sandhu (2014: 12), for example, describe how police officers are trained to repeatedly shout 'stop resisting arrest' when subduing suspects with batons in order to frame the use of force as justified. An important point made by Sandhu and Haggerty (2017), based on their field observations and interviews with officers, is that none of these strategies are used consistently by particular officers; rather, officers tend to choose strategies that they think match particular situations, particular kinds of interlocutors, and particular contexts of policing.

Studies focusing on citizens have found similar attention to the strategic, negotiated dimensions of videoing police officers. Rather than seeing their cameras as objective witnesses to events, citizens use them both as ways to actively make visible particular aspects of what is occurring and as tools with which to negotiate interactional power with police. Bock (2016) argues, based on her fieldwork with activists involved in monitoring the police, that 'cop watching' is a form of 'purposeful witnessing' (p. 14) and 'embodied watching' (p. 26) in which the way participants manage their physical presence on the scene is just as important as the videos they later share over social media. Part of this involves using strategies that produce 'hailing effects' (Neyland & Coopmans, 2014; see also Munro 2004), gestures that function to call people to account and constrain the ways they are able to control situations. Given the suspicion with which police often view people who are recording them, videoing the police always, to some degree, involves citizens negotiating their 'right to look,' which is, to some extent, a matter of asserting their 'legal right' to monitor the police and being prepared to marshal evidence to defend that right (which is why cop watching organisations often arm their members with detailed information about the laws on videoing police in particular jurisdictions). But the 'right to look' is not just a legal right – it is, more importantly, an *interactional right* that needs to be negotiated moment by moment in encounters with authority figures, regardless of what the law says.

On one hand, negotiating the 'right to look' depends upon who is doing the looking, who is being looked at, and how the roles of spectator and spectacle are distributed throughout the interaction, that is, what Neyland & Coopmans (2014: 4) refer to as identifying and managing 'relevant audiences for the discharge of accountability.' On the other hand, it also depends on the 'situated practices of looking and telling' (Garfinkel, 1967: 1) by which people produce *accounts* of their ongoing behaviour and make others accountable for theirs. But the 'right to look' is also a matter of *epistemic* positioning — the right to assert that 'what you see' is 'real.' Mirzoeff (2011: 1) claims that the 'right to look' is not just about claiming a position of objectivity, but rather of asserting ones right to a subjectivity that 'has the autonomy to *arrange the relations of the visible and the sayable*' (emphasis mine).

In this paper I will explore how the 'right to look' is interactionally negotiated in sousveillance situations involving citizens and police using tools from interactional sociolinguistics and ethnomethodology. The data for this analysis is two videos uploaded onto YouTube by citizens involved in encounters with the police. As I will show in my analysis, the 'right to look' does not derive solely from the technological means to record the police nor the 'legal right' to deploy these means, but rather is the result of a complex range of discursive strategies that citizens and officers engage in at the intersection of the micro-history of a particular interaction and societal macro-histories of power, identity and race.

Audiences and accounts

Discussion of how people manage audiences in interactions from a sociolinguistic perspective usually begin with Bell's (1984) important insight that people design their utterances based on the kinds of people they think are listening, and simultaneously use their utterances to 'design' audiences as particular kinds of listeners and define situations as particular kinds of situations. The ways people alter their utterances for particular audiences, according to Bell, applies to all levels of language, including phonology, lexis, and grammar, and others have extended this to include broader discursive features of communication such as politeness strategies (Brown & Levinson, 1987), pragmatic particles (Holmes, 1995), gesture (Galati & Brennan, 2014), and other forms of non-verbal communication such as dress and hairstyle (Giles & Wadleigh, 1999).

Bell's model of audience design builds upon the theory of communication accommodation advanced by Giles (Giles & Smith, 1979; Giles et al., 1972), which emphasises that language is not just a matter of exchanging information but also of negotiating group membership: in social interaction people adjust how they speak, converging to the style of those they want to identify with and diverging from those they wish to distance themselves from. Apropos to the current discussion, one of the main contexts in which Giles tested and refined this theory was in interactions between citizens and police in the form of traffic stops. In such encounters, Giles (2009) observes, both officers and citizens tend to manage the interaction by accommodating to each other's communicative styles, the driver, being less powerful, usually being under more pressure to converge than the officer. The challenges for police offices and citizens in such cases, he says, is to balance being non-accommodative, which might encourage aggression, with being too accommodative, which might seem insincere or encourage complacency.

But such negotiations do not occur in a vacuum; in other studies Giles and is colleagues found that the degree to which drivers accommodate to officers is related to how much they trust them, and trust in law enforcement, not surprisingly, was found to be related to drivers' ethnicity and past experiences with police (Dixon et al., 2008; Giles et al., 2006; Hajek et al., 2006). In particular, they found that the race of individuals involved in traffic stops seemed to have an effect on the ways the parties designed their utterances and managed mutual accommodation, with people using language and non-verbal behaviour to position others in particular recipient roles in relation to specific reference groups based on personal or societal biases. Giles and his colleagues (Anderson et al., 2002: 21) point to social identity theory (Tajfel & Turner, 1986) to explain these effects, noting that when people deal with each other as members of social groups rather than as individuals, it is more likely for them to differentiate from each other rather than accommodate, especially 'when the intergroup identities are embedded in their own longstanding "cultures" ... be they gang, ethnic group, police community, etc.' (p. 21). While such differentiations are rational tactics for enhancing positive identitiy, the creation of communicative distance can also lead to 'misattribution, miscommunication, or even worse' (p. 25).

These negotiations are even more complex when more than just two parties are involved, i.e. multiple officers or multiple citizens. Giles (2009), for instance, discusses how the presence of third parties (for example, friends of the driver sitting in the car) can complicate the situation, putting drivers in a kind of stylistic bind, having to perform both for the officer and for their friends, who in some cases might think less of them for being too accommodative to authority–'while the officer clearly has the most power and the driver is under more pressure to converge than the officer,' writes Giles (2009: 281), 'if the driver does converge, members of her group who overhear might perceive her as a social traitor.'

Bell (1984) calls this phenomenon the 'auditor effect.' It arises from the fact that audiences are often multiple: apart from the person one is addressing, there might also be third party hearers with different roles in the interaction, different rights when' it comes to listening, and different effects on how people talk. Bell, drawing Goffman's concept of 'participation frameworks' (1981), conceives of these other audience members positioned in concentric circles radiating out from the speaker, going from addressee, to auditor, to overhearer, and finally, eavesdropper, each having a different degree of 'legitimacy' in terms of their participation in the primary interaction. In speaking of the 'auditor effect,' the kind of hearers that Bell was most interested in were 'auditors,' people who are not being addressed but are legitimately listening. Citing a range of previous studies (e.g. Douglas-Cowie, 1978; Thelander, 1982), he concludes that auditors can have a profound effect on the way people 'style' their utterances, an assertion that has been confirmed in subsequent studies (e.g. Rickford & McNair-Knox, 1994). People more removed from the interaction, overhearers with less legitimate roles in the interaction, Bell posits, have less of an effect, and eavesdroppers have none at all, since speakers are not aware of their presence.

Others have noted that the auditor effect is not just a matter of style, but also a matter of pragmatics. Hearers positioned in different participant roles can interpret the illocutionary force of utterances differently, and speakers can use this to their advantage. Clark and Schaefer (1992: 281) illustrate this with an example invented by Searle (1969) in which a wife at a party says to the host in the presence of her husband 'It's really quite late.' This single utterances might be heard as an apology by the host and as a request (to be taken home) by the husband, in which case, the husband is positioned as auditor of the apology and the host is positioned as auditor of the request, with each of them likely aware of how the other is hearing the utterance.

Increasingly, however, as in the case of citizens using cell phones to record their encounters with police, the actual auditors of interactions are not physically present, and who they are and what they might think can only be a matter of conjecture. The immediate auditors are the cell phones themselves. There have also been studies, of course, showing how speakers alter their speech when they know they are being recorded. Gordon (2013), for instance, has written about how participants in linguistics research sometimes orient to tape recorders as overhearers, and Haworth (2013) has studied how police officers in interrogations design their utterances both for their immediate interlocutors and for future audiences in courtrooms that might be listening to tape recordings of them. Where the phenomenon of citizens wielding cell phone cameras in their interactions with police differs both from situations considered by Bell (where auditors are conceived of as secondary 'presences' fortuitously introduced into encounters), and from situations where tape recorders or video cameras are more or less static electronic 'presences' (which audit interactions in the 'background'), is that citizens in police encounters *actively deploy* their devices as interactional resources, using them to manipulate the degree of awareness officers have of being audited and the role these electronic auditors have in the interaction. Because of the control citizens have over where to point their cameras and what to do and say when they are pointing them, cell phones (and the imagined audiences behind them) can be positioned in various participant roles, sometimes as addressees, sometimes as auditors, sometimes as overhearers, and sometimes as eavesdroppers, and the different participant roles cameras inhabit can affect the ways police officers (and citizens) can be called upon to account for their actions.

The presence of auditors in interactions alter not just the way people design their utterances, but, more generally, how they are made *accountable* for what they do and say, and how they manage this accountability. Being accountable, however, does not depend on the presence of an auditor. As Garfinkel (1967) has pointed out, people's ability to account for their words and actions and communicate how they are making sense of others' words and actions is the basis for all social interaction. Accountability, from this perspective, is not just a matter of coming to a mutual understanding of what is 'acceptable behaviour' in certain kinds of situations, but develops dynamically within and as part of social situations. It is also not just a matter of language, but includes all of the physical ways people make aspects of the situation *observable* and *reportable* (Garfinkel, 1967).

The presence of cameras alters what I have called (Jones, 2020: 90) the 'infrastructures of accountability' in encounters between citizens and police in at least three ways. First, as I said above, it provides opportunities for those wielding cameras to change the participation framework of the interaction, visibly introducing into the situation additional participants to whom officers and citizens are responsible for producing accounts. Second, it alters the organisation of perception in the situation, giving those wielding cameras and those whose actions are being recorded new opportunities for making certain aspects of what's going on visible, and thus, meaningful. Finally, and perhaps most importantly, it provides ways for both parties to communicate *to each other* what aspects of the situation are subject to being accounted for – that is, what aspects of the situation 'count.'

While these infrastructures of accountability are constructed moment by moment by participants as they negotiate their rights and responsibilities around looking and telling at different points in the interaction, they are built upon a foundation of social relationships that inevitably involve historically sedimented forms of inequality and sets of expectations about who has the right to look and who has the right to be seen in different kinds of circumstances, and it is often these regimes of power and visibility that are responsible for how particular interactions came to occur in the first place (e.g. why a particular driver got pulled over), and what the consequences of the interaction will be after it is finished (e.g. whether or not the citizen – or the officer – will face criminal charges).

Example 1: 'It's my right'

The first example[1] involves an attorney – moonlighting as a Uber driver – who was pulled over by officers from the Wilmington, North Carolina Police Department and the New Hanover County Sheriff's Office on the afternoon of February 26, 2017. The driver, Jesse Bright, was transporting a passenger who had visited an address in a supposedly 'high crime' neighbourhood and was returning home. Upon being stopped, Bright was informed that his passenger was being arrested, at which point he began videoing the proceedings with his cell phone camera. This prompted one of the officers, Sergeant Kenneth Becker, to ask him to stop videoing, resulting in an extended argument between Bright and the officers, who insisted that videoing them was 'against the law' (Schachtman, 2017).

As I mentioned in the previous section, cell phone cameras are very different from fixed recording devices (e.g. closed-circuit TV (CCTV) cameras) in that they allow users to actively and flexibly deploy them as interactional resources, changing what is being monitored by changing the direction in which they are pointed. In other words, the camera can be made visible as auditing the officer, the citizen, or other aspects of the scene, thereby altering

178 *Rodney H. Jones*

Figure 8.1 Excerpt 1: Camera as addressee 1.

moment by moment the ways citizens and officers are called upon to orient to the camera as an auditor.

Although we usually think of the practice of 'filming the cops' as a matter of making visible what police officers are doing, for most of this video the driver trains the camera not on the police officers, but on himself as he narrates what is happening. The video begins, for example, with the driver explaining to the camera that he as been stopped and his passenger is being arrested, briefly turning the camera outward to capture the scene, as if to provide evidence for his statement, before returning it to his own face (Excerpt 1).

The purpose of the driver directly narrating what is occurring rather than simply pointing the camera at the police and providing the non-present audience with a more 'objective' version of events, of course, is that it allows the driver to control what Mirzoeff (2011: 1) refers to as the relationship between the 'seeable and the sayable,' presenting a verbal account of the

Auditor design and accountability 179

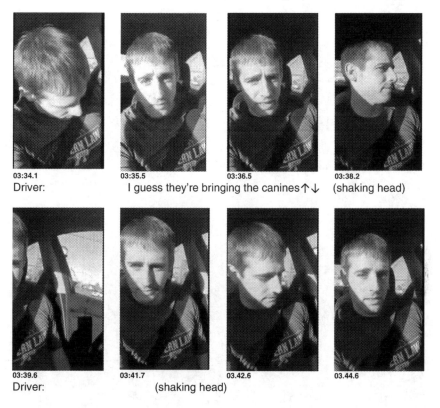

Figure 8.2 Excerpt 2: Camera as addressee 2.

situation and choosing what aspects of the situation to make visible in order to confirm that account. In this way, the driver is able to provide both an account and an *evaluation* of the situation, which is sometimes expressed in words, but more often is communicated through facial expressions and gestures (such as headshaking and eye-rolling) as in Excerpt 2.

Another important affordance for the diver in directly addressing the camera is that it creates intimacy with the non-present audience, who is invited to experience the incident from the driver's point of view – not just 'as it is happening,' but 'as it is happening *to* the driver.' In this regard, the camera is positioned not just as an addressee, but as a confidant and ally.

Finally, by carrying on a conversation with the non-present audience, the driver positions the officers as *overhearers* of a conversation which is, to a large extent, being performed for their benefit. The message such performances potentially send is twofold: First of all, they highlight for officers the presence of the electronic auditor, and second they make clear to them that they are being excluded from the production of an account of the incident.

180   *Rodney H. Jones*

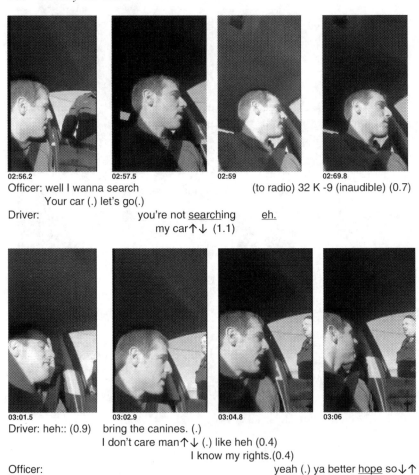

Figure 8.3 Excerpt 3: Driver as overhearer.

Of course, officers also have means of positioning drivers as overhearers by performing conversations with other officers, or with non-present participants through electronic devices of their own. In Excerpt 3, for instance, in response to the driver refusing to allow officers to search his car, the officer conspicuously calls for a K-9 unit[2] to be deployed to the scene.

Another important way the driver uses his camera is as a pragmatic means, a tool for producing a range of different kinds of 'speech acts' such as warnings and assertions. In this video this tactic is particularly evident at the point in the interaction when the officer asks the driver *not* to record him (Excerpt 4), at which point the driver momentarily keeps the camera focused on himself, turning his head as if addressing an interruption from a

Auditor design and accountability 181

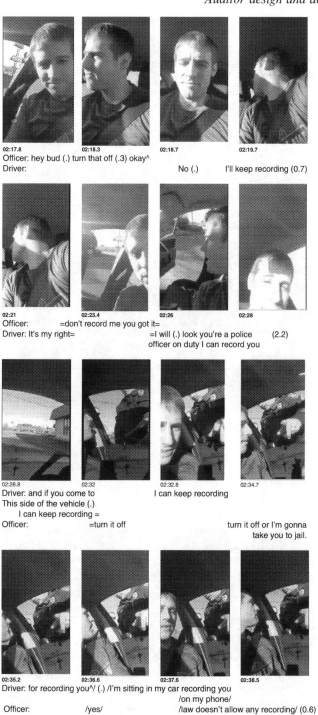

Figure 8.4 Excerpt 4: 'I'll keep recording…it's my right.'

182 *Rodney H. Jones*

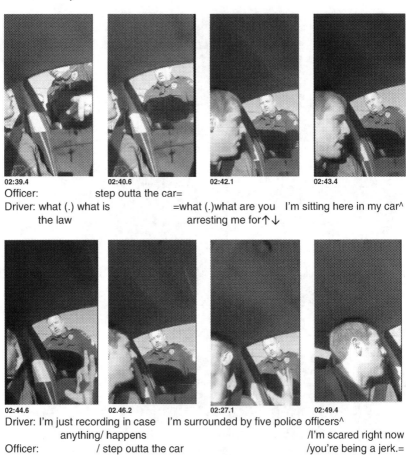

Figure 8.5 Excerpt 5: Non-accommodation.

bystander, and then turns his camera to focus on the officer, tracking his movements from the passenger side of the vehicle to the driver side, narrating his own actions as he does so, saying: 'I can record you...and if you come to this side of the vehicle I can keep recording.'

In this exchange, both the driver and the officer produce justifications for their actions, the driver asserting his 'right' to record a 'police officer on duty,' and the officer claiming (falsely) that it's against the law. What is more important than these conflicting justifications is the lack of accommodation between the two parties, with the officer issuing bald, on record directives using a casual form of address ('hey bud, turn that off,' 'step outta the car'), as well as a threat ('turn it off or I'm gonna take you to jail'), and the driver conspicuously refusing to comply and calling on the officer to account for his actions ('what is the law?', 'what are you arresting me for?').

Auditor design and accountability 183

It is important to remember that such interactions, at least from the point of view of the driver, who is controlling the camera, are also designed as *performances* for the non-present audience. And so the accounts that the driver gives in Excerpt 5 (e.g. 'I'm surrounded by five police officers...I'm scared right now'), and that the officer gives (e.g. 'you're being a jerk') are intended both as responses to their interlocuter's challenges and as framing devices designed to shape the way the non-present auditor might see the situation.

The driver's ongoing consciousness of the auditor and ongoing positioning of the auditor as an ally in his dispute with authority figures is evident in his subsequent staging of performances designed to provoke the officers, to call them to account for both present actions and past statements, and to position himself as the 'reasonable' party in the dispute. In Excerpt 6, for example, the driver makes a point of asking the officer for permission to take a drink – despite the fact that there have been no demands for him restrict his movements inside the car (as there are in the second example below) – and then turns conspicuously to the camera with a slight smirk.

This performative dimension of this encounter is particularly evident in Excerpt 7, where the driver calls upon another officer to account for the pervious officer's insistence that recoding the police is against the law ('can you tell me what this new law is...'). By doing this, the driver puts the second officer in a rhetorical bind, making him choose between contradicting his colleague or supporting him with what he probably knows is a lie. At first, he attempts to deflect the responsibility for accounting for the law to the driver, saying, 'you said you are an attorney, is that correct?' But after the driver continues to press for details about the 'new' law, the officer chooses to lie: '[they've] recently just passed it sir.' Throughout this encounter the driver performs his scepticism through both his tone of voice and his choice

05:23.7 05:24.4 05:25.5 05:26.8
Driver: is it okay with you if I drink my Powerade^ (0.7)
Officer2: °yeah°

Figure 8.6 Excerpt 6: Powerade.

184 *Rodney H. Jones*

Figure 8.7 Excerpt 7: 'Seems like a strange law.'

of words, and he ends the conversation by turning back to face the camera and saying 'seems like a strange law,' as if offering to the non-present audience an evaluation of the veracity of the officer's utterance.

In his encounters with these first two officers, the driver effectively uses his camera as an interactional resource to assert his legal rights and to position them as behaving unreasonably. Later in the video, however, an apparently more senior officer, uses a different strategy with the driver, one that is not just more accommodative, but also more sensitive to the presence of the electronic auditor (Excerpt 8).

This excerpt begins with the officer approaching the driver and addressing him as 'Mr. Bright,' a strategy that both communicates respect and calls the driver to account. Interestingly, the driver immediately answers by addressing the officer by his name – 'Mr. St. Pierre' – which he apparently has read off of the officer's badge, a move which both accommodates to the officer's new, more respectful tone and reminds the officer that he too is being held to account for his behaviour. In the conversation that follows the officer attempts to account for the driver having been stopped with a series of questions ('how long have you been an Uber driver?', 'have you been stopped a lot?') which create the implication that the stop was justified. He then explains to him why the K-9 unit has been called and the procedures that will be followed before the driver can be 'on his way.' This explicit account from the officer for what is being done is delivered with a degree of professionalism not evident in the earlier encounters and results in the driver reciprocating by offering his own account of his behaviour, explaining his fear that he might be blamed for something his passenger left in the car and asking the officer, 'can you understand my frustration?' What is striking about the officer's responses during this exchange is the way he uses metalanguage to create a clear consensus with the driver about exactly what he has said and what he has not said ('I never said that, did I?', 'I asked you a simple question,' 'Negative, sir, I've never said that to you'), a consensus which the officer, of course, knows will be recorded by the driver's cell phone. Another important difference between this exchange and the earlier exchanges with the other officers is that the driver does not turn to look at the camera once, instead orienting his gaze towards the officer the entire time and even appearing to be holding the phone at a lower, less obtrusive angle. In other words, rather than being used as a tool to challenge or exclude the officer, the camera is positioned more as an objective witness, one to whom the officer has an equal opportunity to appeal with his own account of the situation.

Example 2: 'Look at this'

The second example involves two African American brothers, Benjamin and Ryan Brown, who, were pulled over by officers of the Colorado Springs Police Force on March 25, 2015 while driving through a predominantly

186 *Rodney H. Jones*

Officer 3: mister Bright.=   = how long you been an Uber/ driver   /yeah/
Driver: yes=   /mister St. Pierre(.) a year and
                                  half^ two /years/ maybe^ (0.4)

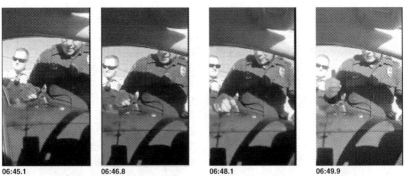

Officer 3: this (.) uh heh have you been <u>stop</u>ped a lot ↓↑ that's
         probably why you've been stopped because you're an Uber driver^
            alright cause there's a lotta <u>his</u>tory on the vehicle (0.6)

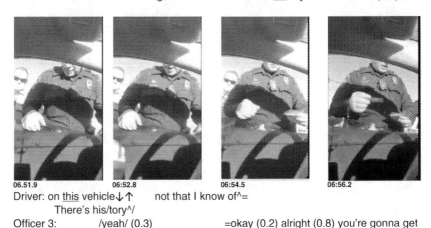

Driver: on <u>this</u> vehicle↓↑   not that I know of^=
       There's his/tory^/
Officer 3:   /yeah/ (0.3)   =okay (0.2) alright (0.8) you're gonna get
                                  your license^ (.) we're gonna wait (.) for a (0.4)

Figure 8.8 Excerpt 8: 'I've never said that to you.'

Auditor design and accountability 187

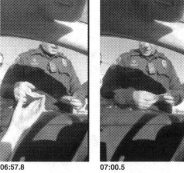 

| 06:57.8 | 07:00.5 | 07:02.5 | 07:04.6 |

Officer 3: canine (.) cause I don't know if he   so we're just gonna have a canine come
mighta dumped something under   out and smell^ (0.5) and if
your seat^ (.) n you don' want us to look^ (0.5)   they do an indication^

| 07:06.4 | 07:07.7 | 07:09.1 | 07:10.9 |

Officer 3: if not↑↓(.) then you'll be on   /okay but it's^ (.)
            your way okay sir^=
Driver: =okay (.) I mean if he threw somethin under the
                                it still (.) it has nothin to do with me. (.) /like^

| 07:12.5 | 07:14.2 | 07:16.2 | 07:17.5 |

Officer 3: I'm not saying it has anything to   I (.) I never said that (.) /I asked you a
            do with you (.) sir ↓↑ (0.6)   did I^ (0.6)   simple question/
Driver: no I/ I feel like some/thing's
                                                                     gonna be under the car

Figure 8.8 (*continued*)

188 *Rodney H. Jones*

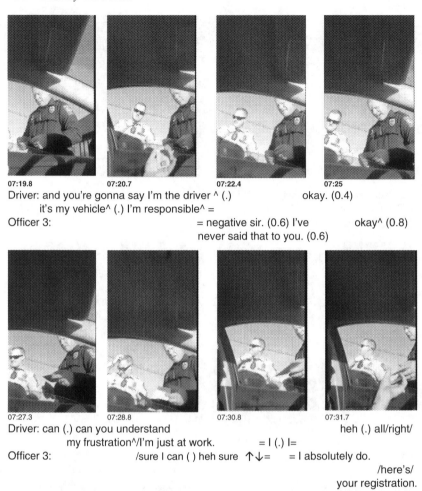

Figure 8.8 (*continued*)

white neighbourhood, ostensibly for driving with a cracked windshield. The driver, Benjamin, was immediately asked to exit the vehicle and was placed in handcuffs, prompting his brother, Ryan, to begin videoing the encounter from the passenger seat. In the moments that followed, Ryan repeatedly asked the officers to explain why they were 'being arrested' in response to officers' requests that he produce his ID and exit the vehicle. The officers finally opened the passenger door, pulled him out of the car and wrestled him to the ground, all of which was captured on the video. Later Benjamin Brown was charged with driving with an obstructed view and Ryan with obstructing and resisting police officers (Roberts, 2015). The video can be viewed at: https://youtu.be/pb4DH4P-7yI.

Table 8.1 Excerpt 9: 'I've got this on camera'

Time	Transcript	Video/Camera angle
00:02	Passenger: what's the reason why you pulled us over officer ↓↑ (0.9) I'm recording this.(.)	Passenger's face (full frontal)
00:06	uh (.) police officer^ (0.4)	Side view of passenger's face
00:07	police officer's pulled us over for no rea/son ↓↑ (0.4) Officer 1: /(inaudible)/	Window with police officer visible outside
00:10	Passenger: I've got this on /camera^Officer 1: /do you have your ID^=	(Camera tilted to landscape view) Passenger's face, window with officer outside visible behind his shoulder
00:13	Passenger: =I have my camera (.) I have my ID and I'm recording this. (.) just to let	Side view of passenger's face
00:15	Passenger: /you know Officer 1: /okay I'd like you pass me your ID please	Front view of passenger's face

While in the video analysed above, the driver did not at first explicitly alert the officers to the fact that he was recording or assert his right to do so until an officer actually told him to stop, in this example the driver calls attention to the fact that he is recording immediately and repeatedly ('I'm recording this,' 'I've got this on camera,' 'I have my camera … and I'm recording this, just to let you know'), using his camera as a means to deliver a warning to the officers that they are being audited and thus, presumably, will be held accountable for their actions (Excerpt 9).

During this exchange, the driver alternates between addressing the officers in ways that demand that they account for their actions ('what is the reason why you pulled us over officer'), and addressing the camera with his own interpretation of the situation ('police officers pulled us over for no reason'). As in the first example, the utterances directed at the officers are designed also to be overheard by the camera, and the words directed towards the camera are designed to be overheard by the officers.

While the camera is, for the passenger, a 'weapon' of sorts, pointed at police in order to constrain their behaviour, police are able to deploy their own (more literal) weapons, in this case, a taser which one officer points in the direction of the passenger window (Excerpt 10). Rather than responding directly to this threat, however, the passenger continues to gaze in the direction of the camera and produces his own account of the officer's actions ('I'm … bein perceived as a threat'), while at the same time displaying for the camera his stationary, non-threatening body.

The last excerpt highlights the fact that often in encounters with police it is as much in the citizen's interest to document their own behaviour as it is to

190   Rodney H. Jones

Table 8.2 Excerpt 10: 'I'm being perceived as a threat'

Time	Transcript	Video/Camera angle
01:01	Passenger: now I'm up per uh (.) bein' perceived as a threat↓↑ (0.1) because () we're bein' pulled over for absolutely no reason^	Passenger's face; window with officer outside visible behind his shoulder; officer pointing taser towards window

Table 8.3 Excerpt 11: 'My hands are visible'

Time	Transcript	Video/Camera angle
00:17	Officer 2: and keep your hands where I can/ see them Passenger: /am I (.) am I under arrest^ you failed to identify yourselves so^ I (0.3) I don't know who you are.	Window behind passenger's shoulder
00:22	Officer 2: (0.4) sir(.) you know I'm a police officer of the city of Colorado Springs^	Passenger's face, oblique angle
00:25	Passenger: you failed to/identify yourself↑ Officer 2: /(inaudible) you need to cooperate I just need your ID now^ (1.0)	Passenger's face, frontal
00:30	Passenger: you failed to identify yourself↑ ↓ (0.9)	Camera moves up and to the left
00:32	Passenger: my hands are(.)are visible↓↑ (1.0)	Passenger's left hand held halfway up

document the behaviour of the authorities in order to refute any possible later claims that they were acting improperly. This can also be seen in Excerpt 11, where, in response to the officer's directive 'keep your hands were I can see them' the passenger both produces a verbal confirmation ('my hands are visible') and turns his camera to *document* the visibility of his hands.

At the same time, the passenger also uses this opportunity to provide for the implied audience a broader perspective on the situation, directing the camera through the open driver side door where his brother can be seen being handcuffed (Excerpt 12), all the while narrating the situation: ('My brother is being put in handcuffs,' 'We're being pulled over for no reason,' 'He still had not identified why he pulled us over').

Slightly over a minute after the passenger starts recording the interaction, one of the officers opens the passenger door, unbuckles Brown's shoulder strap, and begins to pull him out of the vehicle (Excerpt 13). As this is happening, the passenger directs the camera at the officer who is pulling his arms and continually asks the officer to explain why he and his brother have been pulled over, why he is being arrested, and why he is being pulled out of his car. He manages to continue filming as two officers wrestle him to the

Table 8.4 Excerpt 12: 'My brother is being put in handcuffs'

Time	Transcript	Video/Camera angle
00:36	Passenger: I have the recorder recording^ (1.6)	Passenger's torso with his left had held out
00:39	Passenger: my brother is being han (.) put in handcuffs^	Driver's side of car with passenger's brother visible outside open car door
00:41	Passenger: Passenger: we're being pulled over for no reason↓↑ (1.4) he still (.) had not identified	Officer searching passenger's brother, who is in handcuffs
00:47	Passenger: why he's pulled us over^	Camera moves back to passenger's face

ground and press his face into the pavement, and, right before one of the officers reaches over to take the phone out of his hand, he looks into the camera and says, 'You see this? Excessive force.'

As in the other excerpts from this video, the passenger alternates between positioning the camera as an addressee and positioning it as a witness to what is being done to him. But even when he is not providing commentary directly to the camera, he designs his utterances to the police officers in a way that both provides an ongoing narration of what is happening and calls upon officers to account for their actions ('Am I being placed under arrest?', 'Why are you pulling me out of my car?', 'I have no weapons, you have no reason to pull me out of the car'). What is perhaps most striking about this excerpt is the counter narrative that the police articulate as this is going on, saying 'you're not under arrest' and 'I'm *not* pulling you,' even as the officer visibly pulls on the passenger's arm. This verbal 'counter-account' of events, which contradicts both the passenger's narrative and what appears to be actually happening, is reminiscent of Haggerty and Sandhu's (2014: 12) example of police officers shouting 'stop resisting arrest' while beating citizens with their batons. It highlights the fact that the 'right to look' and to call someone to account depends not just on what the camera sees, but also on who can claim the right to interpret what is happening, or as Mirzoeff (2011:1) puts it, who can claim 'the right to arrange the relationship between the seeable and the sayable.'

Discussion and conclusion

Taken together, these two examples highlight a number of common strategies citizens use when deploying video cameras in their encounters with police officers. Perhaps one of the most interesting things to note is how, in both of the videos, the citizens train their cameras *on themselves* much more than on the police. At first this might seem counter-intuitive. In fact, most cop watching organisations advise third parties who are videoing police

192 Rodney H. Jones

Table 8.5 Excerpt 13: 'You see this'

Time	Transcript	Video/Camera angle
01:17	Passenger: am I↑↓am (.) bein' placed under arrest ^ (0.6) Officer 3: you're not underarrest/ (several officers talking at once) Passenger: /what's the I'm (.) I'm	Passenger's right arm, shoulder and lower part of his face; car door opens and officer's arm reaches in
01:24	Passenger: I'm / asking::^ Officer 3: /you're not under arrest= Passenger: =I'm asking for the reason	Close-up of officer's hand grabbing passenger's arm
01:26	Passenger: why we're bein' pulled over. (0.3) you have still failed to identify why you've /pulled us over ↓↑ Officer 2: /(inaudible)	Officer pulling passenger by arm with one hand and by the neck of his sweatshirt with the other
01:31	Officer 2: I'm not pullin' you (.)/youPassenger: /you (inaudible)= Officer 2: =come on out. Passenger: why are you pulling me out ofmy /car↑↓ Officer 2: /I'm not (inaudible) Passenger: sir^ take your hands off of me↓↑	Officer puling passenger by his right arm with both hands
01:39	Officer 2: no you're/ (inaudible) Passenger: /I have not did nothin'↓↑= Officer 3: = (inaudible)	Officer pulling passenger by his right arm and the neck of his sweatshirt
01:43	Passenger: /I have no weapons↓↑(0.2) you have no reason to pull me out of the car↓↑	Close-up of passenger's shoulder
01:47	Passenger: (0.3) this is assault↓↑= Officer 3: = turn around^ (.) turn around^ (0.6)	Officer pulling passenger by the arm
01:49	Officer 3: get down↑↓ (0.9) Officer 2: flat on the/ground Passenger: /you see this↑↓	Camera pointed to the ground
01:52	Passenger: you see this. (0.5)	Officer above passenger, who has been pushed to the ground
01:54	Passenger: excessive force↓↑	Close-up of passenger's face being pushed into the ground

encounters to *avoid* filming the person being stopped and focus exclusively on the officers. A perspective which takes into account the role of audience/ auditor design and the importance of producing and eliciting credible accounts, however, helps to explain citizens' penchant for filming themselves.

Of course, the most obvious advantage for citizens to film themselves is to create a document of their own behaviour to counter future possible accusations of aggression or illegality, a strategy that is particularly clear in the second example. Equally important, though, is the fact that, by positioning the camera as an *addressee* and producing for it a verbal account of the goings on, citizens are able to take control of how what is happening might later be interpreted. It also gives them the opportunity to strategically position the non-present audience either as allies (as in the first example) or as witnesses (as in the second example), and to position themselves as victims by depicting not just what is being done by the police, but what is being done *to them*. Finally, interacting with the camera as an addressee also gives citizens the opportunity to produce conversations designed to be *overheard* by officers, potentially heightening their sense of being both scrutinized and excluded. These observations point more broadly to the fact that one of the main strategic functions of the camera is, as Neyland & Coopmans (2014: 4) put it, to identify 'relevant audiences for the discharge of accountability,' *and* to position those audiences in participant roles that help to support particualr versions of events.

At the same time, of course, the camera is also used to document the actions of the police, and this is done by selectively pointing the camera at officers or panning to provide a broader perspective of the scene. The main advantage here is that the citizen's control of the camera gives them control over what aspects of the situation are *observable* and *reportable* (Garfinkel, 1967). Pointing the camera outward, however, is also a communicative gesture through which citizens can direct 'speech acts' such as 'warnings' towards officers which are designed to constrain the range of action officers can take and signal to them that they are accountable for those actions.

The most important moments in these encounters, however, seem to be those when both citizens and officers are subjects of the camera's gaze and performing their interaction for the auditor, each designing their utterances in order to elicit certain kinds of verbal accounts from the other party, and each designing their accounts to be both heard (by their interlocuter) and overheard by the non-present auditor. It is in these memoments when citizens and officers directly negotiate the relationship between 'the seeable and the sayable,' that is, between what is made observable in the situation and whose account of it ends up counting.

Despite these similarities, there are also obvious differences between these two videos, not least of which is the fact that in one the citizen ends up going on his way after a bit of inconvenience while in the other the citizen ends up with his face planted in the pavement. The important thing to note, in this regard, is that there is nothing in the ways these two citizens used the various strategies discussed above that can explain this disparity. Both asserted their right to video the encounter and wielded their cameras in similar ways designed to signal to the officers the presence of an 'auditor.' And both explicitly refused to comply with requests from the officers and called upon the officers to account for the legitimacy of these requests. The result of this was that one of the citizens (the African American one) ended up being perceived as a 'threat,' whereas the other was simply perceived as a 'jerk.'

The wildly different outcomes can only be explained by the different assumptions about accountability that participants must have brought to these interactions. Both citizens began with the same assumption: that police officers are accountable for informing citizens why they have been stopped and for abiding by certain constitutional restrictions regarding their behaviour towards citizens (restrictions, for example, on search and seizure and on detaining citizens without charging them). In other words, the officers bear the burden of making their intentions visible. The officers in these two cases, however, appear to have approached these two different citizens with very different assumptions about their accountability. At no point, for example, is the Caucasian driver ordered to keep his hands visible, whereas this is one of the first things the African American passenger is asked to do. It is clear, as well, that the passenger himself is well-aware of the assumptions being made about him, to the point that he feels the need to use us own camera to document the visibility of his own hands.

These different assumption about accountability and visibility play out particularly dramatically in the ways officers and citizens negotiate the relationship between the 'seeable and the sayable.' In the first example, the third officer and the driver are able to negotiate a consensus account of the situation, with the driver accepting the officer's justifications for deploying the K-9 unit and the officer acknowledging the driver's 'frustration.' In the second example, however, the passenger and the officers produce contradictory accounts, with the officers insisting that they are not doing things that they are clearly doing.

This last point highlights one of the main reasons why technologies like cell phone cameras are not sufficient to make police accountable for their actions. The ability to make something visible is not enough. One must also have the ability to speak about it, to produce an account which others will regard as legitimate, the power to manage the relationship between 'the seeable and the sayable.' And, as many African Americans who have filmed encounters with police, some of them more deadly than the one discussed here, know, this power is almost always afforded to the powerful – the police, their attorneys, the press and politicians – rather than to the victims or witnesses of police violence. As a result, video evidence of police violence against African Americans, going back to the Rodney King case in 1992, almost never result in serious consequences for the officers. As Beutin (2017: 17) puts it:

> As long as visual evidence of police brutality is interpreted through racialized ways of seeing, the practices of counter-surveillance and the discourse of filming the cops remain circumscribed within a larger cycle of repression that continues to reconfigure itself in ways that uphold the legitimacy of the police, and by extension, the racist state.

Citizen's encounters with police officers are moment by moment negotiations in which sometimes the presence of a cell phone camera can alter the infrastructures of accountability in the situation, changing the power dynamics between participants and constraining the range of actions available to them. At the same time, these encounters take place in the context of larger systems of inequality and injustice which inevitably place practical and discursive limitations on how certain kinds of citizens can use cameras to make police accountable.

This is perhaps what is behind the unrepentant gaze that Derek Chauvin directed towards Darnella Frazier's camera as he took the life of George Floyd, the comfortable assumption that no matter how 'seeable' his crime was, he and the apparatus of police power behind him would retain control over *how* it would be seen.

Notes

1 https://youtu.be/-UQKkYWDUQ4 (Screenshots used with permission of video owner)
2 Dogs trained to sniff out drugs and other contraband.

References

Allan, S. (2013). *Citizen witnessing*. Cambridge, England: Polity Press.
Anderson, M.C., Knutson, T. J., Giles, H., Arroyo, M., & Giles, H. (2002). Revoking our right to remain silent: Law enforcement communication in the 21st century. In H. Giles (ed.), *Law enforcement, communication, and community*, (pp.1–32). Amsterdam: John Benjamins.
Bock, M. A. (2016). Film the police! Cop-watching and its embodied narratives. *Journal of Communication 66*(1), 13–34.
Bell, A. (1984). Language style as audience design. *Language in Society* 13, 145–204.
Beutin, L. P. (2017). Racialization as a way of seeing: The limits of counter-surveillance and police reform. *Surveillance & Society 15*(1), 5–20.
Brighenti, A. (2007). Visibility: A category for the social sciences. *Current Sociology* 55(3), 323–342.
Brown, G. R. (2016). The blue line on thin ice: Police use of force modifications in the era of cameraphones and YouTube. *British Journal of Criminology* 56(2), 293–312.
Brown, P., & Levinson, S. C. (1987). *Politeness: Some universals in language usage*. Cambridge: Cambridge University Press.
Castells M (2007) Communication, power and counter-power in the network society. *International Journal of Communications* 1, 238–266.
Clark, H & Schaefer, E. (1992) Dealing with overhearers. In H. Clark (ed.), *Arenas of language use,* (pp. 248–273), Chicago: University of Chicago Press.
Dixon, T. L., Schell, T. L., Giles, H., & Drogos, K. L. (2008). The influence of race in police–civilian interactions: A content analysis of videotaped interactions taken during Cincinnati Police traffic stops. *Journal of Communication* 58(3), 530–549.
Douglas-Cowie, E. (1978). Linguistic code-switching in a Northern Irish village: Social interaction and social ambition. In P. Trudgill (ed.), *Sociolinguistic patterns in British English,* (pp. 37–51). London: Edward Arnold.

Ericson, R. (1995). The news media and account ability In P. Stenning (ed.) *Accountability for criminal justice: Selected essays* ,(pp. 135–162). Toronto: University of Toronto Press.

Foucault, M. (1975). *Discipline and punish: The birth of the prison*. New York: Random House.

Fyfe, G. and Law, J. (eds) (1988). *Picturing power: Visual depiction and social relations*. London: Routledge.

Galati, A., & Brennan, S. E. (2014). Speakers adapt gestures to addressees' knowledge: Implications for models of co-speech gesture. *Language, Cognition and Neuroscience* 29(4), 435–451.

Garfinkel, H. (1967). *Studies in ethnomethodology*. Englewood Cliffs, NJ: Prentice Hall.

Giles, H. (2009). The process of communication accommodation. In N. Copeland & A. Jaworski (eds.) *The new sociolinguistics reader,*(pp. 276–286). London: Blackwell.

Giles, H., Fortman, J., Dailey, R., Barker, V., Hajek, C., Anderson, M. C., & Rule, N. (2006). Communication accommodation: Law enforcement and the public. In R. M. Dailey & B. A. Le Poire (eds.) *Interpersonal communication matters: Family, health, and community relations* (pp. 241–269). NewYork: Peter Lang.

Giles, H., & Smith, P.M. (1979). Accommodation theory: Optimal levels of convergence. In H. Giles & R. St. Clair (eds.) *Language and social psychology* (pp. 5–65). Oxford: Blackwell.

Giles, H., Taylor, D. M., & Bourhis, R. Y. (1972). Toward a theory of interpersonal accommodation through language: Some Canadian data. *Language in Society 2*, 177–192.

Giles, H., & Wadleigh, P. M. (1999). Accommodating nonverbally. In L. K. Guerrero, J. A. DeVito, & M. L. Hecht (eds.) *The nonverbal communication reader: Classic and contemporary readings*, 2nd ed. (pp. 425–436). Prospect Heights, IL: Waveland.

Goffman, E. (1959). *The presentation of self in everyday life*. New York: Doubleday.

Goffman, E. (1971). *Relations in public: Microstudies of the public order*. New York: Basic Books.

Goffman, E. (1981). *Forms of talk*. Oxford: Blackwell.

Goldsmith A (2010) Policing's new visibility. *British Journal of Criminology 50*, 914–934.

Goold, B. (2003) Public area surveillance and police work: The impact of CCTV on police behaviour and autonomy. *Surveillance & Society* 1(2), 191–203.

Gordon, C. (2013). Beyond the observer's paradox: The audio-recorder as a resource for the display of identity. *Qualitative Research 13*(3), 299–317.

Gregory, S. (2010). Cameras everywhere: Ubiquitous video documentation of human rights, New forms of video advocacy, and considerations of safety, security, dignity and consent. *Journal of Human Rights Practice* 2(2), 191–207. 10.1093/jhuman/huq002

Haggerty, K. D., & Sandhu, A. (2014). The police crisis of visibility [Commentary]. *IEEE Technology and Society Magazine 33*(2), 9–12.

Hajek, C., Barker, V., Giles, H., Louw, J., Pecchioni, L., Makoni, S., & Myers, P. (2006). Communicative dynamics of police-civilian encounters: African and American interethnic data. *Journal of Intercultural Communication Research 35*, 161–182.

Haworth, K. (2013). Audience design in the police interview: The interactional and judicial consequences of audience orientation. *Language in Society 42*(1), 45–69.

Holmes, J. (1995). *Women, men and politeness*. Longman, London.

Jones, R. H. (2020). Accounting for surveillance. *Journal of Sociolinguistics 24*(1), 89–95. 10.1111/josl.12405

Kopak, A. (2014). Lights, cameras, action: A mixed methods analysis of police perceptions of citizens who video record officers in the line of duty in the United States. *International Journal of Criminal Justice Sciences 9* (2), 225–240.

Lyon, David (2001). Surveillance society: Monitoring everyday life. London: Open University Press.

Mann, S., & Ferenbok, J. (2013). New media and the power politics of sousveillance in a surveillance-dominated world. *Surveillance & Society 11*(1/2), 18–34.

Mann, S., Nolan, J., & Wellman, B. (2002). Sousveillance: Inventing and using wearable computing devices for data collection in surveillance environments. *Surveillance & Society*, *1*(3), 331–355. Retrieved from http://library.queensu.ca/ojs/index.php/surveillance-and-society/article/view/3344

Meyer, R. (2015, April 29). Thank God for cell phone video cameras'. *The Atlantic*. Retrieved from https://www.theatlantic.com/technology/archive/2015/04/thank-god-for-cellphone-video-cameras/391688/

Mirzoeff, N. (2011). *The right to look: A counterhistory of visuality*. Durham, NC: Duke University Press Books.

Monahan, T. (2006). Counter-surveillance as political intervention? Social Semiotics, 16, 515–534.

Munro, R. (2004). Punctualizing Identity: Time and the Demanding Relation. Sociology,38(2), 293–311.

Neyland, D. and Coopmans, C. (2014). Visual accountability. *The Sociological Review 62*, 1–23.

Neyland, D. and Woolgar, S. (2002). Accountability in action: the case of a database purchasing decision, *British Journal of Sociology 53* (2), 259–274.

Potere, M. (2012). Who will watch the watchmen?: Citizens recording police conduct. *Northwestern University Law Review 106* (1), 273–316.

Rickford, J. R. & McNair-Knox, F. (1994). Addressee- and Topic- influenced style shift: A quantitative sociolinguistic study. In D. Biber and E. Finegan (eds.), *Sociolinguistic perspectives on register* (pp. 235–276). New York/Oxford: Oxford University Press.

Roberts, M. (2015, May 6). Ryan Brown video: Racial profiling over cracked windshield, ACLU says. *Westword*. Retrieved 22 October 2020 from https://www.westword.com/news/ryan-brown-video-racial-profiling-over-cracked-windshield-aclu-says-6688715

Sandhu, A., & Haggerty, K. D. (2017). Policing on camera. *Theoretical Criminology 21*(1), 78–95.

Schachtman, B. (2017, March 8). Wilmington police officer orders Uber driver to stop filming traffic stop, prompts internal investigation. *Port City Daily*. Retrieved 22 October 2020 from https://portcitydaily.com/wilmington/2017/03/08/can-you-film-on-duty-police-officers-a-recent-incident-may-set-the-record-straight/

Searle, J. R. (1969). *Speech acts*. Cambridge: Cambridge University Press.

Tajfel, H., Turner, J.C., (1986). The social identity theory of intergroup behavior. In S. Worchel, & W.G. Austin (eds.). *Psychology of intergroup relation* (pp.7-24). Chicago: Nelson- Hall Publishers. .

Thelander, M. (1982). A qualitative approach to the quantitative data of speech variation. In S. Romaine (ed.), *Sociolinguistic Variation in Speech Communities* (pp. 65–83). London: Edward Arnold.

Thompson, J. B. (2005). The new visibility. *Theory, Culture & Society 22*(6), 31–51.

Wilkinson, T., & Glazer, M. A. (2016). First amendment under arrest: Photographing police in public places at issue on multiple fronts. *Villanova Law Review Online*: Tolle Lege 61, 55–70.

Transcription Conventions

(.)	Short pause (less than 0.2 seconds)
(0.2)	Measured pause
word	Stress/emphasis
^	Rising intonation
↓↑	Falling-rising intonation
↑↓	Rising-falling intonation

Afterword: Reflexive encounters when speaking across bounded knowledges

Rebekka Friedman

Thank you to the authors for the opportunity to comment on this wonderful book. I am so pleased to see it in print as I was involved in the very early stages of this project, going back as far as 2013, when I first had the pleasure of discussing and learning about some of Constadina Charalambous, Panayiota Charalambous and Ben Rampton's pioneering research on language education in Cyprus. This also led to my involvement in the thought-provoking Language, (In)security and Everyday Practice (LIEP) network, where scholars from sociolinguistics and International Relations (IR) discussed many of the early ideas so powerfully developed in this volume. I have been so pleased to follow LIEP's work over the years and to see it bear fruit in this excellent and timely edited volume.

Security, Ethnography and Discourse: Transdisciplinary Encounters is a highly topical and fascinating collection of pieces. The book uncovers hidden and lived experiences and looks at situated practices, covering a diversity of cases from post-war peacebuilding to Black Lives Matter and US surveillance (often on Muslim communities). The authors help us see both de-securitisation and (in)securitisation processes – and how the two may reinforce each other. The diverse contributions of the volume make clear how these two concepts as well as other concepts such as 'surveillance' have travelled in their translations across disciplines escaping essentialisation. The volume is uniquely reflexive on how being anchored within a distinct discipline may actually hinder us from seeing the world in a different way. The challenge is for scholars to describe practices based on their respective disciplinary baggage and way of framing things, without reinforcing the phenomena they seek to unpack and understand. In this volume for example, Charalambous and Rampton innovatively bring the idea of de-securitisation from Critical Security Studies to a linguistic ethnographic study to speak of processes of peace building and language education. The volume thereby also shows the subtle everyday navigation of risks and 'threats' that may be invisible but are important to people's everyday lives. It makes the basic but profound point that almost imperceptible changes matter.

DOI: 10.4324/9781003080909-102

The book's impact is sure to be far-reaching. The volume demonstrates the importance of combining theoretical reflection with ethnographic research, and makes a strong and radical challenge to the traditional approaches of Political Science, International Relations and Security Studies. It does this by highlighting one of the key contributions of feminist literature in International Relations, in orienting analysis of international problems towards lived experiences and often marginalised and hidden views. As such it resonates with long-standing feminist interventions to International Relations that make clear that 'the personal is political' and bring visibility to spaces, actors and processes previously marginalised and kept invisible as 'apolitical' (Enloe, 1990; Sjoberg and Tickner, 2011). This tradition is continued in the volume, particularly in Nicole Nguyen's chapter. Drawing on feminist geographer Alison Mountz, Nguyen's writing on the US Countering Violent Exremism initiative offers powerful insights about 'embodying the state' and moving away from the idea of the state as a monolithic actor.

The volume will be highly relevant to other disciplines as well. Through its focus on the intersection of micro and macro practices and the use of linguistic ethnography, the book also provides a challenge to those working in ethnographic and anthropological fields, who often tend to focus on the micro level and leave out macro implications and linkages. As such the volume provides a unique transdisciplinary insight into how micro and macro processes affect each other, are interconnected and have an impact in unexpected ways. The intersection of the macro and micro is particularly relevant in terms of the volume's discussion of the emergence of (in)security and its circulation at different scales.

Perhaps most importantly, the chapters combine to make a powerful statement, calling to mind Marilyn Frye's famous analogy of the bird cage. On first glance, it may be hard to see how the pieces of a cage (the wires and bolts) lead to oppression, but when we step back, it becomes very clear. The combined case studies of this volume do something similar, considering examples from different contexts that display similar themes, bringing into question the normative value of policies meant to contain conflict (de-securitisation), and looking at how both (in)securitisation and de-securitisation can enable oppression and violence.

There are three other important contributions that I wish to highlight. First, this volume counters the tendency to treat (non-Western) post-war contexts as very distinctive and different from the Western democracies where scholars are often based. It seamlessly brings into discussion a diverse array of case studies from police practices in the US to peace-building and language education in countries that have recently experienced large-scale intra-state warfare and ethnic conflict. Secondly, building on my comments on transcending the dichotomy between the micro and macro levels of study, the volume emphasises the importance of employing a multiscalar and transdisciplinary focus. Thirdly, the volume raises important insights about broader peace-building and de-securitisation trajectories.

Some examples help to illuminate these important contributions. Roger Mac Ginty focuses on the cumulative impact of micro changes over time and the everyday activities and behaviour of ordinary citizens, looking at a spectrum of everyday peace. Constadina Charalambous, Panayiota Charalambous and Ben Rampton find that more modest Turkish language training in Cyprus can sometimes be more successful in generating de-securitisation than programmes aimed explicitly at peace education. Renata Summa and Milan Puh critically reflect on silence and its many functions in the post-Yugoslav region. The chapters on surveillance and suspicion significantly focus on the social relations connected with surveillance rather than the reification of 'high tech.' They constitute embodied studies of what 'counts' as surveillance and the contingency of surveillant relations.

The contributions in this volume also raise the question of whether, in broader intractable conflicts, we should look at peacebuilding and reconciliation in more modest terms to show that it can take place even in very difficult environments. To go one step further, one might also ask whether these everyday initiatives are a first step, or are they taking place to fill a void precisely in the absence of large scale more substantive peace-building? In my own research in Sri Lanka, for instance, ritual healing after the war became important precisely because formal transitional justice processes were blocked and military disappearances remained unresolved. While informal healing processes provided a much-needed outlet, they also allowed political actors to avoid responsibility for not undertaking formal justice and support processes. This to some extent is an enduring challenge for peacebuilding: if everyday peace-building takes place in contexts of broad scale insecurity that exists in various structures, can they allow large scale insecurity to linger? How transformative is everyday peacebuilding in contexts of large-scale and structural injustices?

To conclude, *Security, Ethnography and Discourse* demonstrates the value of inductive, granular research from the field (so much more relevant now when it is under threat). The book shows us how when one looks beneath the surface, through the insightful eye of scholars who have extensive knowledge of the contexts they write about and the people who live in them, seemingly opposite strategies can play out in different and similar ways in different contexts. As Emma Mc Cluskey powerfully argues in Chapter 5 of the volume: 'Only when placed alongside each other, and outside of disciplinary framings do the dissonances and tensions between how we frame questions, the stories we choose to tell and the labels we choose to give – become visible, enabling conversation and cross-fertilisation to take place across boundaries.' As such *Security, Ethnography and Discourse* emphasises the importance of a diversity of transversal approaches that resists reification and the primacy of the state.

References

Enloe, C. (1990).*Bananas, beaches and bases*. Berkeley: University of California Press.

Sjoberg, L., & Tickner, J. A. (2011). Introduction: International Relations through feminist lenses. In *Feminism and international relations: Conversations about the past, present and future*. London: Routledge. 1–21.

Index

Note: Page numbers in italics denotes figures; bold denotes tables.

access ritual 148
accountability: audiences and accounts 174–7; defined 172; discussion and conclusion 191–5; examples 177–91, *178–84*, *186–8*, **189–92**; infrastructures of 177; public performances of 172; relevant audiences for discharge of 173; strategies of disclosure, involving 172; visibility and 172
accounts 173; audiences and 174–7
acculturation related stress 119
adjacency, principle of 24
Adnan approach, posting up stickers 155–9, *155*, **157**
airport security check, scanning at 159–60
Ajdukovic, D. 91
al-Qaeda on the Arabian Peninsula (AQAP) 134
Ali, Bassem 134
ambiguity, as everyday peace activity *43*
anthropological scholarship 19
anthropology 100, 101; of security 4
Anti-Apartheid Movement 41
anti-immigration Sweden Democrats party 103
anti-Muslim racism 125, 133, 137
anti-people CVE 126
antiterrorism programs 131, 133; domestic 125, 132; police-led 126–7
asylum 20
audiences 174–7; design 174; managing in interactions from sociolinguistic perspective 174
audio-video recording 145, 149
auditor design and accountability 170–4;

audiences and accounts 174–7; discussion and conclusion 191–5; examples 177–91, *178–84*, *186–8*, **189–92**
auditors: effect 175; presence of 176
Austro-Hungarian building 89
avoidance, as everyday peace activity *43*
awareness, kinds of 153

Ball, K. 143, 154
banopticon 162
Beerli, M. J. 19
Bell, A. 174, 175
Beutin, L. P. 194
Bigo, D. 18, 26, 102, 162
Biruski, D. C. 91
blame deferring, as everyday peace activity *43*
'blind' transactions 159
Blommaert, J. 4, 23, 24
Bock, M. A. 171, 173
body idiom 148
'boots-on-the-ground' method 3
Bourdieu, P. 62
Bourhis, R. Y. 174
breaking taboos 100–1; appropriating solidarity as free gift 106–8; demand for reciprocation 106–8; emergence of political communities 101–3; far right 101–3; hidden transcript, voicing of 110–12; indignation and panic 110–12; Oreby, Skåne and transformations of Swedish 'solidarity' 103–6; Swedish decision and changing of stakes 108–10
Brighenti, A. 171

broader implications 161–4
Buzan, B. 17
by-standing 144
bystanders 147

capturing 102
carceral care work 132–3
Case Assessment Management Program (CAMP) 132
c.a.s.e collective 4, 18
Castells, M. 171
cell phones cameras 170–2, 176, 177–91, *178–84, 186–8,* **189–92**
Charalambous, C. 81
Charalambous, P. 20, 23, 81
Christian Science Monitor 89
Cilmi, Bashir 134–5
citizens and police: audiences and accounts 174–7; cell phones to record encounters 176; challenges for 174; discussion and conclusion 191–5; empirical studies 172–3; examples 177–91, *178–84, 186–8,* **189–92**; negotiated dimensions of videoing 173; roles and responsibilities 172; technologically mediated interactions between 171; with video cameras in 170
civil inattention 144, 148
civil society 102
civility between individuals 44
Clark, H. 176
close-up interaction: analysis 3; with surveillance technology 159–60
Closed Circuit Television (CCTV) 1, 153
co-production of national security 126–30
Cohen, S. 111
Cold War 14, 17
collective impact approach 127
communication: features of 174; non-verbal 174; off- and on-line 164; theory of 174
communicative genres 24
communicative interaction, in politics of everyday life 22
community-based surveillance 128
community leaders, conscripting 133–7
comparable interest 53
conceptual instrumentarium 23
conceptualisation of methods 3
conflict-affected contexts: permanent impermanence of 48

conflict disruption 43, 44–5
conflict market 44
contemporary sociolinguistics 26
contemporary surveillance regimes 128
context of violence and exclusion 46
contextualising language 84–6; Mostar 87–90; Vukovar 90–4
conventional counterterrorism methods 119
conversation analysis 22
conversational involvement 26
Cook County Department of Homeland Security and Emergency Management (Illinois) 130
Coopmans, C. 172, 173
cop watching 173
Copenhagen 18
Čorkalo Biruški, D. 85, 91
cost-benefit analysis 47
counter-power 171
Countering Targeted Violence Against Our Communities (CTVAC) 130
Countering Violent Extremism (CVE): actors, interviewing 124; anti-Muslim program 120–1, 124–5; anti-people 126; carceral care work 132–3; challenging 121; conclusion 137–9; conscripting community leaders 133–7; creep of security regimes into intimate and interior spaces 130–3; defined 119–20; domestic war on terror 133–7; examining daily work of practitioners 122–3; funds 135; implementation of 122; key hotspots 123; as national security approach 121; participatory surveillance 127; persistent resistance to local 133; policy making and taking 123–4; practitioners 124–6; radicalization research and co-production of national security 126–30; rethinking research reciprocity 124–6; second generation 136; social service providers 133–7; strategy 119; studying up to map geographies of 123–4; taxonomizing terrorists 126–30
creative destruction 44
creep of security regimes 130–3
critic of notion of everyday peace 37
critical anthropology of security 19
critical methods 3–4
Critical Security Studies 199
criticism 37, 41–2, 49

Croatian Democratic Union (HDZ) 92
Croatian People's Party (HNS) 92
Croatian Ukrainian immigrant community 85
crude religious markers 129
'crypto-focused' interaction 158, 161
Cultures et Conflits (journal) 18
Cyprus: language education in 199; Cyprus Issue 56–9
Cyprus, peace-building through language education in: activity in lessons 64–9; Cyprus Issue 56–9; de-securitisation 69–71; education and introduction of Turkish 56–9; everyday peace 69–71; Greek-Cypriots studying Turkish 69–71; institutional structures, affordances and effects 59–64; language provision at school 59–69; local, vernacular and everyday turns in International Relations/Peace & Conflict Studies 52–4; methods in case study 55–6, **56**; sociolinguistics and linguistic ethnography 54–5

data collection **56**
De Certeau, M. 26
de-colonising anthropology 21
de-disciplinarizing ethnography 3–4
de-personalising avoidance strategies 160
de-securitisation 69–71, 199
De Wilde, J. 17
Dedoose software 123
demand for reciprocation 106–8
diffusing insecurities 19
disattend objects 147
discourse analysis 84
dissociated vigilance 153
doctoral ethnography 149
document analysis 121
domestic war on terror 133–7; initiatives 127
drivers' ethnicity 175

Eastmond, M. 82, 83, 84
economic stressors 119
electronic data, bulk collection of 1
Elmi, Yusuf 134
embodied watching 173
Embodying US security state 119–23, 137–9; conscripting community leaders 133–7; creep of security regimes into intimate and interior spaces 130–3; domestic war on terror 133–7; radicalization research and co-production of national security 126–30; rethinking research reciprocity 124–6; social service providers 133–7; studying up to map geographies of 123–4; taxonomizing terrorists 126–30
emergence of surveillance 162
empathy 40
empirical method 154
encounters between citizens and police 170–4; audiences and accounts 174–7; discussion and conclusion 191–5; examples 177–91, *178–84*, *186–8*, **189–92**
entextualisation 25
epistemic positioning 173
epistemological colonialism 39
Ericson, R. 171–2
ethnographic perspective 4
ethnography 22, 55; of surveillance 162; *see also* surveillance technology
everyday experience of surveillance 143–5; broader implications 161–4; close-up interaction with surveillance technology 159–60; interaction order 145–7; posting up stickers and experience of feeling surveilled 154–9, *155*, **157**; rudimentary model 160–1; surveilled experiences 160–1; unfocused interaction 147–9; walking in street and normalisation of surveillance 149–54, *152*
everyday peace disruption 37–9, 69–71, 82; bottom-up and top-down peace initiatives 48; concept of 40–4, *40*; conflict disruption 44–5; context of violence and exclusion 46; deserving label 'peace' for three reasons 46–8; discussion 48–9; dynamic, social, and context dependent 40; elite-level accord 48; form of negative peace 45; form of peace 45–8; form of power 45; as form of tactical agency 37; indicators of 39; nature of 47; same-sex couples 47; as social infrastructure or prosocial connective tissue 49; types of social practice constituting *43*
Everyday Peace Indicators programme 39, 40

experience of feeling surveilled 154–9
explicitly targeting individuals with psychiatric disabilities 131

family and friends 130
far right parties 100, 101–3
Fassin, D. 27
feeling surveilled, experience of 154–9
feelings of alienation 119
Feenberg, A. 154
'female empowerment' strategies 106
female solidarity 107
Ferenbok, J. 171
'filming the cops', practice of 178
first peace 43, 49
Fleischmann, L. 109
focused interaction 144, 145, *146*; culturally and historically specific 147
foreign bodies, metaphor of 93
foreign language 59
Foucault, M. 163
free gift, appropriating solidarity as 106–8
Freedom of Information Act (FOIA) 123
Friesen, N. 154
full-voiced singing 151

Garfinkel, H. 26, 176
Giles, H. 174, 175
Glickman, Daniel 119
Goffman, E. 143, 172, 175; conversation analysis 22, 55; and everyday experience of surveillance *see* everyday experience of surveillance; observations, walking in street 151–4
Goffmanian approach to surveillance 162
Goldsmith, A. 172
good citizen, performance of 106
Gordon, C. 176
Green, N. 143, 161, 162
growing securitisation, impact of 20
Guillaume X. 82
Gumperz, John 21, 54
Gusterson, H. 100, 101

Haggerty, K. 143, 163–4, 173
hailing effects 173
Haworth, K. 176
hidden transcript 100, 105; voicing of 110–12
Holbraad, M. 101

homegrown terrorism 130
Horgan, John 129
hospitality 105
Hromadžić, A. 87, 89
humanitarian space 19
humanitarian superpower 103, 110
Huysmans, J. 53
Hymes, Dell 21, 54

Independent Democratic Serb Party (SDSS) 92
indexical associations 23
inferencing 23
infrastructures of accountability 177
insecuritisation 20
institutional surveillance 151
instrumentarium 23
inter-group friendship 44
interaction order 145–7; consist of 145–6; defined 145
interactional right 173
International Consortium on Language and Superdiversity 14
International Relations (IR) 2, 3, 13, 38, 82, 100, 199, 200; local, vernacular and everyday turns in 52–4
International Security Studies 17
interruption, defined 44
interview 60–3, 121, 145; in 2006 with secondary students 57; CVE actors 124; Muslim leaders 134; practitioners 133; questions 125; with secondary students in 2012 58; with secondary students in 2013 58
intimate and interior spaces 130–3
IPS approach of international **15–17**

James approach, posting up stickers 156–8, **157**
Jansen, S. 83
Joint Regional Intelligence Center 131
Jones, R. 153

Kaleel, Masoud 134
Kapović, M. 92
Kasunić, S. 91
Khan, K. 81
Khoury, Aysha 135–6
Kolind, T. 83

LA County Department of Mental Health (DMH) 130
language: contextualising 84–6; and

everyday practices 79–95; Mostar 87–90; researching (in)security 27–8; Vukovar 90–4
language education, peace-building through 199; activity in lessons 64–9; Cyprus Issue 56–9; de-securitisation 69–71; education and introduction of Turkish 56–9; everyday peace 69–71; Greek-Cypriots studying Turkish 69–71; institutional structures, affordances and effects 59–64; language provision at school 59–69; local, vernacular and everyday turns in International Relations/Peace & Conflict Studies 52–4; methods in case study 55–6, **56**; sociolinguistics and linguistic ethnography 54–5
language provision at school: activity in lessons 64–9; institutional structures, affordances and effects 59–64
language, (in)security and everyday practice (LIEP) 13–14, 199
large-scale sociological effects 21
Law on Use of Languages and Scripts of National Minorities 91
legacies of conflict 20
legacy carriers 44
Leonardsson, H. 53
liberalism 17
Linguistic Anthropology 4
linguistic ethnography (LE) 3–4 54–55, 20–7, 200; resources 22
linguistics & discourse analysis 22, 55
lived experience 27–8; researching (in)security 27–8
logic of suspicion and othering 102
Los Angeles County Department of Mental Health 131
Los Angeles Police Department (LAPD) 129, 130–1
Low, S. M. 20
Lyon, D. 143, 161, 162, 171

Mac Ginty, R. 53
Mahdi, Abdi 120, 135
Majsec, K. 91
Mangual Figueroa, A. 162
Mann, S. 171
Mannergren Selimovic, J. 82, 83, 84
Mc Cluskey, E. 18, 102
Merkel, Angela 108, 109
Migration Board 104
Milčič, I. 91

Mirzoeff, N. 173, 178, 191
mixed marriages 88
mobilize community members, as terrorist watchdogs 128
Montesinos Coleman, L. 5–6
moral panic 110–11
Mostar 79, 87–90; silence in 84–6
motivation 58
Mountz, Alison 121, 123
multi-ethnic and multicultural city 86
Muslim, CVE actors as 124–5
mutual monitoring possibilities 147–8, 163

National Counterterrorism Center 127
national language in Republic of Cyprus 59
National Pedagogic Standard 91
national security 17; co-production of 126–30
nationalist rhetorics 1
New York Times 88
Neyland, D. 172, 173
Nolan, J. 171
non-escalation of conflict 38
non-focused interaction under surveillance 161
non-verbal communication 174
normalisation of surveillance 149–54
noticing, moments of 153

Ochs, J. 81, 82
off- and on-line communication 164
opening position 148, 153
Oreby 103–6
Orlandi, E. 82, 84

Palmberger, M. 89
panic, moral 110–11
participant observation 121, 144, 145
participation framework 175
participatory surveillance 127, 128
Peace & Conflict Studies (PCS) 20, 38–9; local, vernacular and everyday turns in 52–4
peace-building through language education 52, 199; activity in lessons 64–9; Cyprus Issue 56–9; de-securitisation 69–71; education and introduction of Turkish 56–9; everyday peace 69–71; Greek-Cypriots studying Turkish 69–71; institutional structures, affordances and effects

59–64; language provision at school 59–69; local, vernacular and everyday turns in International Relations/Peace & Conflict Studies 52–4; methods in case study 55–6, **56**; sociolinguistics and linguistic ethnography 54–5
'Perspektiva' 89
Political Anthropological Research in International Sociology (PARIS) approach 100, 102
Political Anthropological Research on International Social Sciences (PARISS) 20
political communities, emergence of 101–3
political science 200
post-conflict societies 94–5; silence and/as security in post-conflict 82–4
post-Yugoslav region, silence as practices of (in)security: contextualising language and silence in two contested cities 84–6; language and everyday practices 79–95; Mostar 87–90; post-conflict societies, silence and interdicts and possibilities for 94–5; segregated and 'reunified' school system 87–90; silence and/as security in post-conflict societies 82–4; silencing spaces of coexistence 90–4; Vukovar 90–4
posting up stickers 154–9, *155*, **157**
practical reflexivity 2
pre-criminal dilemma 127
professionalized mental health approach 127, 130
Providing Alternatives to Hinder Extremism (PATHE) 130–2
provisional perches 48
psychiatric disabilities, explicitly targeting individuals with 131
public and academic discourses 22, 55
public transcript 100, 105, 106
purposeful witnessing 173
Pütz, O. 144, 159, 160, 161

qualitative analysis software 123
qualitative research 121

racial profiling 157, 162
racialised insecuritisation 157
racialization, terrorism 128–9
Radicalization in the West: The Homegrown Threat 128

radicalization theory 121, 126–30
Rahman, Tanvir 126, 133
Rampton, B. 81
ratified participants 147
realism 17
reciprocation, demand for 106–8
reciprocity 38, 40, *40*; rethinking research 124–6
recontextualisation 25
reflexivity: researching (in)security 27–8
refugee crisis 101, 103
remedial ritual 148
researching (in)security: international and the transversal 14, 17–20; IPS approach of international **15–17**; language, reflexivity and lived experience 27–8; language, (in)security and everyday practice 13–14; linguistic ethnography 20–7; sociolinguistic studies of superdiversity **15–17**; working at interface 27–8
Richmond, O. P. 53
right to look 173–4
risk assessment strategy 131
ritualized politeness, as everyday peace activity *43*
Rosenow, D. 5–6
Routledge Handbook of Surveillance Studies 143
Rudd, G. 53
rudimentary model 160–1
Russian Revolution 45

same-sex couples 47
Sandhu, A. 173
scene recorded by the video-glasses *152*
Schaefer, E. 176
school system, segregated and 'reunified' 87–90
Scott, J. C. 100, 105
Searle, J. R. 176
Secondary School of Machinery and Traffic 88
Secondary School of Traffic 88
securitarian 1
securitisation theory 17, 18
(in)security: concept of 2; 'critical methods' to transdisciplinary encounter in 3–4; discourses and institutions, trajectories 14; as emergent, contingent, unexpected 4–5; examining 14; international and transversal 14, 17–20; IPS approach of

international **15–17**; language, reflexivity and lived experience 27–8; language, (in)security and everyday practice 13–14; linguistic ethnography 20–7; sociolinguistic studies of superdiversity **15–17**; trap 4; working at interface 27–8
security scapes 5, 19, 49
(in)security, silence as practices of 78–9; contextualising language and silence in two contested cities 84–6; language and everyday practices 79–95; Mostar 87–90; post-conflict societies, silence and interdicts and possibilities for 94–5; segregated and 'reunified' school system 87–90; silence and/as security in post-conflict societies 82–4; silencing spaces of coexistence 90–4; Vukovar 90–4
security situation 42
segregated and 'reunified' school system 87–90
shared humanity 40
silence: and/as security in post-conflict societies 82–4; in contested cities 84–6; and interdicts 82
silence-as-doing 82
silence as practices of (in)security 78–9; contextualising language and silence in two contested cities 84–6; language and everyday practices 79–95; Mostar 87–90; post-conflict societies, silence and interdicts and possibilities for 94–5; segregated and 'reunified' school system 87–90; silence and/as security in post-conflict societies 82–4; silencing spaces of coexistence 90–4; Vukovar 90–4
silencing spaces of coexistence 90–4
situational proprieties 148; violation of 148
small-scale interactions 21
Smith, G. 154
Smith, P.M. 174
Social Democratic Party of Croatia (SDP) 92
social identity theory 175
social organisation, lowest level of 46, 47
social service providers 133–7; as terrorist watchdogs 128
social structure 145
socialisation 40
sociality 38, 40–1, *40*; in urban spaces in South Asia, Hoek and Gandhi 48

societalization 40
sociolinguistic studies of superdiversity **15–17**
sociolinguistics 3, 13, 54–5, 143, 199
solidarity 38, 40–2, *40*, 100; appropriating, as free gift 106–8; female 107; transformations of 103–6
sousveillance 9, 163; surveillance vs. 171
speech economy 21
stakes, changing of 108–10
Stefansson, A. H. 83
Steinhilper, E. 109
stickers, posting up 154–9, *155*, **157**
superdiversity, sociolinguistic studies of **15–17**
surveillance technology 20, 199; broader implications 161–4; close-up interaction with 159–60; community-based 128; interaction order 145–7; large-scale generalisations about 164; non-focused interaction 161; participatory 128; posting up stickers and experience of feeling surveilled 154–9, *155*, **157**; rudimentary model 160–1; sousveillance vs. 171; subjective experience of 154; surveilled experiences 160–1; unfocused interaction 147–9; walking in street and normalisation of surveillance 149–54, *152*
surveilled experiences 160–1
surveilling intimate space to counter violent extremism: conclusion 137–9; conscripting community leaders 133–7; creep of security regimes into intimate and interior spaces 130–3; domestic war on terror 133–7; radicalization research and co-production of national security 126–30; rethinking research reciprocity 124–6; social service providers 133–7; studying up to map geographies of 123–4; taxonomizing terrorists 126–30
Sweden, xenophobia as acceptable in: appropriating solidarity as free gift 106–8; demand for reciprocation 106–8; emergence of political communities 101–3; far right 101–3; hidden transcript, voicing of 110–12; indignation and panic 110–12; Oreby, Skåne and transformations of Swedish

'solidarity' 103–6; Swedish decision and changing of stakes 108–10
Swedish decision 108–10
Swedish-for-immigrants (SFI) policy 103
System-Wide Mental Assessment Response Team (SMART) 132

taboos, breaking 100–1; appropriating solidarity as free gift 106–8; demand for reciprocation 106–8; emergence of political communities 101–3; far right 101–3; hidden transcript, voicing of 110–12; indignation and panic 110–12; Oreby, Skåne and transformations of Swedish 'solidarity' 103–6; Swedish decision and changing of stakes 108–10
tape recorders as overhearers 176
taxonomizing terrorists 126–30
Taylor, D. M. 174
technology: not as causing accountability 171–2; power of 17; technologically mediated interactions 171; of visibility 171
telling, as everyday peace activity *43*
temporary toeholds 48
territories of the selfbring to scene 146
terror, domestic war on 133–7
terrorism: homegrown 130; racialization 128–9; -related arrest 134; scholars 129
text trajectories 24
textual 'projectiles' 25
thick descriptions 2
time to time scanning 153
'top-down' approach 102
Toplista Nadrealista 79, 80
transdisciplinary dialogue, setting foundations for: international and the transversal 14, 17–20; IPS approach of international **15–17**; language, reflexivity and lived experience 27–8; language, (in)security and everyday practice 13–14; linguistic ethnography 20–7; sociolinguistic studies of superdiversity **15–17**; working at interface 27–8
transdisciplinary encounter 3–4
Turkish: education and introduction of 56–9; Greek-Cypriots studying 69–71; language lesson 64–9; secondary curriculum 59
Tutu, Desmond 41
two school under one roof model 89

2006 Fieldwork 56, **56**
2012 Fieldwork 56, **56**
2018 OSCE report 87

Umwelt 157–8
undocumented migrants, positioning of 20
unfocused interaction 143, 146, *146*, 147–9, 160–1; culturally and historically specific 147; involving 149; key elements in 144
United States Attorney's Office for the District of Massachusetts 129–30

vernacular (in)security 19
video cameras: as objective witnesses 173; proliferation of 170; role in encounters 172; strategies citizens use when deploying encounters with police officers 177–91, *178–84*, *186–8*, **189–92**
video-glasses, scene recorded by *152*
violence, indirect into direct 37
visibility: accountability and 172; technologies of 171
Vukovar 79, 90–4; silence in 84–6

walking in street, normalisation of surveillance 149–54, *152*
Warabe, Aeden 120, 125–6
Waver, O. 17
Wellman, B. 171
'*Wir Schaffen das*' policy 108, 109
witnessing, purposeful 173
World Organization for Resource Development and Education (WORDE) 129

xenophobia as acceptable in Sweden: appropriating solidarity as free gift 106–8; demand for reciprocation 106–8; emergence of political communities 101–3; far right 101–3; hidden transcript, voicing of 110–12; indignation and panic 110–12; Oreby, Skåne and transformations of Swedish 'solidarity' 103–6; Swedish decision and changing of stakes 108–10

Yugoslavia 79–81

Zurawski, N. 143, 161, 162